A *Good* Ending

A Compassionate Guide to Funerals, Pastoral Care, and Life Celebrations

DAVID SPARKS

UNITED CHURCH
PUBLISHING HOUSE

A Good Ending
A Compassionate Guide to Funerals, Pastoral Care, and Life Celebrations
David Sparks

Library and Archives Canada Cataloguing in Publication

Sparks, David, 1938-, author
    A good ending : a compassionate guide to funerals, pastoral care, and life celebrations / David Sparks.
Issued in print and electronic formats.
ISBN 978-1-55134-216-0 (pbk.).--ISBN 978-1-55134-217-7 (pdf)

    1. Church work with the bereaved. 2. Church work with the terminally ill. 3. Bereavement--Religious aspects. 4. Death--Religious aspects. 5. Funeral service. 6. Memorial service. I. Title.

BV4330.S58 2014   259'.6   C2014-901630-1
                                                             C2014-901631-X

United Church Publishing House
3250 Bloor St. West, Suite 300
Toronto, ON
Canada M8X 2Y4
1-800-268-3781
www.united-church.ca/sales/ucph
Design: Diane Renault-Collicott, Graphics and Print
Cover image: © Bvanduijl | Dreamstime.com

UCPH is a ministry of The United Church of Canada, supported by the Mission and Service Fund and readers like you.

Dedication

This book is dedicated to Patricia Gilmore who gave me the idea
and who, over several years, reminded me of the need.

The purpose of human life is to serve,
and to show compassion
and the will to help others.

Albert Schweitzer (1875–1965)

Contents

Good Advice

A great piece of advice can be like a great book, growing in value and importance the more you use it. I received lots of wonderful advice (and books) during seminary that unfortunately stayed packed in boxes and shelves; I did not realize how valuable they were until I needed them. One such piece of advice was "Be careful, don't drop the baby" (during baptisms). I shelved this gem for years between "absurd" and "redundant," until along came a nine-month-old baby in a satin christening outfit! Another gem that I mistakenly filed, this time between "obvious" and "duh," was "Whatever you do, do not mess up a funeral!"

As worship leaders we all know the importance of ritual. And as pastoral care providers we know the emotional significance of a well-crafted funeral or celebration of life service. We know that leading a memorial service is a privileged, sacred trust that is never to be taken lightly. Obviously, no one would purposely mess up a funeral. I think what the person was really trying to say was "Be your best always, but *do* your best *to be* your best at a funeral."

During a funeral or celebration of life service, we worship leaders have the potential to be of either great help or great harm to the people who are saying their goodbyes. We are at our best during funerals, and we do our best (using all of our skills and training) to create spaces where good endings are possible. However, every so often we need a little help to do our best, because funerals are hard work.

Funerals are hard work because for many of us, the congregation does not change (much) between funerals, making it increasingly difficult to find fitting words to honour the deceased that have not been used before. It is hard work because often we are grieving with the people whom we are attempting to comfort. It is hard work because sometimes between council meetings, pastoral visits, weddings, and sermon preparation, there is simply no time. And sometimes we are thrown into situations (suicides, murders, tragic accidents) that are hard to imagine and seemingly impossible to prepare for. At all such times, pull out this book! David can help you work toward a very good ending.

A Good Ending is filled with useful advice from a variety of different people, sound instruction, and powerful liturgies that walk the worship leader through everything needed for them to do their best at a funeral or celebration of life service (from caring for the dying and meeting with the family before the death through to follow-up after the service). When you do not know where to start, but want to do your best, this book will help you get there.

I wish I had had this book on my desk 10 years ago. David's pastoral skill is evident in his writing and liturgy; reading this book feels like consulting with a trusted friend or mentor. For people starting out in worship leadership, *A Good Ending* will help to alleviate any anxieties they might have about leading a service. For seasoned worship leaders, this book will act like a refresher course, offering new ideas, new perspectives, and new liturgies.

Dearest worship leaders, pull out your tabs and sticky notes, and trust me, do not file this book away! You will want it close by for quick reference. This book, like good advice, is an invaluable gift. Thank you, David.

Alydia Smith
Program Coordinator,
Worship, Music, and Spirituality
The United Church of Canada

This Is Not about What You Must Do

In this book I deliberately paint a broad canvas. The areas covered range from a theological basis of bereavement through a consideration of secular celebrations, to pastoral care and onward through services and their component parts, to meditations. I make no claims of covering the whole territory. If you want a complete treatise on pastoral care for before and after bereavement, there are books that cover this aspect. If you want to find out in detail about childhood grief, there are books and articles out there. If you want to obtain a comprehensive set of liturgies for funerals and celebrations of life, you can do it. And if you want to specialize in secular celebrations, there are excellent handbooks for this area alone.

A Good Ending arose from my pastoral experience as a minister, called on many occasions to be with dying persons and their families, to conduct services for members of my pastoral charges, and to conduct many more for individuals who had little or no Christian faith.

It is the sort of book I would dearly liked to have had at the beginning of my ministry. So it is primarily for those who are beginning in Christian ministry, both lay or in one of the ordered streams of ministry. It is also for those who are facing the death of a well-loved family member and want insights about what is going on, how the death of their loved one might be celebrated, and how they might seek help if the grieving process is not going well.

This is not a handbook about what you *must* do or what you should say to a dying person or their family members; rather, I hope it will help you find your own path and your own words. The same goes for the service, memorial, or celebration. There are many examples of prayers and meditations that you may wish to use exactly as they are printed here, or you may want to revise and modify them to meet the different situations that you encounter.

I hope this book will challenge you to think about the meaning of death and what happens after a person dies; and I hope it opens you up to concepts and ideas that are new and surprising. I also hope that the book will encourage you to work out your own pastoral practice around dying and death and to write your own prayers and meditations. If you say, "I have a prayer that is much more appropriate in this situation than the one in the book," or "The prayer on page 48 has given me an idea that I am able to develop on my own," I will be very happy! You are at liberty to use any of the material printed here for your pastoral situation. However, if you wish to reprint poems and passages for which copyright permission has had to be sought for the purposes of this book, I refer you to those copyright sources at the end of each chapter. If you want to republish portions of this book in another book or article, you will have to seek permission from the United Church Publishing House (see page ii).

A note about names: Since many of my stories are based on true events and experiences, I have changed all names and some situations to ensure the privacy of individuals.

And a note about language: It is my practice in liturgy and in meditations that the language should be inclusive of male and female genders in spite of the Hebrew and Christian scriptures being full of male references and pronouns. In this book I have mostly avoided the awkward "he/she" way of indicating personal pronouns and attempted to balance the number of she's with he's. If I have failed, and you the reader will be the judge, I ask your forgiveness, but my aim was equality of gender reference.

You only have one opportunity to celebrate and mourn the end of a person's life, and each opportunity is unique and challenging. May you find as you are compassionately with a dying person and their family, as you prepare and offer the celebration or service, and as you work with the grieving family afterwards, that the Holy One is with you.

David Sparks

ACKNOWLEDGEMENTS

Thanks for Your Help

I am deeply grateful to those many individuals who have helped me throughout the process of envisaging, researching, and writing this resource. The book would never have happened if Pat Gilmore had not given me the idea and kept reminding me of the need for a "funeral book" over the years.

Mike Schwartzentruber and Ellen Turnbull at Wood Lake Books encouraged me in the early stages of writing and helped me shape the manuscript. Then the resource in its first draft form was sent out to a series of educators and ministers who gave their comments and answered my questions. I am grateful to John Young of Queen's University and William Kervin of Emmanuel College, who put me in touch with former students who have been so helpful in looking over the manuscript. I am grateful for the cooperation of Jennifer Janzen-Ball, Coordinator of the Designated Lay Ministry Program, for reviewing the manuscript and for suggesting former students from her program who could help me.

My thanks also go to Susan Lukey, editor of *Gathering*, who has provided me with resources from that wonderful publication, and to Alan Gaunt, who allowed me to use and adapt some of his prayers. Alan's writing inspired me early in my ministry to move from using other people's resources to writing my own.

The staff of several funeral establishments have contributed from their experience, and I am particularly grateful to Brent Trudell of Jenkins Funeral Home, Craig Sandberg of Blake Funeral Chapel, and Ronald Baker of the Northwest Funeral Alternative, all of Thunder Bay, Ontario, and to Brenda Hamilton of the Providence Funeral Home, Summerland, British Columbia.

Kelly Phipps of the Penticton Bereavement Centre in British Columbia provided me with resources and valuable contacts. I learned a whole lot from Sam Mercier, a celebrant, and from Andrea Turner of the Andy Moog Hospice in Penticton and Michelle Webb. Susan Kast was a great source of information about the grief of children, and I drew on the experience of Tom Melvin (in his article in *Gathering*) in this same area. Thanks, too, to Maria Ling for some good suggestions.

The core of insights and inspiration for the book came from those who, week by week, are called on to stand beside those who are dying and their families and then have the challenge of conducting the service or celebration for them. I was encouraged and learned so much from Lynda Goy-Flint and Gordon Flint, Doreen Hewitson, Armand Houle, Wayne Jarvis, Roger Manuel, Don Stiles, Wanda Stride, and Laura Turnbull.

Bob Root has provided many inspiring prayers and other liturgy, while thanks are also due to Cynthia Breadner for her liturgical pieces, which, she says, are "inspired and rooted in the spiritual direction of the late Fred Joblin of Orillia, Ontario." Thanks also to Linda Sobottka of the Suicide Prevention Resource Center for her help and permission to use the excellent resources of that organization, while it has been most useful to consider the non-Western context of bereavement in the African context through the eyes of Emmanuel K. Ofori. And thanks to Robert Wright, Minister of Goodfish Lake and Saddle Lake, Alberta, for his help.

Last, but not in any way least, thanks to my wife, Kathy, who has lost me on many occasions when I was researching or writing the book. Her quiet, loving support and considered judgment have been strength to me over the nearly two years of writing.

David Sparks

The Reason for This Book

My own first experiences in ministry and my conversations with those new to this challenging vocation have made it clear that when a person is dying or when a death occurs, ministers are expected to help in a way that no one else is able to help. To do this they need a variety of resources to guide them through the stages of suffering, loss, and grieving, and as they prepare for a funeral service or life celebration. The same need for resources is a reality for the person who is called on as a good friend to help family members when a loved one is dying or has died. This book brings a wide range of resources together and is offered to all those who stand ready to help families at the testing time of bereavement.

But what does this mean in practice?

Consider these situations: You are new to ministry and you receive a call from someone in your congregation: "My wife, Sara, is in the hospital; the doctor has just told me there is nothing more he can do for her. Can you help us?" Or a staff member of the local funeral home calls with news that one of your members has passed away and the family has asked, "Will the minister take Alfredo's service?" Or a member of your congregation comes to the office and confides, "Alice, our youngest, is behaving strangely. Did you know that Gavin, her brother, died six months ago? What shall we do?"

The news that a church member does not have long to live or that a family needs you to take a funeral or celebration of life service, or that you are needed to deal with feelings around the loss of a brother or sister present major challenges in ministry. My sense from talking and working with the committed and compassionate individuals who are fresh to ministry is that they want to gain all the skills and confidence they can to comfortably and confidently carry out these tasks. This resource is designed to make their pastoral care and worship leadership tasks easier and to encourage them to create their own resources.

However, you do not have to be in an order of ministry to be called on to help in a pastoral way or with the service when someone is dying or has died. For instance: You have a friend who is dying; the family members are gathered but are not sure how to face up to his approaching death. They are exhausted through being constantly at the bedside and are in danger of becoming ill themselves. This question is posed to you as a good friend: "We are worn out and are looking for some practical help. What can we do?" Are you able to respond in an appropriately pastoral way?

Another situation: You have been asked by the family of a person who has just died to lead the service. You have led Sunday worship before and have had some training in this area, but realize that a memorial service or funeral is something very different. What is the order for the service? What prayers should you use? What do you say at the graveside? What else will the family expect of you? Where do you turn to for the help you need?

Or a family member asks you to give a talk (or eulogy) about someone whom you knew well who has died. You have the public speaking skills, but what should be included in the talk and what left out? You are not sure.

Or again, you are approached by a family who did not have an interment for their loved one's cremated remains at the time of the funeral. They ask, "We want to scatter our loved one's ashes respectfully, but do not know how to do this or what we can say. Can you advise us?"

For the good friends who are asked to patiently be with dying persons and their families, to preside at funeral or interment services, and to provide pastoral care after the services are over, help is essential and it has to be given in simple and understandable language.

There are programs for instructing both lay and ordered ministers during their training and internship times, but they are necessarily limited in scope and duration. There are also good resources for the specific stages of dying and bereavement. For lay persons who are asked to help with the bereavement experience, there are the same printed and video resources available and courses for those who search them out. What is lacking is the simple, comprehensive, one-volume resource to supplement the training. It is this need that I have attempted to meet with *A Good Ending*.

There is also a need for a resource that family members can use, one where they can look for readings for a funeral service, for prayers for the bedside of a dying person, and for insights they can glean to help them with a person whose time of grieving seems endless. The book will prove a valuable resource for them.

Pastoral Basis

There are many resources that centre on the funeral or celebration of life service. They are concerned with preparing and writing the meditation or sermon, the order of service, the prayers, scripture readings, and sometimes how the eulogy is to be prepared and delivered. The focus of these books and other resources begins with the time when the officiant is asked to take the service and ends when the remains of the person who has died are committed to God's eternal care at the cemetery. Similarly, there are books that focus on the compassionate skills of pastoral care.

These resources are excellent in meeting the questions surrounding specific stages of death and dying, but my experience gleaned from many years of ministry is that the bereavement experience needs to be considered as a whole; you cannot separate the funeral service from the pastoral care given to the dying person and family members and friends before and after he dies. There are three key stages that form an essential entity: first, pastoral care for the dying person and his family; then the funeral, memorial, or celebration service; and finally, the post-service pastoral care. Together they make for a good ending.

You will see later that the pastoral element of compassion is key to the meditation or sermon, and that the person who is pastorally caring to the family is the one who is in the best position to officiate at the service.

Death, the Ever-Present Reality

There is no "Get out of Death Free" card. Each one of us will die, and as the years go by and our bodies age, the reality of death is something we increasingly come to terms with, or choose to ignore. Neither is there any immunity from death for our well-loved family members. Some have lived good and fulfilling lives and have died at a ripe old age feeling good about the work they have done and the relationships they have established. On the other hand, some have died well before their time, never having achieved any sense of direction or a satisfactory relationship during their brief human existence.

The way we face the reality of our own coming death and how we have faced the bereavement experience in our own family circle will make a significant difference to the way we care for families who turn to us in times of bereavement. It was 15 years after the death of my own father that I was forced, during a pastoral care course, to confront the fact that I had failed to adequately grieve his loss. I came to realize that this was a factor affecting the way in which I ministered to those who had suffered losses of their own. If you find that your own bereavement experience is a barrier to helping others, then it makes good sense to look for skilled help in order that your ministry is effective and relevant.

Difference between a Funeral, a Celebration of Life, and a Memorial

The terms "Funeral," "Memorial Service," and "Celebration of Life" are used interchangeably in common practice. They do, however, have different traditional meanings:

A funeral is a ceremony or service for celebrating, respecting, and remembering the life of a person who has died, with the body present at the ceremony.

A memorial is a ceremony or service for celebrating, respecting, and remembering the person who has died, without the physical body present. There may be cremated remains present during the ceremony or service.

With **a celebration of life** there may or may not be cremated remains of a loved one present, but the emphasis in the service or ceremony will be on a tribute to the person who has died.

In future years, I envision the further blurring of the three terms and that the term "funeral" will commonly be used whether the physical body is present or not.

CHAPTER 1

Rites of Passage in a Secular World

Love, like a carefully loaded ship,
crosses the gulf between the generations.
Therefore we do not neglect the ceremonies
of our passage, when we wed, when we die,
and when we are blessed with a child.

Antoine de Saint-Exupéry (1900–1944)

The following scenarios are familiar to many people in the Western world:

- A group of youngsters gather around a decorated cake; the candles have been lit, and the birthday boy or girl takes a big breath and blows out the candles.

- It is a wedding, and a speech by the best man has just ended. The guests stand and raise their glasses. "The bride and groom!" is the toast.

- A mother has recently given birth to her first child, Adam, and there is an informal family gathering. The father has bought an apple tree and dug a hole in the ground. As the family members watch, the mother plants the sapling, and younger members of the family enthusiastically fill in the hole. "This is for Adam and for all of us to enjoy," the mother says.

- A small company of family and friends gather around an open grave, and an urn containing the last earthly remains of one loved by them all is lowered into the grave. A worship leader says the ancient words "Into God's keeping we commit our sister here departed."

The birthday, wedding, birth, and funeral ceremonies of which these scenarios form a part are found in the life patterns of peoples all over the world. In rural India, a family group gathers around the body of a loved one who died earlier in the day. A priest and family members join in prayers to mark the end of his life. They will meet again following the cremation for a final rite of farewell.

The rituals are different, the religious content or lack of it varies, and the cultural, economic, and geographic circumstances of the participants may be poles apart. There will be, however, the same need to gather and to mark with words and actions the key moments in the life of members of the human race. The metaphor of "life as a journey" is a good one. As on a road trip you travel from one place to another—stopping for refreshment, to meet friends, and to sleep for the night—so in the journey of life there are significant stopping places along the way and a final destination.

For thousands of years, these rites of passage—the entry of a child into this world; attaining adulthood; marriage of two people for love or for the economic good of their families; and the death of a person—were marked first and foremost by religious rituals. Even those with little or no religious faith or without allegiance to a church or faith group would seek to be married in a "sacred" sanctuary and to have their child baptized in the gathering place of a faith community. They would also expect to have a religious service when they died.

Times have changed, and with the growth of secularism and with a loss of the fear, respect, and love of God (Holy One, Higher Power), the long-felt need for religious ceremonies to celebrate the rites of passage has declined. And so in the West the baby shower is more likely to be a family feature around the birth of a baby than baptism by a minister or priest; the marriage ceremony is more likely to be on a beach in the Dominican Republic than in the local church; and a celebration of life will often be a gathering at a sports or community centre rather than at a church.

The need to celebrate the rites of passage, however, is as important as ever, and the death of a person will be significantly and ceremoniously marked within the family and friendship circle even if it is not accompanied by religious rites as in former days. A recent visit to our small-town post office where all deaths are posted revealed five notices of deaths and five celebrations either designated or planned, but not a single religious service or celebration.

Non-Religious Services

The contemporary worship leader has to be ready with an answer for the person who asks, "Can you help me with a celebration of life that has no religious content?" or "My friend/loved one/family member specifically said that she didn't want a church service, but we want to remember her as family and friends together. What do you suggest?"

To abandon the religious funeral service with its hope of a blessed life after this one ends for a simple time of thanksgiving and leave-taking is nothing less than a radical change in the way human beings have regarded death for countless centuries. The worship leader is challenged by this situation. The expectations of those who call on him to help them through the bereavement experience may not match the worship leader's expectations or training. Worship leaders will expect to respond to the dying person and to the celebration or funeral service with a Christian approach, but may find that this will be all right "As long as you don't mention God or Jesus in all this" (to quote a family member who approached me to conduct a service).

One valid response is simply to affirm your roots in a specific faith tradition, e.g., "I am trained as a worship leader in the Christian church and am not comfortable with conducting secular services or celebrations. I will try to find you someone who is able to help."

If there is a person in the area who conducts non-religious celebrations, then you can make a referral to this secular celebrant. She will have the non-faith resources appropriate for an end-of-life celebration and the experience of celebrating without a specific faith perspective.

If you are new to a community, it is good to make enquiries with area clergy, local funeral homes, and at the central hospital to see if they have names and contact information for secular celebrants. Unfortunately, in many areas it will be difficult or expensive to find a secular celebrant, so this approach may not prove practical.

The request to preside at a secular celebration may come from a family member who is a long-time member of your faith community. "Other family members are not religious, but I know you and I trust you, and we don't want a 'stranger' presiding at this final ritual of our loved one. What can *you* do for us?"

The request may come from someone who has been a congregant at one of the services where you were the officiating minister and has felt that it was an inspiring or meaningful rite of passage, or the person asking for your help may be looking for someone/anyone who is willing to preside at a celebration in memory of their loved one.

These and other approaches for a secular celebration all need to be taken seriously. There is value in telling the family members that you may be willing to help them, and that you may *or may not* be able to create a suitable service or celebration, but that you need to check out what this means for them and for yourself before you decide. Some of the questions you pose directly or indirectly to the family may be these:

- What are the most important elements in the funeral or celebration of life for you?

- What are the most important elements in the funeral or celebration of life for close family members?

- What elements of the service—readings, hymns, theological concepts or words describing God—would you not want to form a part of the service? (Do you believe in an afterlife or heaven, for example?)

- Was your loved one a member of a faith community? What were his expectations for the service marking the end of his life? Has he left any verbal or written instructions about his funeral/celebration of life?

- At what location do you see this celebration taking place and why is this location significant?

- Would a time of celebration following a meal, at which family members or friends speak about their loved one, be an appropriate way to celebrate her life? (In this situation the need may be for an emcee rather than a celebrant.)

Some of the questions that you pose to yourself might be these:

- Are there service elements that the family want to discard that are essential to my own understanding of a funeral, memorial, or life celebration? If so, can I explain this in simple terms to the family members? For example, "It is essential for me to speak of the loss that people are feeling; I can't just talk of thanksgiving for happy times" or "For this to be a meaningful celebration for me as well as for you, I need to include at least one reading from the Christian scriptures. Shall we look over several of these together?"

- Are there words for God or theological terms that can be stated in simpler language? (e.g., "Resurrection" replaced by "life after death")

- Bearing in mind the faith community involvement (or lack of it) of the person who has died, what would be a faithful response in terms of the service content and location? How does this mesh with the needs of family members? For example, "Mom was a pillar of the United Church, but her sons who don't attend worship are more at home in the curling club bar and would like the celebration there. How can we work this out?"

- Is this a celebration of life that would be best carried out by family and friends informally speaking of their loved one after a good meal with a sensitive emcee in charge of the gathering?

- Is there a vital life theme that has a strong theological or biblical basis, but can be developed without making connection to its root in faith? For example, the person who has died may have been the dependable rock of the family circle. If it were a religious service, the connection might be made to the man who built his house on a rock in the parable of Jesus (Matthew 7:24), but where the celebration is secular the powerful theme of a "rock-solid foundation," with large rocks present in the celebration area and small rocks given to participants could be used to make the point.

This is by no means a comprehensive series of questions, but it will be good to have some at the back of your mind as you talk with the family. You might also ask family members to take a look at examples of secular celebrations you have used in the past. Alternatively, you might show family members elements of a secular service such as those in "Secular Celebrations" on page 178 or the non-religious celebrations in the "Meditation" on page 198 and get them to comment on the selections they like and the selections they do not like and why. Their responses as you review the liturgies together might be something like "This reading is useful," "I don't like that affirmation," or "I would like to modify this committal."

Through this process of choice, elimination, and modification, you will likely find the form of service that would be helpful for the particular family group you are working with and one that you are comfortably able to use. At the end of the day, if you are able to find a combination of words and readings (sacred and secular), objects and actions that meaningfully celebrate the life's end of a person in your local community, you will have served that community well and brought recognition to your faith community.

This does not mean that you have to abandon the Christian foundation to which you have been called. It may be helpful, for example, for the family to hear that the theme of loving kindness central to the Christian and Abrahamic (Jewish, Muslim, Christian) traditions will form an integral part of your celebration or service and will be an often unspoken but essential part of the pastoral care as you work with the bereaved family after the service is over.

It is also important to point out to family members that if you are making a statement that arises from your Christian tradition, you will declare it openly in the service. So, "From the viewpoint of the Christian tradition, the work that Louis did in promoting the cause of low-cost housing in our town would be seen as just and vital work."

However, it will be necessary to assure the family members that the contribution that the deceased person made to his social groups—Rotary Club, Lions Club, his colleagues at work, his friends who have the same hobby—and his family circle will also find a place in the celebration. It is also good to tell family members that the central values that governed their loved one's life, e.g., generosity, lifelong learning, will also be reflected in the service.

The family will be reassured if you make it clear that although you will be approaching the celebration through the essentially Christian lens of your faith community, you will not be using specifically Christian prayers, readings, or language. They also need to hear that you will not be going out of your way to convert anyone through the celebration or service that you will be creating.

The Importance of Language

It is all very well and good to discuss secular celebrations in general terms, but what does it mean in practice? A key factor is the language used.

We often use the sung grace "Johnny Appleseed" when our grandchildren are with us:

> Oh the Lord is good to me
> and so I thank the Lord
> for giving me the things I need,
> the sun and the rain and the apple seed,
> the Lord is good to me,
> Johnny Appleseed. Amen.

Imagine our surprise when Nathan, my grandson, said that they had sung the same song before snack time at playschool, "But," he claimed, "you have been singing the wrong words. They should be…"

> Oh the Earth is good to me
> and so I thank the Earth
> for giving me the things I need,
> the sun and the rain and the apple seed,
> the Earth is good to me,
> Johnny Appleseed. My friend.

The difference is to whom or to what we give our thanks. Is it "God," or "The Lord," or is it "Mother Earth," or simply "The Earth"? If we thank "The Lord," some would say that we are thanking Jesus who is "The Lord," but most would say that we are ascribing our thanks to God, whom we sometimes call "The Lord" and who is the creative source of all things—the Mighty Creator who cares for us all and has gracefully given us all we need without asking us for anything in return.

For people of faith, it is traditionally important to name the Name. It is important to give our thanks to God, the Holy One, or the Higher Power, for the life of a family member. For those without a formal faith, thanksgiving does not have to be directed to the Holy One. It is enough to come together with other friends and join in a common thanksgiving time for someone who was a significant person in their lives.

And so, if the person is a member of the Christian faith community, this would be appropriate:

Preface to the Service
We have come together to worship God,
and to give God thanks for (*name*),
whose life is over.
We have come to share our sense of loss
over a well-loved family member and friend.
His/her presence was there for us in times of testing,
and we are here for *his/her* loved ones
as they feel their loss.
Give us a good remembrance today,
and send us out encouraged with the hope of the life
that begins when this one ends.

Whereas, if the person had no Christian faith, the following preface, which does not name God or refer to a life to come, would be more appropriate:

Preface to the Service

Celebrant: We have come to this service to celebrate the life of (*name*) whose life has ended.

All: It is good to be here.

Celebrant: We have come to join with others who knew *him/her* and loved *him/her,* to share our memories, and to tell our stories.

All: It is good to be here.

Celebrant: We have come to tell of all we have lost in (*name*)'s passing, to put our grief into words, and to follow words with actions.

All: It is good to be here.

Celebrant: We have come as family and friends to remember the effect of (*name*)'s life on each of our lives.

All: It is good to be here.

As worship leader you will not seek to impose a Christian or other faith on anyone at this difficult and vulnerable time. You will prefer to meet the grieving family where they are and with the belief system that they rely on for their life's journey. Though you will personally see God as the focus of thanksgiving, you will be glad to respond positively to others who are telling stories, finding readings, and remembering the person who has died without mentioning the Holy One or praying in the name of Jesus the Christ.

I have included a section for secular celebrations at the conclusion of chapter 17 and non-religious meditations in chapter 18.

The Grey Areas

Don't be surprised if the self-declared, non-religious folk talking to you about the service mention that they would like Psalm 23, or verses from Ecclesiastes chapter 3, or the Gospel of John chapter 14 to be included in the order of service. And don't be surprised if they request The Lord's Prayer. These religious staples go beyond their words and content and for some families are part of what makes a "real" funeral. Indeed, the suggestion that these items be included may be the beginning of a fruitful conversation about the faith component of the service.

The same goes for music. The request for "Amazing Grace" does not mean that there is a group of "wretches" in the family longing to be saved. The John Newton favourite is well-known from popular music, and its stirring, haunting melody touches the emotions and brings back memories of past services in ways for which words would fall short. And be ready for requests for modern music that has a strong faith component, e.g., "We Rise Again" by The Rankin Family.

But how will your faith community leadership feel about secular celebrations? A key factor here is your willingness as a worship leader to be open. If you fail to explain your theological position to those you serve as minister or pastor, then there may be unfavourable comparisons made between the way you conduct secular services and the way you conduct religious ones. If, on the other hand, you bring examples of the secular celebrations to the board/council, give an explanation of the implicit theology, and invite questions, it is unlikely that there will be any problems. It would be beneficial to invite one or more of the board or council members or a member of the worship committee to attend one of the secular celebrations and report back to the leadership group about how it met the family's needs and how it differed or was the same as the conventional funeral or celebration service.

One of the side benefits of this process will be to open up your faith community to readings that, though outside of the canon of Hebrew or Christian scriptures, are inspirational and meet needs of the mourning group in a way that the traditional readings cannot do.

In the next chapter, I examine the theological underpinning of the bereavement event: the pastoral care of the dying person, the funeral or celebration service, and the post-funeral pastoral care. This I have characterized by loving kindness and believe that if this loving kindness is integral to the pastoral care and the funeral service or celebration, it will be possible for both the Christian and the secular approaches to be used with integrity by the worship leader.

Chapter 2

Biblical Roots

We start our quest for biblical roots with the nature of the Holy One, who is at the centre of the experience. The primary image of God that gradually but unevenly emerges in the Hebrew scriptures is of a loving, compassionate, and just God.

> **Psalm 23**
> The Lord is my shepherd, I shall not want.
> [God] makes me lie down in green pastures;
> [God] leads me beside still waters;
> [God] restores my soul.
> [God] leads me in right paths
> for [God's] name's sake.
> Even though I walk through the darkest valley,
> I fear no evil;
> for you are with me;
> your rod and your staff—
> they comfort me.
> You prepare a table before me
> in the presence of my enemies;
> you anoint my head with oil;
> my cup overflows.
> Surely goodness and mercy shall follow me
> all the days of my life,
> and I shall dwell in the house of the Lord
> my whole life long.

The psalm most frequently used at funerals and celebrations of life, in both Christian and Jewish faith communities, is Psalm 23. The writer of the psalm portrays God as the Loving Host at whose table the writer is safe and cared for with compassion. This may originate from a time when the psalmist felt most deeply and personally the presence of God during a service of worship.

The primary metaphor used in the psalm is of God as the Good Shepherd, and though the psalm is written in the first person, the Shepherd is herding a flock of sheep, so there is the sense of a community relationship with the Holy One. God is to be trusted, the psalmist writes, and the diligent followers of God will go the faithful way and be refreshed in spirit. More than that, in the toughest times, in "the darkest valley," the compassionate company of the Holy One will be a strength and a comfort in the deepest spiritual sense. And the final thought is one of hope for a fulfilling and faithful life.

The way of the Loving Host, then, is compassionate action, and the strong hope is of a good life with the Holy One at the centre of it. As you go about your pastoral care with the dying person and her family, as you prepare and write the service, and as you care for the family after the service is over, it is this grace-full compassion that you will bring to your work.

Hosea 2:19–23

[Israel,] I will make you for my wife forever; I will take you for my wife in righteousness and in justice, in steadfast love, and in mercy. I will take you for my wife in faithfulness; and you shall know the Lord. On that day I will answer, says the Lord, I will answer the heavens and they shall answer the earth: and the earth shall answer the grain, the wine, and the oil, and they shall answer Jezreel; and I will sow him for myself in the land. And I will have pity on Loruhamah, and I will say to Loammi, "You are my people"; and he shall say, "You are my God."

The prophets are not usually thought of as leaders and conscience keepers who emphasize the love of God. Justice, yes, but love, no. It is something of a surprise, then, when after some hard verses about the relationship of God to Israel, the prophet Hosea uses the analogy of loving wedding partners to make clear how it will be between God and God's people. The verses read like a series of wedding vows and give substance to the love that God affirms. The prophet says that God's love is permanent, just, loyal and true, compassionate, and faithful and is a personal relationship. It is a love that is seldom returned by the people of Israel, but includes within it the ideas of forgiveness and mercy. There is nothing sweet or sentimental about this loving kindness. Like authentic love in a human marriage, it endures the strongest challenges and is there to encourage in the most difficult times.

It is interesting to note that in the Jewish tradition, the preparation of the dead for burial is sometimes referred to as *Hesed shel emet,* which translates as "true loving kindness." This is so because there is no way in which the dead are able to repay the persons who perform this service. In the Christian tradition, we would also see this as a love overflowing with grace, and it can work itself out in some practical ways. In one pastoral charge, I remember a traditional, non-domestic husband being in a major crisis when his wife died suddenly. It was a compassionate neighbour and church member who came to his rescue with some elementary cooking, washing, and ironing lessons.

And then there are the many kind friends who bring casseroles to families when a loved one has died. Sometimes the appetizing food says more than an eloquent letter of condolence. These practical actions are in tune with the compassionate attitude of the writer of Psalm 23, for the profound love of God, God's loving kindness, is at the heart of all you do when you work with a dying person and with her family.

It is not just in the Hebrew scriptures common to the Jewish faith and Christianity that the sense of a fully loving God is shown, but also in the Muslim faith. Each section of the Qur'an and all followers of Islam starting a project, endeavour, or journey begin with the words *Bismillah Rahmaneh Rahim,* which mean "In the name of Allah, the Compassionate, the Merciful...." All life to a Muslim begins and ends with Allah. Allah, God, is the Beloved; humankind is the lover; and the process is love.

Which brings us to God's anointed one, Jesus. Jesus had his own way of talking about the loving kindness of God. One of the stories he tells is about a son who whines until he gets his inheritance in advance, and then goes off and wastes it on the high life (Luke 15:11–32). The cash is soon gone; he needs a bailout; and his good-time friends are not there for him. So he goes back to his dad ready to become one of his hourly paid workers. He expects to be shunned and reviled by his whole family, and his brother treats him that way, but his father welcomes him home with a huge hug, a new outfit, and a party. That's what God's love is like; that's loving kindness for you.

There are several instances where Jesus was called in to help those who were dead or dying, like the widow's son at Nairn. He showed compassion to those who had lost a life's partner or family member, in this case a beloved son.

Luke 7:11–17

Soon afterwards he went to a town called Nain, and his disciples and a large crowd went with him. As he approached the gate of the town, a man who had died was being carried out. He was his mother's only son, and she was a widow; and with her was a large crowd from the town. When the Lord saw her, he had compassion for her and said to her, "Do not weep." Then he came forward and touched the bier, and the bearers stood still. And he said, "Young man, I say to you, rise!" The dead man sat up and began to speak, and Jesus gave him to his mother. Fear seized all of them; and they glorified God, saying, "A great prophet has risen among us!" and "God has looked favorably on his people!" This word about him spread throughout Judea and all the surrounding country.

The bringing back to life of those who are dead, as in the account of the raising of Jairus' daughter in Mark's gospel, are present in the gospels along with other miracle stories, but the relevant question is not "Did the raising from death actually happen?" though this is a fair question. The relevant question is "What sort of person would do this?" And the answer is there within the account; it is the compassion of Jesus that marks him out and calls for a response from those of us who are concerned for dying and grieving persons today.

This is not complicated theology; the gospel accounts speak for themselves of Jesus, God's anointed, living out this loving kindness to a remarkable degree. But it is not enough to restrict loving kindness to the Hebrew scriptures and the Christian gospels, for these wonderful qualities are apparent in the saints of the ages, those who have taken their inspiration from the compassionate Christ and work in his spirit.

I suspect that many, if not all of you, will have been on the receiving end of the extreme kindness of someone whose actions never made the newspapers or TV. I think of a statistics lecturer who in my studying days didn't just concern himself with the statistics problems of his students, but would sit down beside each class member and ask the question "What would you *really* like to be doing with your life?" The response to his question was dramatic as students felt freed to train for fulfilling work they had never considered themselves good enough to do, and courses at colleges and universities that they had never known how to apply for.

On the world stage, I think of individuals like Jean Vanier, the founder of the L'Arche communities for those who are mentally challenged. Vanier had been distressed by the scandalous conditions he had encountered in institutions. His now worldwide movement began when Vanier invited two young men with developmental disabilities, Raphael Simi and Philippe Seux, to live with him in a small village in the French village of Trosly-Breuil. His loving kindness shone out in the simple response of creating a warm and accepting home environment.

On a political level, one pastor who made a world of difference, but is seldom credited with the change he brought, is Christian Fuhrer, the pastor of St. Nikolai church in Leipzig, who with a series of prayer meetings for peace hastened the fall of the Berlin wall and the end of Soviet repression in East Germany. His loving kindness was lived out when he and a group of church members took their candles over to the tanks and troops that confronted them and prayed for them and with them.

We keep this concept of the ultimate loving kindness of the Holy One in mind as we consider the resurrection. Of all the ultimate questions, the most often thought about and the least expressed is "What happens to me when I die?" And along with this question comes a raft of others: "Will I see my loved ones (and my not so loved ones) in the afterlife?" "Will I be judged by God for all the bad things I did in my human life?" "Is there a hell where I go for all eternity if I am found guilty?" "Will I have a renewed human body, and if it is a not a human body but a spiritual body, what will it feel and look like?"

For the Christian, however, it is the resurrection of Jesus that is the pointer toward the ultimate reality of a life graced by the compassionate God that begins after this one ends. The four gospels speak in some very different ways of this life.

Mark 16:1–7

When the sabbath was over, Mary Magdalene, and Mary the mother of James, and Salome bought spices, so that they might go and anoint him. And very early on the first day of the week, when the sun had risen, they went to the tomb. They had been saying to one another, "Who will roll away the stone for us from the entrance to the tomb?" When they looked up, they saw that the stone, which was very large, had already been rolled back. As they entered the tomb, they saw a young man, dressed in a white robe, sitting on the right side; and they were alarmed. But he said to them, "Do not be alarmed; you are looking for Jesus of Nazareth, who was crucified. He has been raised; he is not here. Look, there is the place they laid him. But go, tell his disciples and Peter that he is going ahead of you to Galilee; there you will see him, just as he told you."

In this, the earliest account of the rising of Jesus from the dead, the reader is called on to take note that the tomb is empty and there is the promise that if the disciples go to Galilee, they will encounter the risen Christ. The mention of Galilee is no accident as this is the place that the mission of Jesus began. The account in the Gospel of Luke expands on the Mark account.

Luke 24:36–47

While they were talking about this, Jesus himself stood among them and said to them, "Peace be with you." They were startled and terrified, and thought that they were seeing a ghost. He said to them, "Why are you frightened, and why do doubts arise in your hearts? Look at my hands and my feet; see that it is I myself. Touch me and see; for a ghost does not have flesh and bones as you see that I have." And when he had said this, he showed them his hands and his feet. While in their joy they were disbelieving and still wondering, he said to them, "Have you anything here to eat?" They gave him a piece of broiled fish, and he took it and ate in their presence. Then he said to them, "These are my words that I spoke to you while I was still with you—that everything written about me in the law of Moses, the prophets, and the psalms must be fulfilled." Then he opened their minds to understand the scriptures, and he said to them, "Thus it is written, that the Messiah is to suffer and to rise from the dead on the third day, and that repentance and forgiveness of sins is to be proclaimed in his name to all nations, beginning from Jerusalem."

In this account, Jesus appears in human bodily form, eating and drinking with the disciples. Scholars tell us that we have in these accounts both history, which records what Jesus said and did, and metaphor, which is a reflection by the faith community of the time on the events following the death of Jesus. They remind us that truth can emerge from both history and metaphor and point toward the ultimate loving kindness of God that is worked out for us in a life that begins as this one ends.

It is this ultimate hope that you will make clear to those who are dying and those who have been bereaved, but it is also an ongoing challenge to live out the resurrection quality of life in the now. As Harry Williams puts it, "Resurrection as our final and ultimate future can be known only by those who perceive resurrection with us now encompassing all we are and do. For only then will it be recognized as a country we have already entered and in whose light and warmth we have already lived."[1]

So we see from the Christian scriptures that there has been no end to God's loving kindness for Jesus, nor will there be for us or for those we meet in the shadow of death. The words of the apostle Paul in Romans, chapter 8, which I often use in end-of-life services, echo these thoughts.

> ### Romans 8:18, 31, 35, 37–39
> The sufferings of this present time are not worth comparing with the glory about to be revealed to us....If God is for us, who is against us?...Who will separate us from the love of Christ? Will hardship, or distress, or persecution, or famine, or nakedness, or peril, or sword? ...No, in all these things we are more than conquerors through him who loved us. For I am convinced that neither death, nor life, nor angels, nor rulers, nor things present, nor things to come, nor powers, nor height, nor depth, nor anything else in all creation, will be able to separate us from the love of God in Christ Jesus our Lord.

Or as the last lines of A New Creed of The United Church of Canada succinctly phrase it, "In life, in death, in life beyond death....We are not alone."

---

[1] © Harry Williams, 1972, *True Resurrection* and Continuum, by permission of Bloomsbury Publishing Plc.

Chapter 3

Pastoral Care for the Dying Person

The person who spiritually cares for the dying person and her family will be the appropriate one to conduct the funeral service for her, irrespective of their position in the hierarchy of the religious group, and will offer pastoral care following the service.

Where the dying person does not profess a Christian or other faith, there may be a person who gives compassionate and friendly support to the dying person who is willing to be the one to lead the celebration of her life. These secular celebrants will need to have had training and practice, and feel confident in their own ability to lead the common act of thanksgiving and grieving of the group, but with these qualities will do an excellent job.

What follows in this section are some practical suggestions about how to care in a pastoral way for the individual whose life is coming to an end. But first, a consideration about whether the person is dying.

Is the Person Dying? How Long Will It Take?

The judgment call on whether or not the person is dying is a subjective one. I recall being present in an intensive care unit where a patient was hooked up to several life support devices, including one that assisted him to breathe. The family members were called in to say their last goodbyes, and as chaplain I was called on to pray for the person and to give him God's blessing for his final journey on earth. This I did and went on my way to await the buzz of my pager, which would summon me to the ward after he had passed away. It never came. The patient, a man in his seventies, resumed breathing on his own and was discharged the next day to the joy of his loving family members. Skilled doctors, nurses, and palliative care workers are often right when they say that the patient is dying, but not always; the patient is often the best judge, and it is good to listen and take note when the dying person says that his time has come.

The same problem is apparent when one asks the question "How long has he got? How long will she live?" It is difficult for those who have medical and palliative care skills to tell, and though some are experienced and often close in their estimate of days or weeks, others may be way off. Life goes on for the family of those who are dying, and it is extraordinarily helpful to have some idea of when their loved one will pass away. Employers are asking family members to tell them when they will be back to work; friends are pressuring them to let them know when they can go on that promised holiday together; there is daycare to organize; and a need to catch up on neglected work around the house and yard. All the loved one of the dying person is able to say is "The doctor says it will be around…days or weeks; she also says it may be a whole lot longer (or shorter). I'm sorry, but I'm simply unable to make firm plans to be with you in the near future."

If the dying person does not die as soon as is anticipated, which often happens, then the caregiver may encourage the family to cut back their intense presence at the bedside and be good to themselves. Part of the encouragement the caregiver gives should include the options of taking sufficient time to have nutritious meals, going home to rest and sleep at night, and taking time for a shower or relaxing bath in the morning. If nursing staff have already mentioned this to the supporting family and friends, then the role of the caregiver should be to reinforce the suggestions of the staff and draw attention to members of the family who are looking very tired or exhausted.

However, at the end of the day, the loved one's family members will make their own decisions about time spent at the bedside, and you will continue to support them in their presence, whether it is good for their physical and mental health or not. It is good to continue prayers for strength of the family and prayers for those who cannot be at the bedside of the dying person because of ill health or work commitments.

It is also useful to stress the reality that some family members will miss the time of death and that if they do, they will not have cared less for their loved one in his eyes or in God's eyes.

What Is Going on with the Dying Person and Their Family?

For many of those who are dying, the primary feeling is that of fear, though this is often not expressed. "There is the fear of change, fear of losing our separate self and all we seem to possess, and fear of the unchartered territory we're entering."[1] There is the loss of family, friendships, and participation in the communities that have sustained her over the years. The dying person no longer has the roles she had in her active life: membership in a health club, one of a group that met regularly at the coffee shop, cherished grandmother to youngsters with whom she read bedtime stories and treated to ice cream against the express direction of their mother.

And there is the fear of moving into the uncharted territory that follows the end of this life, fear of a future that she cannot possibly anticipate. The person who is pastorally with the dying person need not deal specifically with these fears unless asked, but needs to be aware of them. She needs also to be aware of the fears and other feelings that are present in the family members who are around the one who is dying. There may be the permanent loss of a supportive and encouraging loved one, and the need to re-balance the family or friendship circle. On the other hand, there may be the relief that suffering and emotional struggle that has drained the family is coming to an end, and that forgiveness has been given or received.

Every death situation is different, and every dying person is unique; the challenge for the pastoral caregiver (worship leader in a pastoral role) is to evaluate the emotional and practical needs of both the dying person and her family and respond with compassion.

A Positive Presence with the Dying Person

There are some general guidelines to follow when you are with those who are dying, and a key one is to not let the fact of the upcoming death of the person dominate your approach to the conversation. If you have been asked to see this dying person and have never been a part of his life before, there will be a getting-to-know-you period, and during this time, you will explore his family and friendship circle; his interests; the books he enjoys; the movies he has been to see; whether he is a gardener or a stamp collector. This is not the time to resort to platitudes such as, "Well, you have had a good long life anyway...your family and friends will never forget you...be strong...I know you can be." Focus on giving the person the dignity he deserves, and this means encouraging him to live his life as fully as he can in spite of his limited lifespan. So you don't talk about how he was a skilled carpenter, but how he *is* a great carpenter; not how he had such fun with his grandchildren, but how he *is* having so much fun making the Lego models with them even though he is in hospice.

Life did not change with the diagnosis; life goes on, with the only difference being that there is a finite, approaching, and certain end point. More than this, the enforced time in bed or the time with reduced mobility gives the dying person the opportunity to do a whole lot of reminiscing, and you can be the one to encourage him to look back over his life and get him to talk over those times and those situations that were significant and meaningful. It is likely that during the review he will talk about those times when he struggled and overcame some tough situations.

A significant question might be, "How did you deal with a challenge such as this?" It could be a challenge in a work situation, or in a relationship, or with a fraternal group, and this may be a way of preparing the person for dealing with the challenging struggle that lies ahead as he dies. There will be weakness and discomfort as he deals with medical treatment, but you can encourage him to live life to the fullest extent that his pain and limited mobility allow.

The one difference would be the way in which you concern yourself with her life of faith. You will want to know if faith for her is a living, vital experience or something that was left behind in Sunday school many years ago. If the dying person is a fellow church member or an individual who is a member of the faith community where you minister, then the "getting to know you" will already be done, and you will bring to the bedside many weeks or months of relating to her. She is not essentially different because she has received the diagnosis that her life will end in a specific period of time, so begin by picking up from where you left off the last time you met. Chat about family members; talk about knitting or hockey or cooking; or discuss whatever interest it is that you share. Ask about the food and how she is finding the hospital experience; relate to your family member, church member, or friend in the same way that you always did. The fact that she is dying hasn't changed her as a person, just given her the certainty of an experience that awaits each one of us, the fact that we all will die.

Talk, but more importantly, listen to what is on his mind. Give the person the time to say what he wants to say; it is often helpful to directly refrain from talking, leaving a clear pool of silence, so that he is able to talk into it— whatever is on his mind. And who knows what that might be? It could be his physical discomfort, difficulty with breathing, or the fact that he is lying on the same spot in the bed and feels sore. It could be that he is worried about a family member who will be left without support when he dies. It could be he is worried about his cat and how she is faring without him. The agenda is that of the dying person and not yours. Respect their concerns above all else.

What the dying person will appreciate as she talks is your undivided attention. It is very easy to let your attention stray and consider the get well cards on the notice board, the petunias in the flower vase, or (especially) your watch. What the person will value above all else is your careful listening to what she shares with you, so give clear signs that you are listening. A forward, positive posture will do this as will nods of the head. Deliberate eye contact will signal your full attention as will verbal indications that you have heard what they have been telling you, e.g., gentle "er" and "um" sounds on one level and some unobtrusive rephrasing of what you have heard on another. For example, after a long description of treatment that has been physically gruelling or emotionally challenging, a remark like "Well, Edith, you certainly sound as if you have been having a dreadful time" will dovetail in with the feeling component of Edith's experience and will be appreciated.

Be aware of physical clues shown by someone who is unable or unwilling to put something into words. Continual movement of arms and legs may indicate considerable discomfort related to the physical condition of the person or it may indicate that they are anxious to contact the nurse and get her to bring a bedpan. Above all, be aware of the person's need to rest or sleep. Watch the person's eyes; if they close, stop talking for a while.

If you are visiting with a friend or fellow family member, be sure that you do not stray from the agenda of the person you are visiting to your own agenda unless she asks you to do so. While I was bedridden for two months in hospital following a bike accident, I had a couple of church members come to visit me. They talked to each other across the bed for 45 minutes about their own ailments, enjoying the visit immensely, but treating me as a bystander. I spent the last half hour hoping that they would go away. And this reminds me that a short visit is usually better than a long one, and it is good to check in to see how the person is feeling about you being there. Some comment like "You are probably feeling like some rest now" will facilitate a move toward a prayer and the end of the visit. If the person is anxious that you stay, she will probably not be shy in saying, "I wish you would stay a little longer" or ask you a question about a family member or mutual friend to prevent you leaving.

A Conversation Where There Is Little Response
If the dying person is so sick that he is not able to keep a conversation going or if he speaks weakly or hesitatingly, don't assume that there is no point in continuing the visit. Hearing is the last sense to go when a life is coming to an end, so if necessary, carry on a one-sided conversation, and don't be afraid to hold his hand. You are there because you care for that person, and your physical presence is the most important thing. So stay around, even if you get little response. Don't be afraid to speak of your love or friendship, for the words that arise from deep relationship and caring will be words the dying person longs to hear.

If there is little response to the questions you put to the dying person and you are in the room with other family members, there is a tendency to talk about them in the third person as if they are not present at all. "Mal is sure looking pale today. Did you talk to the nurse? I think he is going down." Mal may not be communicating much; Mal may not be able to speak at all; but he may be taking in every word. It is a good and sensitive practice to treat the patient, whether he is able to speak or not, as if he can hear the conversation and include him even when there is no verbal response. If there is a need for a family discussion, make sure that this is done outside the room, preferably in a lounge or conference area.

Talking to the Dying Person about the Service
It is a huge gift to the clergy person/worship leader if the dying person is willing to share her thoughts about the rite that will mark the end of her life. Support the dying person if she raises the subject and explain how it will help, not just you, but the whole family. My experience is that you seize the moment to talk about the funeral, memorial, or celebration, even if it is most inconvenient for yourself. The opportunity may not come again.

If at all possible, have the person include one or more family members in the conversation and explain to the person who is dying that the family members left behind are the ones who will be reminded of her and will be feeling their loss deeply. Briefly range over the whole area of the service:

- Where would the person like the service/celebration to be held?

- Whom would she prefer to give talks (eulogies)—family members, friends, or persons from her workplace? And give the caution that more speakers and longer eulogies would not be better; quite the reverse.

- Whom would she choose to be involved as readers of scripture or other readings?

- What items symbolizing her life or photographs would she like on the communion table, or would she like a video of her life to be made? If so, whom would she like to create it, and what place might it have in the service/celebration?

- What music would she like played, including popular and inspirational songs, and what hymns would she like sung? (If you feel that one or more of the choices would be difficult for the congregation to manage, be up front about it. It will save you from a tough solo on the day. An alternative is to contact a competent soloist known to the dying person or her faith community.)

- What scripture readings or secular readings are especially meaningful for the dying person, and does she have any thoughts about the theme of the meditation? One typical approach is "You were always so involved with young persons in your life—teaching school, involved in the activities of your own children, and helping with the summer church camp. You were one of the best teachers and guides of young people that I know. I wonder if I could use 'Jesus the Teacher' as a theme for your service?"

- The subject of the interment service could usefully be raised. What will be the service content and where will it be held? This is an opportunity to encourage the person to tell the family that she wants to have a service at the graveside and that the service should be on the same day as the funeral/celebration.

It is also a time to remind the dying person that it is the family who will be arranging and be present at the service and that their needs will be sought out and heeded in the arrangements.

Prayer with the Dying Person

If the person is a person of faith and you are the representative of the faith community, questions about prayer arise: "Should I pray?" "When do I pray?" and "If I pray, what do I say?" The answer to the first question is a simple one: Ask! If the person is not comfortable with prayer on this occasion, ask at another time, and if it is clear that prayer is not going to be a positive experience, a gentle "God bless!" or "Peace be with you!" as you go out of the room is enough. Some people will expect your visit to begin and end with prayer. Most will want you to pray at the end of the time spent together.

Where persons have no formal faith, you can still ask if they would like a prayer and you will be surprised how many will say, "Yes, please!" But it is important not to impose prayer on those who don't want prayer. References to God and the Holy One should be used with caution.

However, if no prayer is offered at the end of a visit, it will be helpful to summarize the key points in the way you would do in a prayer but with no ascription to God, i.e., no thanks to the Higher Power and no blessing or offering of peace.

Having made sure that prayer is in order, ask the person if she would like to pray with you. The person may have issues to bring before God that you have no idea existed, and the invitation to pray gives her an opportunity to put any concern that has been troubling her, any anxiety about a family member or friend, into words before someone who will not share it with another living soul.

I remember wondering whether to visit Jack, who came to church at Christmas and Easter only and was seriously ill in the local hospital. There was no indication that he was dying, so I struggled with the need to make the visit: it was out of my way; it would mean that I would be home late for dinner. I rationalized I could easily leave it until next week. The problem was the nagging conviction that I must go, and so I made the diversion. After a good conversation, I asked Jack if he would like to join me in prayer, and he was keen to do so. It turned out that he had a confession to make, a need to get off his chest a happening from years back that still haunted him. I listened to his words, assured him of God's pardon, and was aware of the sense of peace that permeated that place. I was soon on my way home. Jack died that evening.

The prayer at the end of a visit should be in preparation throughout the visit. If there are worries about family members, friends, or a pet, these should find a place in the prayer. If there are anxieties about treatment or thanks for the attention of a doctor or particular nurses, then they should have a place in the prayer. If there is regret for actions in the past or fear for what comes after death, then this should also find a place in the prayer.

At the end of the prayer, there should be an affirmation of the love of God for the individual and the assurance that in time or beyond time God's love is with him and will never leave him.

Sometimes, it is difficult to keep track of all the people and situations to be included in the prayer. My experience is simply to do your best and be ready for the moment in the car coming home when you realize that the person's daughter wasn't Brenda but Bertha or that you forgot to pray for Dr. Verana who had been particularly kind. It is not crucial to remember everyone, and if the dying person says, "We should have prayed for Grandma Hoskins," just respond, "You are right. Well, let's pray for her now... Caring Creator, be with Grandma and give her strength for this difficult time. Amen."

A prayer might be offered like this:

> Loving God,
> we thank you for the time we have shared together.
> It has been good to be here.
> We thank you for those who are strength to *Eva,*
> her well-loved husband, *Paul,*
> and her children, *Lisa and Jason.*
> We thank you for those who have looked after *Eva.*
> Especially we remember *Dr. Ranic* and night nurse *Julie,*
> who talked with *Eva* when she was afraid and in pain.
> Holy One, be a companion with *Eva* in the struggle that
> is hers now and in the journey beyond this life that lies
> ahead.
> We pray in the name of Jesus, for whom dying was a
> faithful but tough experience. Amen.

Or when other family members are present:

> Let's join hands.
> Holy One, you are with us all the time,
> and in these times of sickness and frustration
> you are with us, a loving and sustaining presence.
> When *Richard* goes for tests and treatment, you go with
> him, and your limitless compassion is with Sally
> (*Richard's wife*) when she feels lonely and anxious.
> Be with those family members (*names*) who are troubled
> because they cannot be here today, and with those friends
> (*names*) who long to see *Richard* but cannot do so because
> of work or family commitments.
> In all the uncertainty *Richard* feels at this time, O God,
> be the solid ground beneath his feet, and may he know
> your peace, the peace that lasts forever. Amen.

It is sometimes helpful to share in the Lord's Prayer. It isn't the words that are important, but the fact that it is a shared prayer and the "mantra" that links the person to the rest of the faith community.

Readings, Sacred and Secular

There will be times when it is appropriate to read some passages from the sacred writings of the faith group to which the person belongs. Again, it is both sensitive and appropriate to ask the person whether she wants you to read and whether she has a favourite passage. The place for the reading is usually before prayer is offered, and the passage should be chosen by the dying person or have relevance to the spiritual or practical needs in that situation.

Psalm 23 is a reading frequently requested and with good reason as it is well-known and speaks directly of God's sustaining presence with those who are going through "the darkest valley." I remember being with a man who was dying and in great pain. "Would you like me to read anything from the Bible?" I asked. "I would like you to sing Psalm 23 with me," he replied. So I held his hand, and we sang Psalm 23, not very tunefully, but he told me he felt so much better at the end of it. Whether the three other patients in the room felt better I rather doubt! With older persons it may be more helpful to read this psalm of comfort from the King James version that they would have been taught as children.

There are several types of readings that may be helpful. There are readings that speak of a hope of life after death and a community of the saints, readings that speak of God's presence when the dying person feels most alone, and readings that are especially relevant to women or to children. Some of the scripture passages that I have had requested or have read are:

> In the darkest valley God is with you (Psalm 23)
> Out of the depths (Psalm 130)
> God the eternal presence (Psalm 139)
> I lift up my eyes to the hills (Psalm 121)
> God will wipe away the tears (Isaiah 25:6*a*, 7–9)
> Come to me, all of you who are weary (Matthew 11:25–30)
> Jesus blesses the little children (Mark 10:13–16)
> I go to prepare a place for you (John 14:1–9)
> God's loving presence (Romans 8:31*b*–39)
> The spiritual body (1 Corinthians 15:20–22, 51–58)
> Eternal glory beyond all measure (2 Corinthians 4:13–18)
> A new birth into a living hope (1 Peter 1:3–9)
> A new heaven and a new earth (Revelation 21:1–7)

On the secular reading side, the readings in appendix 2, page 267, provide inspirational material that may be appropriate.

You may want to check out whether the dying person would like something read out of the newspaper or a passage from a favourite book. If the person is a sports fan, then a report of the previous evening's football or hockey game might go down very well. Also, talking books with audio buds or headphones are a wonderful way of passing the night hours and require little assistance to set up and keep going. If the person has an iPod or similar device, there may be music or text that he would like to tune in to.

The Sacrament of Holy Communion (Eucharist)

During the two months I was in hospital following my cycling accident, I was visited by clergy of my own and several other denominations, and for the most part they were empathetic, sensitive, and friendly. It was four weeks into my hospital stay when a lay trainee chaplain asked the question "Have you received the sacrament of Holy Communion?" and I realized that this sacrament was something I had been missing. For many denominations it is only ordained clergy who are permitted to celebrate the eucharist, so I was hesitant and asked, "Can you celebrate with me?" "Sure," she replied, and as we prayed and as I received bread and grape juice, I felt the challenge and the joy and the peace that come from this common act of the Christian church.

What different people receive as the eucharist varies enormously, but the sacrament is especially meaningful for those who are going through the valley of the shadow of death. For the dying person, taking the bread and wine is a way of being one with the faith community of which she is a part, but cannot physically join at the table. And more than this, it is a way of sensing that she is a part of that community of saints present and past who have unity in Jesus Christ. The dying person may remember parents or grandparents with whom she shared Holy Communion in time past and sense that before long she will once again know their presence.

There is usually space in the service to come humbly before God and confess those things that are on the communicant's mind, believe that God hears what she says in the silence of her own heart, and receive an assurance of total forgiveness. This may be a significant time for the dying person (and for family members if they are with them). The dying communicant will have an opportunity to bring to God the deepest feelings that she has and the fears that are hers about the fact of death that lies just ahead. Again, she can do this believing that God hears her prayer and will give her strength for the days of dying and the time of death itself.

Both the communicant and the person celebrating will bring before God the family members who are supporting this person and the friends who have shown their care. There will be much gratitude here and hope that those who are giving help will receive the spiritual and physical help they need.

Participating in the eucharist will hopefully bring peace to the dying person, peace that passes all human understanding. This is the bridge time when human life is ending and another life is beginning, and in the experience of communion, the merging of humanity and new life in the spirit becomes a reality.

So, if you are a worship leader and are trained and ready to offer the eucharist, then this is something to consider for each dying person. As always, the key question to be asked is "Will celebrating the eucharist (or Holy Communion) be helpful to you?" If you are not prepared to do this, or if your denomination restricts the celebration of this sacrament to those who are ordained or commissioned, then you should ask the person if she would like to receive the bread and grape juice (or wine) and then arrange for a suitable ministry person from the denomination to come round and be the celebrant.

Remember to check that taking the bread and wine will be in accord with her treatment and nutrition plan. If the dying person is not able to ingest the elements, they may be touched gently to her lips. It will be good if the spouse or other family members were asked to join in the eucharistic celebration and, as long as this is fine with the dying person, then the invitation should be extended.

In some traditions, such as in those of the Roman Catholic Church, elements are set aside by the priest at the mass for serving to the dying person at home or in the hospital by a deacon, chaplain, or other authorized church celebrant. In this situation, the reserved elements should be used.

I cannot stress too strongly that celebration of the eucharist can open spiritual doors that is not possible any other way. It can be the place where "heaven" and earth momentarily meet. Most dying persons of faith will welcome the opportunity to celebrate. One word of caution: do not delay the invitation too long as it is better for the dying person to have a reasonable understanding of what is happening.

Permission to Die

Sometimes the person who is dying may hold out against all the odds, waiting for a family member significant to him to arrive before taking his last breath; and sometimes he is waiting for permission from family members to die. Or the dying person may be hanging on, worried about how the family members will be when he passes away, worried about how they will be able to manage without him. He is ready, his body is ready for the peace that comes with death, but he needs a word from a significant family member.

The more sensitive family members may be aware of this, but as pastoral caregiver you may also be the one to alert them to the need to say, "It's okay to go now. We are going to miss you so much, but we are ready for God's peace to enfold you. Just let go." As pastoral caregiver, you will be ready to reinforce this in the prayers you offer.

A Person of Little or No Faith

There will be times where the pastoral caregiver may be called on to help a dying person of little or no faith background, but one or more of their family members will have a connection with you, the pastoral caregiver. It could be a spouse of a good friend of a church member or it might be someone who was married in the church, or has a vague or perceived connection. Several times I have been asked to visit a dying person or to conduct a funeral where the request has come from someone who has told me, "My grandmother/father was married in your church." And again, the request may come out of the blue from a family member who knows his loved one is dying, will be looking for someone (anyone) to lead a funeral service, and wants to get to know the celebrant/worship leader who will be doing it.

Many of the approaches and attitudes in the above sections are common to those with no faith or with some Christian or other faith, and a compassionate worship leader will be aware of the need for a positive and affirming attitude, the need to encourage open expression of fear and other feelings, and the need to follow the agenda of the person who is dying and not your own.

The answer, "No" to the question, "Do you want me to pray with you?" is a good indicator that the person being visited is not a person of faith, though this may not necessarily be the case. It is also useful to remember that if a prayer is not offered to "God" or "The Holy One," it may be helpful to voice the same sentiments at the end of your visit in a calm and peaceful way. The person who is dying may appreciate that her family are with her at this time of weakness and despair, and what was originally a prayer offered to the Loving God may be reframed into a series of positive statements:

> Let us all join hands around *Eva*'s bed.
> We are thankful for this time we have shared together:
> the talk, the laughter, the stories.
> *Paul, Lisa,* and *Jason,* you have been strength to your *wife,*
> to your *mother,* in these tough times.
> We are thankful for those who have looked after you, *Eva.*
> We especially remember *Dr. Ranic* and night nurse *Julie,*
> who talked with you when you were afraid and in pain.
> We realize that the next few days will be not be easy, but
> (*you will be able to face the journey from this life knowing
> that*) your close family members are with you every step
> of the way.

At the end of these statements the worship leader could put her hand on the brow of the dying person and say, "Peace be with you, *Eva*." The family members would then speak, hug, and kiss their goodbyes.

Usually, it will not be helpful to read scripture with the one exception of Psalm 23. This may be called on because of family use in childhood or because, even with its references to God, it remains the testimony of one who is going through an exceptionally hard time and is ready to put his feelings into words. "I feel like that, too, and I would like that sense of assurance," may be the spoken or unspoken response of the dying person hearing this piece of ancient scripture. This passage of scripture (and any others) would only be read with the dying person's permission. A general question such as "Would you like me to read something to you?" may be a useful one to ask.

It will be helpful for the worship leader to have non-scripture readings ready to use. He might say, "I have found this reading very helpful," offering one or two like the following:

> You would know the secret of death,
> but how shall you find it unless you seek
> it in the heart of life?
> The owl whose night-bound eyes are blind unto the day
> cannot unveil the mystery of light.
> If you would indeed behold the spirit of death,
> open your heart wide unto the body of life.
> For life and death are one,
> even as the river and the sea are one.
> For what is it to die but to stand naked in the wind and
> to melt into the sun?
> And what is it to cease breathing, but to free the breath
> from its restless tides, that it may rise and expand
> unencumbered?
> Only when you drink from the river of silence
> shall you indeed sing.
> And when you have reached the mountaintop,
> then you shall begin to climb.
> And when the earth shall claim your limbs,
> then shall you truly dance.
>   Kahlil Gibran [2]

For a creative person, validating their attitude to life:

> Thousands of years of history have passed...and during that time human beings have fought, killed, plundered, and wronged each other in every possible way. Of such stuff history is made.
>
> But also during that time other human beings have quietly and patiently persevered...in the development of the arts, crafts, inventions, ideas, and programmes. From these millions of creative persons, most of them unnoticed and unknown in the upheavals of history, have come the good and lasting things in the sum of human culture.
> Barbara G. Walker [3]

For one who is aware of an indescribable source:

> I was not aware of the moment when I first crossed the threshold of this life. What was the power that made me open out into this vast mystery like a bud in the forest at midnight! When in the morning I looked upon the light I felt in a moment that I was no stranger in their world, that the inscrutable without name and form had taken me in the arms in the form of my own mother. Even so, in death, the same unknown will appear as even known to me. And because I love this life, I know I shall love this death as well. The child cries out when from the right breast the mother takes it away, in the very next moment to find in the left one its consolation.
> Rabindranath Tagore [4]

A key factor here is for the worship leader to develop her own library of readings that she can call on to suit the situation. For those without a recognized faith, the books *Earth Prayers from Around the World* and *Life Prayers from Around the World* by Elizabeth Roberts and Elias Amidon have been found to be especially helpful by some. The ability to search the Internet enables worship leaders unlimited opportunities to find poems and readings that are appropriate for various situations and for the outlook of the person who is dying, but you have to have the determination to carry out this task.

Another good question is "Is there something you would like me to read? A passage from a book or a magazine that is especially significant to you?" The response to this question may be surprising.

A Service of Saying Goodbye

Where a loved one has a diagnosis that suggests death will happen within days or weeks, it is possible to craft a service that is held in the home or hospital, includes many of the elements of the funeral/celebration, and has the dying person present. This is a true "goodbye" (God-be-with- you!) service.

In this situation, family members and good friends have the opportunity to publicly talk about the joy and wisdom that the dying person has brought to their lives, and the worship leader is able to offer a strong note of resurrection hope to her and to her family members and close friends. In the prayer of thanksgiving as well as the thanks given for aspects of the dying person's life, there is an opportunity for her to voice her own thanks to God, especially for her family and friends, but also for areas of life that have given her especial joy and fulfillment.

The act of committal has a whole fresh impetus and meaning if the loved one is aware of her life being committed to the love of God for all eternity. And at this service, the sacrament of Holy Communion could naturally be offered to a person of faith.

Clearly the length and content of the service would have to be tailored to the strength or weakness of the dying loved one. And it should be noted that this service would in no way replace the one-on-one farewells of family and friends or a service after the person has died.

How Will We Live on after Death?

What will happen to our loved one after she dies? Where will she go? What will it be like? How will she live on? If these questions are not asked, you may be sure they will be on the minds of those around the bed of the dying person. The life that begins (or does not begin) when this one ends is of huge interest to the vast majority of people and becomes a major concern as life draws to an end.

There have been myriad forms of speculation, a raft of lurid near-death experiences told, but nobody has come back to give us the definitive answer. Do we live on? Will we have individual existence? Will we meet our loved ones and our not-so-loved ones again? These are good, relevant questions, and as a pastoral caregiver you will need to be ready with an answer at the bedside of the dying person and as you write the meditation.

Inevitably there will be mention of heaven, but what is this heaven like? Talk to a dozen people, and you will get a dozen different answers—everything from a shining city with golden paved streets to a tranquil fishing hole. And is heaven the most important aspect of what happens after we die? I like to start with the belief that no one is lost to God. As the old Jewish prayer puts it:

> We remember those who have departed.
> They have not died into the grave,
> but into the love and eternity of God.

The love and eternity of God, who was our Creator, will have the last word with us. How we don't know, in what location we can't be sure, but the loving God in the end will see us through: In life, in death, God is with us.

There are some certainties as we think of how we will live on. We will continue in the memory of our loved ones and in the memories of those whom in our lives we have touched in many different ways. And among those who will remember us, it will be family members and friends who will remember us best of all. That is why the eulogy and the thanksgiving prayer in the memorial or funeral service are so important, because they model and inspire the remembering that will continue long after the service is over. When we celebrate the eucharist, we remember and are inspired by Jesus, whose life on earth ended 2,000 plus years ago. More than this, we will be remembered in the communities of which we have been a part and may be missed. We will be remembered in the church of which we have been a member, and the business, fraternal, and sports groups in which we had a significant place.

I was sent last year the CD of the memorial service for Ron, a "pillar of the church," who helped and supported me when I was an intern and had died after a long illness. You could tell in the family and church stories during the service the faithfulness of this man, but also in the enthusiastic and spirited singing of the old, familiar hymns how much he meant to the faith community. I remembered how he always kept a sermon in the glove compartment of his car in case the Sunday morning worship leader failed to show. He will be remembered in his home church for many years. Eventually though, Ron's faithfulness and his contribution to the faith community will fade from memory, and as the years go by, he will be remembered by fewer and fewer people. Shakespeare was right when he wrote "The good men do lives after them...." (*Julius Caesar*). And the following words (adapted) of St. John

Chrysostom are true: "The person whom we lose is no longer in the place she was; she is now wherever we are." This *is* true, but memory is not forever, and it is our mortality that puts limits on our remembering.

However, if the community lives and is effective, then the memory of Ron lives on in different ways. If the community cares for those in need in his church and cries out for justice for persons in the locality who are denied a fair wage, and writes in support of political prisoners, then in this just and merciful group the spirit of Ron lives on. Though his name might be forgotten, his influence is alive. The same community influence would hold true if the aim of the group was to protect the environment, or support persons released from jail, or give shelter to those in danger of being abused.

Some would say that this is avoiding the issue: "We know that we will live on in the memory of our loved ones, but (answer the question) will we have a separate and self-conscious existence after we have died? Or is death the terminus of it all?" I have touched on this issue in chapter 2 "Biblical Roots," but it is worth reinforcing with reference to Paul whom we meet in the Christian scriptures. If you had asked the apostle Paul the question about a conscious existence after death, there is no doubt he would have answered: "I have known the love of God through the work I have done and the relationships I have made. On the road to Damascus I realized I had to change my allegiance and follow Jesus; when in prison I was given the strength to witness to the jailor; when shipwrecked I found the strength to endure; when death was in prospect for me I was inspired to put fear behind me. What was the common denominator in all this? It was the active, practical love of God as we understand it in Jesus Christ, which knows no limits of time or space."

Look again at the reading from Romans 8 at the end of chapter 2 (page 26). The love of God that Paul writes about is not a time-limited love, nor is it a space-limited love, and this is a love we are able to take to heart. It won't show us what "heaven" looks like, or confirm whether when we die we will see our loved ones who have died; it won't tell us how it feels to be alive again, to be resurrected. But if we are held fast with God's love how *can* it fail to work out?

This is my way of looking at how we live on after death, but you will have your own concepts. The important factor is that you are ready with a well thought out answer when someone says, "I've been wondering about heaven," or "My grandma said she would be waiting for me when I die, will she?"

or "I'm afraid of what happens when I die. What does happen?" These questions will come your way, so be ready!

On a more practical level, we have the ability to live on through our body parts donated to others after death.

Organ Donation

There is a long list of persons waiting for replacement organs and tissues. There is a huge demand for kidneys, livers, corneas, and lungs among others. Most provinces and states have a card that is given to those who have a driver's licence issued or reissued on which they may give permission for these body parts to be used, if the person has an automobile accident for example.

In a situation where a person is dying, but has not filled in a donation card or expressed a wish to donate organs or tissues, the pastoral caregiver may have the opportunity to raise the subject. Both the dying person and the family may have views on the need for the card to be completed (or permission to be given in writing for donation), and the pastoral caregiver can act as a catalyst in making sure that if there is a wish for organs to be donated, this wish is carried out and that the document is signed and witnessed.

It is useful to talk to the medical professionals before the person dies about how the donation of tissues and organs may be facilitated in that institution. In a situation where a baby or a young person has died, the donation of organs and/or tissues may be seen as a direct way in which the person who has died lives on, and can be a powerful aid to the grieving process.

A good friend died recently, and a year after her death her spouse was visiting us and showed us a certificate and medal acknowledging the donation of corneas that had been given to restore good sight to a stranger. The corneas were the only useful parts of her body that could be harvested, but that they were transplanted into the eyes of another person was a factor that significantly aided the grieving process for family members left behind.

Self-Care for the Worship Leader in a Pastoral Role

Being with those who are dying is intense and demanding work. In her book *Being with Dying*, Joan Halifax reminds her readers that as caregivers we are called on to offer loving kindness not only to those with whom we work, but also to ourselves: "Just as a mother can care best for her child after her own needs have been met, it's crucial that we recognize our own limits of compassion, in the same way (as in an airliner emergency) we're instructed to place the oxygen mask on our own face before we try to help those around us."[5]

This means that all the advice you give to family members about taking time to get enough to eat and sufficient sleep and time away from their loved one also applies equally to yourself. You need to pace yourself and to realize that there are others who are able to give care to the person who is dying, and to have the confidence that they will do a good job. You may also need a friend or colleague with whom you can talk out your options and concerns around the bereavement. Military authorities are now waking up to the fact of post-traumatic stress in soldiers and the need to take it seriously. It is a reminder that those who wait beside the bed of a dying person may be exposed to a traumatic situation and the stress that comes with dying and death.

This is also a time when it is crucial to adhere to our regimes of both physical and spiritual exercise, especially as it will seem that there is little time to be about both forms of personal renewal.

[1] Excerpts from *Being with Dying*, by Joan Halifax, ©2008 by Joan Halifax. Reprinted by arrangement with The Permissions Company, Inc., on behalf of Shambhala Publications Inc., Boston, MA. www.shambhala.com.

[2] From "On Death" by Kahlil Gibran (1883–1930). In the public domain.

[3] "Thousands of Years of History" by Barbara Walker, from *Life Prayers,* Elizabeth Roberts (ed.) (Harperone, 1996).

[4] Rabindranath Tagore (1861–1941). In the public domain.

[5] Excerpts from *Being with Dying*, by Joan Halifax, ©2008 by Joan Halifax. Reprinted by arrangement with The Permissions Company, Inc., on behalf of Shambhala Publications Inc., Boston, MA. www.shambhala.com.

CHAPTER 4

At the Time of Death and After

With Family Present

As we've seen in chapter 3, the time of death is often hard to predict. If a clergy person or pastoral caregiver is there for the last moments of the person's life, one of the helpful actions that they may carry out is to pray with the family and with their dying loved one. The prayer is to give the family strength and hope that their loved one will be safe and at peace as they finally leave this world for the next. If the dying person is conscious or even if she is not, she should be addressed directly and assured of God's presence with her as she dies. She may be reassured that it is all right to die. Both the family and the dying person should be assured of God's blessing at this time.

The prayer might read like this:

> Loving God,
> we do not want to let *Ruth* go;
> she is so loved by all of us here:
> so loved by all her family, so loved by her friends.
> We want her to stay with us,
> but we realize that her time on earth is ending.
> We realize that she will not get better,
> so we release her to you, our God,
> knowing that with your love around her
> she will be safe, cherished, and at peace eternally.
> Receive, O God, *Ruth* into your eternal care.
> Embrace her and look after her, because we cannot do
> that any more.

(*Then the pastoral caregiver/clergy person asks the family to join hands around the bed.*)

> Loving God,
> be with each family member here (*if you know all the names, use them one after the other*).
> Give them courage for *Ruth*'s dying and for her death.
> Strengthen them in mind and spirit and enable them
> to be a strong support for each other.
> Be with *Geoff* who cannot be here and, O God,
> be with him in any of the anxiety, frustration,
> or hopelessness he feels.
> When they feel downhearted comfort them,
> when they feel without hope encourage them.
> God's blessing be with you in the hours
> and the days ahead.
> God's peace be your peace. Amen.
> (*The pastoral caregiver/clergy person may then put her hand on the dying person's forehead.*)
> Loving God, go with *Ruth* on her journey from life to
> death and from death to life again.
> She is not alone on her journey because you go with her,
> and your love will never leave her.
> Bless her journey and accept her into your eternal peace.
> We pray in the name of Jesus the Christ. Amen.

The Secular Approach

Where the dying person is not a person of faith, the emphasis should be on the dying person living on in the memories of those who love them. Faith references and mention of God's name are not helpful here. The caregiver might ask the family members to join hands and say:

> We are glad that soon *Ruth* will not be suffering any more. We know she will be at peace and we are glad of that. Though she will be gone from among us, we know that she will live on in the memories of each person here and in the memories of so many friends and family members far from here. *Ruth* was a person who loved and cared deeply; she will not be forgotten.

If the pastoral caregiver/clergy person is present when the person dies, then her role will be to offer a listening ear to each and all family members, so that their sorrow, guilt, and distress are deeply heard. The person may encourage each person to have time with their loved one alone and to say their personal goodbye. The pastoral caregiver/clergy person may also facilitate a family goodbye without necessarily being a part of this process, such as: "Maybe you family members would like to have your own time together saying your goodbye to *Ruth*."

The pastoral caregiver/clergy person may also encourage ("give permission" for) the family members to leave the area when the goodbyes have been said.

If the friend or family member dies at home and the pastoral caregiver/clergy person is present, then he should encourage the family members to contact their doctor and wait with them until she arrives.

Most times, the pastoral caregiver/clergy person will not be present when the person dies. He may at the time of death receive a phone call asking him to come to the hospital or the home. The expectation is that he will offer a prayer and final blessing with the person who has died and a prayer with the family members, e.g.:

> Loving God,
> we thank you that for *Ruth* the struggle with sickness/
> cancer/her heart problems is over,
> (*or if Ruth has died quietly and naturally of old age*)
> we give thanks for *Ruth's* long and good life.
> We rejoice that your love is with her now
> and always will be.
> We pray for the family members who are here
> (*name each one*).
> We realize how much each one has lost in *Ruth's* death,
> but we rejoice that *Ruth* is at peace now,
> your peace that passes all human understanding,
> and that within that peace, she is safe and happy and
> renewed. Amen.
> (*The pastoral caregiver/clergy person will put her hand on
> the deceased person's forehead and offer a blessing.*)
> As God has blessed you in this life, *Ruth*,

so God's blessing goes with you as your new life begins.
God's love will surround you,
God's Spirit will receive you,
and God's peace will enfold you,
now, and beyond all time. Amen.

The clergy/caregiver may also give compassionate pastoral care and offer advice about calling the doctor and notifying the chosen funeral home.

When the Pastoral Caregiver Is Not Present at Time of Death

Usually, the family will notify the clergy person or caregiver at some point after death has occurred with a request for that person to conduct the funeral or celebration service. This call provides the caregiver with the opportunity to offer her sympathy and affirm that she is ready to come round to give support. If not, some simple but essential questions should be asked: "When and where and at what time will the service take place?"

If there is a request for the service to be at the worship place of the person called, there will be some further comments and questions, including: "I will make sure that the sanctuary is available when you need it. Will you want refreshments after the service? If so, would you like me to contact the person who handles this job, or give her your number?"

The pastoral caregiver/clergy person will tell the family member that she would like to come round to their home or meet in the worship place with family. She will also give advance notice that she will be asking the family members whether they or the person who has died has any favourite scriptures, songs, or hymns and will tell the family member that she will be contacting the musician of the faith community to alert him to the approaching service. The caregiver or clergy will also ask about calling on a family member or members willing to give a eulogy or tribute to the deceased.

Contact with the Funeral Home When the Pastoral Caregiver Is Not Present

It is unusual for the family to ask the caregiver or clergy to contact the funeral home on their behalf. Most often, the clergy person will receive a call from the funeral home asking whether she would be willing to conduct the service and giving her the date and time. The funeral home will usually provide the name of the person who has died and give her age. They will also provide the name and telephone number or cellphone number or e-mail address of the family member who is the main contact for the service. It is useful to ask who the funeral home person responsible for the service will be, for this may not be the same person making the call.

If there is to be an interment after the service, the date and time will usually be passed along by the funeral home representative. If there is no mention of the interment, then this should be checked out with the encouragement to fix a "final disposition" date. For services these days, the interment will often be at a place and time of the family's choosing, and the public information will be "at a later date."

If the service is to be in the sanctuary of the caregiver or clergy's faith community, then it is the responsibility of the caregiver or clergy to check with the administrator/secretary or "keeper of the church date book" to determine whether the sanctuary is free and if there are to be refreshments and whether the hall or reception room is available. If there are date conflicts, then it is the responsibility of the caregiver or clergy to talk with the funeral home representative about an alternative date or place.

Contact with Faith Community/Church (your own)

As mentioned above, it is the clergy or caregiver's responsibility to check out the availability of sanctuary and hall or reception room. If there is a person specifically responsible for catering to funerals, she will be asked if her group is available to provide food and drink following the service. If group members are unable to do the job, then the funeral home representative will be contacted to find an alternative.

Where catering is done by the faith community, then it is important that the group contact person is given the phone contact number of the family member responsible for the service and is ready for the question, "How much will it cost?" The cost per person for the lunch/tea or other meal should be determined ahead of need by the official board/council/catering group of the faith community. The caregiver/clergy will also call the church musician or music director and determine if she is able to play at the service. If so, he will tell the musician that the songs or hymns and the "coming in" and "going out" music will be communicated following the meeting with the family.

The musician is usually a good judge as to whether the music is well-known or obscure. If songs or hymns are meant to be sung by the congregation, the musician will usually know if they are well-known or will result in a quavering solo by the worship leader!

The church sound/video technician is increasingly involved in services and will want to know what he will be asked to do well in advance. The technician will be responsible for the sound and visual aspects of the service. He will be able to help the worship leader by enabling the family to play non-religious music before, during, and after the service by feeding tracks from CDs and computer files into the sound system. Families sometimes produce a photo or video history of their loved one's life in digital form for playing before or after the service, and it is the responsibility of the technician to make sure that the format is compatible with the equipment in the sanctuary.

Some churches have a full-time or part-time custodian, and it is useful to alert him to the forthcoming service. The custodian may have the responsibility for cleaning the sanctuary, moving chairs, reserving parking spots, providing music, and many other duties.

If the church administrator/secretary is not the keeper of the church date book, she will still want to know about the service, as she may have to prepare cheques for the participants, run off a bulletin, or update the Register of Deaths.

There are churches where there is a congregational member who volunteers to organize a funeral (or a wedding). This person, if trained and competent (he may be called the funeral coordinator or celebration organizer), can take much of the effort off the shoulders of the worship leader by carrying out many of the practical tasks. This is especially significant when there is no funeral home involved.

Contact with the Faith Community/Church (not your own)

If the person who is asked to conduct the funeral/celebration has been carrying out the pastoral work for a dying person who is the member of another faith community, or if the person who has died wants the service to be in the sanctuary of another faith community, you have to show the greatest respect to the current clergy person of that faith community.

The minister (ordained, diaconal, or designated lay) has the right to conduct all the services in her church and sometimes this right is clearly stated in the board or council policies of the church. So what is to be done? Where there is a will, there is a way, and with goodwill on both sides, the service can be conducted in a way that honours the pastoral care that has been shown to the dying person and her family and the right of the home church clergy to conduct funerals in her own faith community in her own way.

Clearly, the welcome will be given by the home church clergy and the final blessing will be theirs to offer. Apart from these parts of the service, my sense is that those service items that are not personal or pastoral may be offered by the home clergy person. So the sentences and opening prayer can quite naturally be offered by the home team. However, it makes sense for the readings to be chosen by the guest worship leader and the meditation to be given by him, too. The prayer that follows the meditation can be offered by either the home clergy or the visitor. The thanksgiving prayer format that I normally use is one that includes a series of specific thanksgivings that relate to the life of the person who has died, so if the prayer is offered by the home clergy, she needs to be supplied with a short list of the personal reasons to give thanks.

To determine music for the service, there needs to be a consultation with the home clergy, the guest clergy, and the local faith community music director. Sometimes the deceased will have given instructions about what he wants played and sung, and it will be good to follow these ideas as much as possible, but usually this is an area where songs and hymns that reflect the theme of the service need to be combined with the hymns and songs familiar to the local congregation. Again, with goodwill and discussion this should present no problem.

If the home minister insists on leading the service in her own way with her own materials, then the worship leader will have to consult with the family and give them the choice: "Do you want the service to be in the faith community building as asked for by the dying person? If this is the case, the service will be conducted by the home clergy person in her own way. Or do you want the worship leader specified to conduct the service? If this is the case, we will have to find another location."

CHAPTER 5

A Good Death

Sensitive and appropriate pastoral care that includes attention to spiritual needs, together with sensitive medical treatment, are elements of what is often described as "a good death." Existing is not living, yet some medical caregivers still confuse an extended length of days—more existing time— with good living time.

I remember during my time as an intern chaplain to an intensive care unit working with a 90-year-old mother of two daughters who was a patient. Hilda was on life support and hooked up to a series of tubes and wires; she was very uncomfortable, with no quality of life at all. The daughters were understandably upset by the way their mother looked and felt, but the young physician thought there was a chance that with another round of treatment, Hilda's life might be extended, so he went in to talk with her.

The young man carefully explained how the extensive and likely painful treatment would be carried out. He was detailed, he was considerate, and he was careful. Hilda had a breathing tube down her throat and so she couldn't voice a reply to the doctor, but her gesture with her one good arm was very clear. She pointed upward with her fingers three times. It wasn't more treatment she wanted; it was her release to go to her "heaven." She was taken off life support, and in a few hours she had died. Her death was the compassionate way for her and a huge relief to her daughters.

The compassionate doctor will be ready to let her patient go and make her comfortable with appropriate drugs. As a pastoral caregiver you will want to encourage the physician in this course of action.

A good death is what is looked for when it is most likely that a person's life is coming to an end. For the clergy person or worship leader in a pastoral care role, there will often be an opportunity to play a part in this process.

A key factor in the process of moving toward a good death is that wherever possible *the dying person is in charge of her own dying.* She calls the shots when it comes to treatment, especially the painkilling drugs that she takes— the amounts that are administered to her or that are available to her for self-administration.

It is the dying person who decides which visitors will come to see her and how long they will stay. It is the dying person who determines her priorities for the limited time she has left on this earth and, as far as is possible, where she will end her life. It is easy to spend a lot of time and energy bemoaning the fact that a human life is ending and so many things are no longer possible: holidays that cannot be taken, friends that cannot be visited, hobbies that cannot be pursued, and grandchildren who cannot be seen growing up. These are incalculable losses that a death deadline renders inevitable, but the effect of this deadline is to make other events possible that could not possibly happen if life without a limit continues.

During my ministry I have from time to time been one of those persons who hears the fifth step of Alcoholics Anonymous. This is the time when the addicted person writes down those hurts he has inflicted on others in great detail and having completed the list to the best of his ability, reads it aloud to one other person. Having completed this step, he does his best to make amends to every person he has harmed or slighted.

For the dying person, there is the possibility of asking forgiveness from those whom he has harmed and getting together with those with whom he has been in conflict. The new factor, the approach of the death deadline, makes it more likely that resolution will be achieved.

This is particularly true of major disagreements in the family circle, which can be bitter and prolonged. The upcoming death of a family member can be the incentive necessary to end the harsh words and to enable the participants to forgive and forget. The clergy person or pastoral caregiver can be the one who hears of the conflict and gets the process of reconciliation underway. He can be a good death initiator and catalyst. A useful question that he can put to the person who is dying is "Now that you know your life will end soon, what is it you need to do? Who is it you need to see?"

There is an often used phrase at this time: "You need to get your affairs in order," and this is usually thought of in financial terms. Have you got an up-to-date will and do you know where it is? Have you got joint bank accounts with your spouse, and are you ready to talk to your bank representative about how his life will change financially? Are your life and other insurance documents in an accessible place? Does your partner know what investments you have and where they are held?

The death deadline is a major incentive to get your financial house in order, and sometimes the dying person needs to be reminded of this. However, there are less practical aspects that come at the end of life that come under the category of "Things I have always wanted to do, but never quite got round to." It may be something as simple as having a soft ice cream with chocolate and lemon swirls or as major as going to Paris to see the Mona Lisa; as easy as calling up an old school friend to see what he did with his life or as momentous as taking a helicopter ride over the Grand Canyon.

One of the observations of dying people is the way taken-for-granted experiences take on fresh and vivid meaning: how the rolling clouds seem so wonderfully shaped and compelling as they move; how the smile of a grandchild is suddenly so full of meaning; and how the touch of a friend brings back a multitude of past experiences. As one of the caregivers for the person whose life is ending, you might ask the person dying a question that gives them the opportunity to express some of these deep feelings:

"I saw a smile come onto your face when you took a sip of water just now," says the pastoral caregiver.

"You know, I have just realized how good a sip of cold water tastes on my tongue," responds the dying one.

"You surely were paying close attention to those flowers the last visitor brought," says the pastoral caregiver.

"It's a long time since I looked at a rosebud and realized how delicate were the petals, how glorious the scent, how beautiful the delicate shade of pink," responds the dying one.

CHAPTER 6

Response to Wishes of the Person Who Has Died

We have seen in chapter 3 how it is useful to talk to the dying person about the sort of service he would want after he dies. There is value in knowing his wishes. However, his needs have to be balanced with the needs of family members.

The dying person's instructions may have been recorded some time before and left with a family member, with a lawyer, in the church office, or at a funeral home. If the instructions are current and reasonable, they will be easy for the family members to carry out. The person who has died may have requested that the worship leader of his own church conduct the service, and he may have stated his choice of place: church, funeral home, or graveside. He may have suggested hymns and scripture readings, poems, photos, and other media ideas, and named family members who might speak (eulogize) at the service. All of this is useful information for the worship leader and will enable her to create a meaningful celebration or funeral service.

However, the instructions may be out of date or unreasonable; they may be challenging or even impossible for the family to implement. For example, the minister or priest of the church may be retired or may now be at another church, the hymns or songs may be no longer familiar to the congregation, and the photographs may be lost.

The key factor for the responsible family members to keep in mind is that it is they and not the person who has died who are responsible for the service. Though they will do the very best to respect the wishes of the deceased person, some of the instructions may not be possible to carry out, and some may not be wise to follow. If the family has to make changes to the instructions, this will probably make for a better service, and they need not feel badly about it.

No Service

In these secular times, it is not unusual for the person who has died to leave instructions that there is to be no service. This may seem like a full stop to the family. "Fred said that he wanted no service so we will carry out his wishes; we won't have one." For you as the pastoral caregiver or worship leader the no service directive will lead to some additional questions: "What was the reason for these instructions? Was Fred a person who had no time for religion?" He may have had a set of beliefs forced on him that were doctrinaire or unfeeling, or he may have met a person of faith who crossed him in love or business and so he put up barriers between him and a specific church. Or he may have been a most faithful person but with huge modesty, and knowing the work required to organize a funeral, have wanted to spare the minister and the catering group the time and trouble. In my pastoral experience, I remember Lucille. She had been a key person in organizing over a hundred funerals, but had left the specific instruction of no service for herself in a bid to save members from the same work that she had faithfully carried out for others.

Another reason (sometimes unstated) is the belief that the funeral will be expensive, and the deceased person had wanted to save family members the not insignificant expense.

Often the person who has died will have shared his reasons for no service with his next of kin. Take the trouble to talk with this person. It is essential to keep in mind that the family is not obligated to go without a service because their loved one has given these seemingly clear instructions. It is important to explore together with the family member how family members and good friends will feel if there is no opportunity to grieve together, to meet in a sacred place together, to worship together, and to have food and fellowship together. It is essential to point out that grief will not be denied, and often the service in church or funeral chapel provides an excellent opportunity to get started on the grief journey—essential if there are not to be emotional consequences in the future.

It is also helpful to make clear to the primary family member that as she has much to be thankful for in the life of her loved one, so there will be many others who will want to express their thanks and will want to hear thanks expressed on their behalf.

If the person has been a long-time member of the church, fraternal organization, or veteran's group, then these communities will want to corporately give thanks and corporately grieve someone whose loss will diminish their community. To deny this expression in a public way is to deny a fundamental need when a loved one dies. You only have one life and one chance to give thanks for the whole of it, and the service provides this opportunity for family, friends, and for the communities of which she was a part to say goodbye.

However, if a religious service will not be meaningful to family members, then it may be appropriate to suggest that a secular celebration of life (such as those that follow in this book) or some secular/religious hybrid service may be the way to go.

If you discover that it is the expense of the funeral or celebration that is the reason for the no service directive, then there are ways in which the cost may be reduced. A first approach might be a discussion with the funeral home staff member. Some ways of reducing costs may include using family resources rather than those of the funeral home, e.g., flowers from a friend's garden rather than the florist, family cars rather than the funeral home limos, and potluck food provided by friends and family members for the meal after the service. An additional way is having the minister and her helpers direct the service in the church rather than having the staff of the funeral home present during the service. Most ministers and pastoral charges will be ready to reduce fees or will be ready to receive no payment at all if the family is able to show need. Many funeral homes will also consider deferring payment.

With both funeral home and church it is helpful to be up front about the need to have an inexpensive funeral. The worship leader may be able to facilitate this.

The worship leader will sometimes encounter a situation where family members are determined to follow the no service directive whatever the reason for this instruction. If the person has been a significant member of the church family, then the faith community may choose to remember her in the Sunday service (e.g., including a eulogy and prayer of thanksgiving) or in a special service on another day of the week. In talking to the family about this, it will be helpful for the clergy or worship leader to relate the importance of the work and service that the person who has died gave to the faith community and the need for church members to grieve the loss of a valued member. The family will then be invited to the church celebration of life.

CHAPTER 7

Changing Roles of Worship Leader and Funeral Director

Mention the word "funeral" in North America some 20 years ago and the images that would have come to mind would have been of a coffin or casket, a service in a church or funeral home chapel, and an earth burial in a cemetery. Fast forward to today, and we see significant changes on the funeral scene.

A large number of funerals today are paid for in advance. There is often a "pre-need" interview with family members at which the wishes of the family members for the whole funeral experience are determined. So, for example, the wish for a gathering before the service is noted, as is the type of casket or the preference for cremation. The location of the service, at a church or funeral home chapel, is specified as are the needs for transportation. Some funeral homes also ask the family for details of the service, such as favourite hymns and scripture readings, but this practice is by no means the rule. As the worship leader, you can take a proactive stance by asking your faith community members to consider their wishes for the memorial, celebration, or funeral experience in advance, to be ready to talk it over, and to have the needs recorded in the funeral home, or church office, or both.

Today, there is a popular move toward choosing cremation rather than an earth burial. An urn containing the cremated remains is present in the church or sometimes just a picture of the person who has died is placed at the front of the sanctuary. In earlier times, the interment always followed the service; now it is often carried out at some other time or place while the funeral or celebration is directly followed by a gathering for a meal.

As the nature of the funeral has changed, so has the relationship between the funeral director and the worship leader in a pastoral care role. The pastoral caregiver will work with the family and the person who is dying and has the responsible task of making sure that the process of dying and the death are handled compassionately for all concerned. But as soon as death and the act of saying "goodbye" are over, their responsibilities cease for a while.

A funeral home or memorial society (see "No Funeral Home" on page 64) usually has the central and legal tasks of picking up the body from the home or hospital and bringing it to an area where it is stored and embalmed. A licensed funeral director is responsible for ensuring that the legal requirements of the province or state are followed, both from the viewpoint of the paperwork that has to be completed and the respectful disposition of the remains. The duties of the funeral staff member, in conjunction with the executor or next-of-kin, include: how the body will be disposed, earth burial or cremation; the type of service to be held; and who will lead the service. In the days when earth burial was the norm, the storage and movement of the remains of the deceased was a major undertaking. The coffin or casket took up significant space, and if it had to be moved around for public viewing before and after the funeral service and for the burial, there was a requirement for several persons to do it. This was usually led by a team from the funeral home, all of whom had to be present at all stages of the service.

In comparison with a large and heavy casket, the urn containing the cremated remains of the deceased person is easily portable, and there is no need for a team of funeral home workers to move the remains before and after the service. Much of the moving can now be done by family members. Once the urn is handed over to the family member responsible, he is able to take it wherever he wants it to go. There may be a gathering of family members on the night before the service in the funeral home, but it might just as easily be in a family home, or in a restaurant, or in a church hall.

The responsible family member is able to bring the urn to the church or social hall before the service. He can surround it with a picture or pictures of the person who has died and significant objects from her life's work or pastimes. And he is able to readily remove it from the place of worship or celebration when the service is over and take it to the place of interment.

If there is a staff member from the funeral home present, then she will be able to supervise the placing of the urn and its movement at significant times. She will also be responsible for the other tasks, e.g., placing the registers for guests to sign, bringing and placing holders and vases for the flowers, ensuring the sound system is working efficiently, and making sure the grieving family members are cared for. If there is no funeral home representative present, the responsible family member will look to the worship leader to guide him in doing these tasks.

Worship Leader as Funeral Coordinator

In some situations, the worship leader may coordinate the whole funeral as well as lead the spiritual service. My experience is that the worship leader in this role can provide a celebration experience just as moving, as care-full, and as significant to the family as one where the funeral home staff take a traditional supervisory role at all stages. However, it means that as well as focusing on the worship for the day, he has to remember the many other tasks that have to be done. Some worship leaders will have no difficulty in taking on the additional load; others will find themselves overburdened.

I have detailed the duties of the worship leader as a funeral coordinator in the "Worship Leader's Checklist" in appendix 1, page 253.

Ushers and Funeral Helpers

One of the ways in which the worship leader's responsibilities may be lightened is by the family providing ushers to help with the jobs that have to be done before, during, and after the service. A group of one to four ushers can make a huge difference to the flow of the service.

I have detailed an "Usher's/Funeral Helper's Checklist" in appendix 1, page 256.

An alternative is to have someone from the congregation act as an assistant (funeral helper) to the worship leader. This person carries out all the tasks that usually fall to the funeral staff member and sometimes the tasks of the ushers. This may be a paid or voluntary position, but if paid, the fee needs to be made clear to the family (with other fees) ahead of the service.

Role of the Worship Leader (other location)

Where the worship leader is taking the service in a funeral home or church that is not her own, there is less to think about ahead of the service and when she arrives. However, she will still have to make sure that she is prepared, that she cares for the grieving family members, and that she has established communication with the funeral home and the representative of the hosting faith community.

See "Worship Leader's Checklist (other location)" on page 258

No Funeral Home

It is possible for a family to carry out some or all of the tasks usually carried out by the funeral home or memorial society. These include washing and preparing the body for burial, clothing the body, and keeping it in the family home for people to visit prior to burial. It is also possible for family members to transport the remains of their loved one to the place of burial and for arrangements to be made for them to bury his body. It is also possible for the family to take the body to the crematorium, be present during the cremation, pick up the ashes after the cremation is over, and dispose of them as they wish.

However, there are specific regulations covering this process, and these vary from province to province and from state to state.

If you encounter a family who is taking on the tasks usually carried out by a funeral home, make sure that the family is planning ahead carefully. It is worth checking that the family is aware of the necessary provincial/state regulations and is following them.

Green Funerals

There is a move toward burials where only non-permanent materials are used. One can request that the funeral home uses environmentally friendly embalming fluid and purchase a coffin without metal fastenings.

It is also possible in some areas to bury the body in a designated wood or forest glade with no marker.

Most funeral homes will be happy to advise families about how the loved one's remains can be treated in a respectfully green way…"earth to earth, dust to dust."

CHAPTER 8

Concerning the Family

Gathering Information

Over the years, the silent prayer I offer before I meet with the family has remained constant in my preparation for a funeral, memorial, or celebration service. You have no idea who will be in the family group that awaits you and what the needs or the mood of that group will be. So I place my meeting with them in God's hands in the hope that together we will be able to arrange a faithful service or celebration worthy of the person who has died. It has often proved to be a stressful and difficult process, but I have never come away from a family meeting feeling that I have given less than my best to the preparation of the service or celebration. With the benefit of hindsight, my best has not always been good enough, but you can only go with the people available to you and the information they provide.

There is work to be done before the conversation with the family, and some of it will have been done in the course of pastoral visitation at the time of death or in the normal course of faith community life. If you have known and visited the person who has died, then you will already have established your own picture of her.

If you didn't know the person, check out the information given to you by the funeral director or the family member with whom you first speak. At least you will be able to tell if the death was expected or sudden, whether the person who has died was old or young, and probably whether she was a member of a faith community or not. You will know whether there has been a decision on the final disposition of the body or cremated remains of the deceased or whether they will be in the keeping of a family member. If you know a friend of the person who has died, a quick conversation with him might be helpful.

It is useful to jot down some of the qualities that come to mind, such as how she appeared to you and whether other people's opinions validate your own. My notes might look something like following:

> Death expected, 75 plus; Grace; always had a friendly smile; husband Bert died five years ago—I did funeral; member of the woman's group, went out of her way to welcome newcomers; had a green thumb... loved roses; one grandson, Matt, her pride and joy; terrible singer and loud; commented unfavourably on my ties—"Why doesn't he wear a collar?" Helped at Shelter House. Others saw her as one who helped without any fuss; had a terrible, loud voice; arranged the church flowers; taught Sunday school 20 years ago; was a member of the Rebecca Lodge; sometimes spoke her mind without thinking.

The comments of the funeral director and the comments and voice tone of the family member whom you contacted will alert you to the family mood following the death of the loved one. If the service is to be held in a sanctuary/reception area that is not your own, then you will have contacted the clergy person or hall administrator, who may have made some comments or challenges for you to bear in mind at the meeting. You may have other information from the musician to pass along. You will have made some notes; check them over before coming to the meeting with the family. This preliminary work is worth the time.

The family members often have no idea what you will want to do in your time with them or what you will say. I usually invite the family members to tell me their names and where they come from and write down their relationship to the deceased. I mention to them that I will take notes of the conversation, adding, "My memory isn't so hot!" I then look for common ground to reduce the stress level, for example, I may discover that they live close to a city where I have lived or have children the same ages as my children. Then I explain the elements of the funeral /celebration service, the thanksgiving, the sense of loss experienced by those at the service, and finally the gospel hope that the Christian faith makes clear for those who are members of the faith community. If the Christian—or another—faith is not a significant factor for them, then I make the point that the person who has died will live in the hearts of those whom she loved for as long as they live and I share with them that we will talk about that.

Rather than ask a whole lot of direct questions at the start, I encourage the family to carry on a conversation about the loved one, with me, the worship leader, as the friendly but quiet observer. An open-ended comment, such as "Could you talk for a little while about your mother...tell me what she was like and maybe share a few stories about her?" may get the conversation going. Some family members will be more willing or able to talk about their loved one than others, so a little encouragement to the reluctant members will not go amiss. If this indirect approach doesn't work, some direct questions like "What did your loved one enjoy doing?" or "What have you learned (or not learned) from your loved one?" may help.

Another good question to provoke discussion is "What gave your loved one's life purpose and meaning? What was really important to her?" Or a question like "What three words best describe your mother?" or "What have you learned from your loved one?" will often stir the memories of family members and get them talking.

It is important to establish at this point whether someone from the family or someone on behalf of the family will be offering a eulogy, memorial, or tribute about the person who has died. If this is the case, the worship leader will have less information to gather, though she still needs to have a feel for the person before she writes the prayers and prepares the meditation and service.

What Was She Like?
Going through the worship leader's mind as the family members reminisce will be a number of questions: What were the characteristics of the person? What did your loved one enjoy doing? Was she naturally shy or an outgoing person? Did she work outside the home or was she a homemaker? And was the homemaking more important than the work or the other way round? What work did she do and did she enjoy her working time? In what ways? And was she appreciated for the job she did?

How did her family see her? A caring mother and grandmother? A matriarch? One who got along with everyone? A great cook? A person who played well with the grandchildren? Was she liked within the family circle? Was she loved? Was she respected? Was she tolerated? Was she a gardener? Handy with the needle? Was she on Facebook and Twitter? What did she do for fun and further education? And what was her level of education or trade training? What sports did she play and what satisfaction did she get from her participation? Did she play a musical instrument? Play in a band or group? What music did she enjoy? Jazz? Classical? Pop? Elvis? What were the challenges in her life, the troubles she had to go through? How did she help other people? Locally or overseas? What were her regrets in life and what did she see as her accomplishments? What did her friends see as her accomplishments?

How was her life of faith? Was she a regular or occasional churchgoer? Was she active in Christian education? Did she take a leadership role in church life? Did she sing in the choir? Was she a leader in raising social justice issues? How would she like to be remembered for her church life? How will others remember her? Was she spiritual rather than faithful? Did she practise a spiritual discipline? Did she meditate?

Did she have a significant place in the local community? What did she give to local life? Were there groups for seniors or fraternal organizations where she was a member or leader? Was she a much-treasured member of a seniors' home? How was she seen in these communities, and how will the groups be poorer for her death? Was she a golfer, a walker, or a cyclist? How will the teams she was a part of miss her skills and abilities, her contribution to the life of the group?

If you were to set the loved one's life to music, what would be the theme tune? What is the central theme running through her life?

The family conversation will not reveal the answers to all these questions; neither is it supposed to.

What the worship leader needs is a picture, an accurate sketch, of the person who has died so that thanks may be offered for her specific life. Each person is unique, and each is worthy of a unique thanksgiving. Friends and family members will be encouraged during the service to remember the person in their own way and, perhaps more importantly, to continue to remember her long after the service is over. It is useful to think of the meditation as a catalyst that gets people remembering and keeps their memories strong.

As you consider what you will say in your meditation, reflect back especially on the stories that speak of the core values and the loves of the person who has died. What activities were most important to her? What did she spend her money on? More significantly, what did she spend her time doing, and on what did she use her most treasured skills and energy? What did she love doing? And whom did she love most?

Life Story

An alternative to the above "theme approach" is for the worship leader to work with the family to draw up a short life story of the person who has died. Family members may have a head start on this if they have had to produce an obituary for the newspaper, but a "life story" is not just the factual account of the life. It can be one with humour and anecdote added to make the person live in the minds of the hearers, and it will be best if family members can augment the narrative with stories from the family storehouse as the life account proceeds.

On the day of the celebration, the life story may be told by a family member if he is able to cope emotionally or by the worship leader. The advantage of the "life story approach" is that the whole spectrum of the person's life will be covered, and many in the congregation will learn about aspects of their friend and loved one that they would never have imagined from their limited experience of her. The disadvantage is that time will be spent on not missing an important *stage* in the life's journey rather than on the key stories that make clear the *core values* and the *central theme* of the person's life.

Family Relationships

As you listen to the family conversation, you are challenged to think about the relationship of each member to the deceased because their relationship will colour their stories and their memories. Did they get along? Were they the favoured sons and daughters or did they do the lion's share of chores in the family home and receive little thanks?

What will also be apparent at the time of a parent's death and during the interview with the family are the relationships between the family members. Is it an easy relationship with lots of leg pulling and inside jokes or are there tensions from childhood that emerge and are magnified? Do siblings like or positively dislike each other?

The worship leader will usually be unaware of the rivalries between family members before the family meeting. Such rivalries may cause disagreements about the service content and what happens to the remains of the loved one—way out of proportion to what one would expect. These service or celebration items have the potential of becoming the battleground where long-standing rivalries are played out. If you have trouble working it all out, don't blame yourself! Your role in this situation is not to determine who is right and who is wrong, but to keep your eye firmly on the end result, that is, a service that is worthy of the person who has died and the prompt and mutually agreed final disposition of her remains.

Writing the Service Material

To practise the art of writing service material, you could work with another worship leader and imagine that each of you has been given the task of writing material for the celebration of life or funeral of the other. You might have a session where you imagine that you represent your family members, gathered after you have died, and answer the questions needed to create the theme of the service, the meditation, and prayer of thanksgiving. You could choose hymns and scripture readings and put together a whole service for review by each other or a sympathetic friend. An alternative might be to work together on a service for a well-known fictional character or cartoon star. Dagwood from the *Blondie* comic strip would fit the bill or maybe Ellie from *For Better or for Worse*.

Either practice idea would be a great training exercise for deciding what constitutes the core values of the person and which characteristics and achievements should be highlighted.

Family Disagreements

The worship leader should be ready for disagreements about the service that have not been worked out ahead of the family interview. On one occasion, I had two sisters strongly disagree at the beginning of our meeting about whether the service for their mother should be in the church where I was minister or in the local community hall. One sister said, "I hope I don't have to listen to a whole lot of religious propaganda from you during the service. Can't we have the service at the Legion without any of this God stuff?" The other sister took the opposite view: "Mother was a faithful member of this church for 55 years, and for her the Christian faith was a guiding light. This is where the service should be held."

Clearly this disagreement should have been worked through before the family members came to see me. I told the two sisters to go to another place in the church and work out their differences and then return if their points of view had been reconciled and tell me whether this faith community (including myself) would be able to help them. They did just that, and the service went ahead in our sanctuary.

Family Feelings about the Death

The worship leader should be aware of the feelings of the family members around their loved one's death. This is often not straightforward and may depend on the circumstances of death or a relationship that changed over the years. Here are examples of different circumstances and the feelings that arose from them:

> Marie, 10 years old, was killed as the snow machine she was driving turned over in rough terrain. Her parents had a rule that she was not to go out on her own, but Marie, a kid who did not listen if it didn't suit her, had disregarded the parental instruction and to make matters worse did not wear her crash helmet. She picked up the keys to the machine, went out at the end of the day, and accidentally hit an obscured tree root in the trail. The parents had a huge sense of loss in the death of their only daughter and *major guilt feelings* about the snow machine and its keys being easily available. However, the guilt feelings were mitigated by the fact that Marie was disobeying direct instructions, and they slowly came to terms with her death after joining a grief group.

> Flora was in her nineties; she had fallen, broken her hip, and contracted pneumonia. She had enjoyed a good life and had two children and five grandchildren. She had been a widow for eight years. It soon became clear that she would die from complications from the pneumonia. Jeff, her eldest son, lived close by and had always been a support to his mother and recognized that her death was inevitable. He thought that only drugs that eased her pain should be administered, and no oxygen. Jeff was quite at peace with his mother's death. "I think Mom should be allowed to slip away," he said. Frank, the youngest of the three, lived a day away by plane and had seldom come to see his mother. Now she was dying, his *guilt* came to the fore. "I don't think the doctor is doing enough for Mom," he complained. "Why doesn't he insist on using oxygen and tell the nurses to feed her? I think she could live a few more months yet. I am going to report

that doctor." Even when she died peacefully Frank continued his tirade, but his feelings stemmed from personal neglect of his parent, and in reality her death was handled carefully and with compassion by medical staff.

May was in her late fifties and was dying from ovarian cancer. Her death was painful and long-drawn-out. May's older sister, Freda, took charge of her dying and enabled May to die where she wanted, at home. Caring for her was a major task, and she called on a good friend of May, Hilda, to stand in when she needed a break. At first, Hilda seemed to be doing well, but her sense of humour and her level of care began to deteriorate. Eventually, Hilda had to be replaced by workers from a care agency and when Hilda and Freda talked about this, the reason became clear. "My mother died of ovarian cancer," Hilda said. "Being with May reminded me of my mother's death and made me terribly afraid. I went to the doctor because I thought I might have cancer as well."

An Unpleasant Person Dies

As one sees from the above examples, the feelings that arise when someone dies may result from events and situations beyond the knowledge of the worship leader. One time, I was talking with family members who had lost their mother and, for lack of any positive information or funny stories of family life, I asked them what good things we might share about their mother. There was an awkward pause, and then one of the three children spoke up for them all: "Our mother gave us a very rough time as kids—and after. Today, they would say that she abused us emotionally and verbally. We are all glad she is gone."

In this case there were no *good* feelings. On the contrary, there was joy in her passing. Although this is an extreme situation of dislike, there are many situations where there is little sorrow engendered because the person who has died was sarcastic or angry or mean-spirited or cruel. How is the worship leader to deal with this situation?

The first and obvious factor is that if there are few or no feelings of loss, there is no need to speak of the loss and how to deal with it in the meditation. Yet a note of caution needs to be sounded here, for there may be those outside the family circle who were close to the deceased in a friendship, social, or intimate relationship who will be missing her very much. Their loss needs to be taken seriously. And this leads to the question of who judges the worth of the individual.

The group meeting with the worship leader may have little or nothing good to say about the person who has died, but there may be those who have experienced the care, good humour, or skills of the person in an area of which the family is unaware. The family members may also be unaware of a traumatic event or childhood relationship that was at the root of the unpleasant character trait. In a situation of unrelieved family negativity about the deceased individual, the worship leader would be well to cast his net wider for others who are able to speak about her in a positive vein.

Perhaps the most important questions to be asked are "How does God see this unpleasant person? Does God see a person as one who is to be punished or excluded from eternal life? Does God see an evil influence to be erased and a sinner to be condemned?" Those who, like me, have the vision of a God of ultimate loving kindness, a compassionate God, will see the unpleasant person as one whose dark side is to be acknowledged, but whose ultimate destiny as one of God's children is secure. If everyone is aware that Frieda had a sharp tongue, or was mean, or disliked her children, then this may be mentioned in the service, but this negativity may be balanced by talking about some of her good talents or kind ways with friends.

A particular situation sometimes encountered is where there was an addiction to alcohol or drugs. Some families will want to cover up the use of alcohol or drugs both in the interview and in the meditation given at the service. However, if the addiction is well known to the family and friendship group and influenced the behaviour of the individual, the "elephant in the room" will be obvious and will bring a sense of unreality if not mentioned in the service.

Death as Relief

A huge sense of relief may be experienced where the dying person's life partner has been under strain due to caregiver duties that he took upon himself or caregiving that was thrust upon him. Those on the outside may be critical and comment on his lack of grief in a negative way, but the insiders will be sensitive to the pressure sustained in the weeks of responsibility prior to the loved one's death and the relief he now feels at being able to get back to "normal." Superficially, his feelings might seem to be those of indifference and lack of grief, while the true feelings will reveal a joy that the struggle is over. In the service it will not be wrong to articulate the joy and relief alongside the grief that is being felt by friends and will be experienced in due time by close family members.

We Could Have Done More

A counter to the relief that the struggle of the loved one is over and that "We did all we could," is the complaint "We could have done more…" "We could have spent more time with her when she was ill; we could have been more persistent with the doctors when they were passing the buck from one to the other; we could have tried different treatments or the herbal remedies our neighbours recommended."

Sometimes these feelings of guilt have a foundation in fact, but most often there is little basis for them. My experience of being with families of dying loved ones is that there are at least one or two family members who compromise their own health by staying beside the dying person. During the family interview there is a good opportunity to affirm their loyalty and caring and invite them to relax and take it easy for a few weeks.

If the feelings of "I could have done more" persist, then the person should be referred to a psychologist or counsellor for help. In the service, it may be useful to include a prayer of confession and assurance of pardon.

Another common regret is "We were not with Dad when he died and we always promised we would be there for him." The fact of the matter is that 24-hour presence at the bedside of the dying person is not possible, and constant attendance at the bedside would have compromised the family member's own health. The worship leader in the pastoral care role has the opportunity to remind the family members of the reality of the situation and to affirm the high level of visiting that they have maintained throughout the final illness.

Other Family Members

Is this the main family grouping or are there other members? I remember being taken on one side at a reception after the service for a well-loved mother and grandmother of several children by one of the children and told, "My wife and I appreciated the words you spoke, but we didn't recognize the person you were talking about, my mother." To be on the receiving end of words such as these is not a good feeling! It was a reminder to me that one child, one group of children, or one extended group of family members may have a radically different set of memories, underlying emotions, and family priorities from the family members who contacted you, with whom you visited, and from whose memories and relationship you spoke.

A key question here is, "Are the family members who have contacted you the major family group?" Usually there is no doubt; however, it is good to keep an open mind, and if for instance you find that another family group is writing the obituary, or that the next of kin or trustees are not present, then be prepared to contact them directly.

I often ask, "Are there other family members whom I should contact?" Or noting that one significant family member has been purposely ignored in our discussion, I will ask, "Do you have John's phone number or e-mail? I would like to be in touch." If there is a best friend who has been close to the deceased, sometimes closer than family members, maybe an old service buddy with whom the person who died went fishing over the years, then I will ask for contact information and follow up. Someone like this could give the eulogy. Watch carefully though, as some of the stories may need censoring!

Sometimes the need to arrange a service is a great opportunity to get feuding members of a family together. As they reminisce about childhood happenings, holidays, and eccentric characters, there is an opportunity for old animosity to be put on one side and slights to be forgotten as the work of creating a worthy tribute proceeds.

You should not rely on this good outcome happening, however, for long-standing divisions may run deep and not only may the family be unwilling to work together on the service, but the death of a parent and especially the division of family property may intensify rivalries. I was contacted 15 years after conducting a service for a parent by a son of a deeply divided family with a request that made it clear that distrust of one side of the family for the other was alive and well.

The Service Content

There is a need during the time spent with the family to discuss the service format and any requests for music, scripture, or other readings. My experience of non-church families is that they are often happy to leave the choice of scriptures to the worship leader, and this simplifies the process. In this situation you are able to fit the readings, songs, and hymns to the person as revealed in the pastoral situation prior to death or by the family members in the planning conversation. With regard to hymns and songs, they can be those that are familiar to the potential congregation.

A challenge comes when the scripture selection requested is not in accord with the person whom you have come to know when he was dying and/ or the hymns chosen were more popular (and relevant to) the beginning of the last century than the beginning of this one. What is to be done? As far as scripture is concerned, you can always have the passage requested by the family read in addition to the passage that you feel is in tune with the person who has died—and be up front with the family about why you are including another scripture. If there is a secular reading that the family would like, then you have the options of having it read before the scriptures or including the reading, or a portion of it, in the meditation. You may also use it at the interment portion of the service.

The same goes for music. The tune of an unsuitable hymn may be played but the words not sung, and there is the option of having the music that is significant to the family members or to the deceased played as the family enters the church or chapel or as they leave. (See chapter 14 "What Makes for a Good Funeral?" page 113 "Good Music.") If there is a strong family wish for a reading or for a song or hymn, I always try to find a way to include it somewhere in the service. Where there is a will there is a way!

With church families, there is likely to be more of a sense of the scriptures and secular readings that the person would like. It is wise to check in the church office to see whether the person who has died has left instructions about the readings and hymns she wanted for her funeral or memorial service. Often there is a Funeral Services file, and if not, it is a prudent move to establish such a file and to invite church members to register their funeral requests for hymns and readings and to talk to you about them.

At one church where I ministered, I was cautioned by a faithful member, Flora, that she would come back and haunt me if the reading, "Gone only from our sight," was *not* read at her funeral. It was!

In terms of songs and hymns, there will often be a select number that are known and loved by the congregation and thus sung with heart and soul and voice. It is wise to suggest to the family of church members that two or more of these be used at the service. Some may have special meaning to the faith community. So, at a lakeside church I served, the hymn, "Jesus You Have Come to the Lakeshore," was a favourite. When it is a church member who has died, it is good to remember that the faith community is grieving the loss as well as the family, and their wishes are to be considered in the service planning.

Fees

Traditionally, there are fees associated with a funeral, memorial, or celebration. The minister is usually given a fee and so is the organist or pianist. If there is a technician, she will be paid and so will the person who is responsible for putting the bulletin together. If there is a funeral coordinator, he will receive a fee and if the janitor or church cleaner has work as a result of the service, she will be paid for her time and effort. In addition, many churches charge a fee for the use of the building, which has to be heated in winter and cooled in summer. There may also be catering fees.

It is the responsibility of the church board, council, or administrative body to set these fees, and the worship leader should ensure that the fees are available before the first service she conducts and that they are kept up to date. It will also be her responsibility to make sure that these fees are paid on the day of the service to all those who have a part in the memorial, funeral, or celebration.

Talking about fees is one of the most awkward tasks of the person responsible for the service. Often a family member will raise the question "How much should we pay you for the service, Reverend?" The most satisfactory response is to have a list of fees available on a sheet of paper and respond to the family member with "They are all listed here. Take a look, and if you have any questions, ask me."

Alternatively, the worship leader should detail the fees or refer the person to the church office where the administrator will have the list of persons to be paid and the fee amounts. Sometimes, there will be no request for fees and fee amounts and then it is the responsibility of the worship leader to inform the family of the persons who have to be paid and the amounts. The fee for the use of the sanctuary is sometimes a surprise for family members, and in this case the worship leader may refer to the heating and cooling and the high costs of maintaining the building.

In some churches there is a difference in fees depending on whether the person who has died is a member of the church or not. I have been the minister of several churches where the fee for the sanctuary has usually been waived for church members. The problem here is the definition of the term "member." Is an adherent a member? Is a person on the church mailing list a member? Where do you draw the line? The key here is that the issue of what defines membership has been discussed by the administrative body, has been documented, and is available to the worship leader.

Often it is useful for the council or board to sound out local churches in their area about fee amounts before coming to a decision for their staff and building. It is helpful if the fees are reviewed every two years.

Where there is a funeral home involved in the service, it is important that the worship leader checks to see if payment for all fees is facilitated by the funeral home before informing the family of costs. It is also important that current fees for church staff and the sanctuary are communicated directly to local funeral homes and that the funeral home is clear that in the case where their fees are below the church's schedule of fees, it is the church's schedule that will be used.

There are times when the family members of the person who has died will not have the money to pay the fees. In this situation, all or the major part of the fees should be waived.

Pastoral Care to the Grieving Family

You come to visit the family at their request to prepare for the service/celebration. This is a significant task and one that has been the preserve of clergy over the ages. You will do the best job you can to make the service liturgy for the person who has died meaningful and comforting. However, there is an unstated task when you meet with the family and that is to enable them to speak of their loss, and you will be ready to provide pastoral care and prayer if this is appropriate. You bring to this task all the skills that you used when you visited the dying person in their home or hospital. You will listen to their words and you will be sensitive to the feelings that different family members have and share between themselves. You will be ready to speak to family members not present, especially grandchildren. You will be ready to speak to any individual who has special needs or refer them to an experienced counsellor or grief group if need be. Only in the situation where you are conducting the service at the direct request of the person who has died and there is another clergy who is responsible for the pastoral care of the family will you let this crucial task go.

It requires much patience, endurance, and skill to stay with the family when the service is over and the friends and wider family are no longer dropping by. In visits with the family, it is important that you continue to talk about the person who died by name and encourage family members to talk of him and tell stories about him. Where a family has lost a child by accident or illness or if the person has taken his own life, the sense of grief is deeper and more acute, so be prepared to allocate more of your pastoral time to families who have lost loved ones in these tragic ways.

You will offer prayer to the family at the end of your time with them. The prayer might be like this:

> Eternal God,
> we are glad that *Ruth* is with you now,
> is fully loved by you,
> and has nothing to fear.
> We pray for this family (*all names*)
> as they feel *Ruth's* loss from amongst them.
> She loved them so dearly; they will miss her so much.
> Grant them strength for the days ahead, and especially
> be with them and with everyone who comes to the
> celebration on *Tuesday*.
> On that day, may they find old memories
> and discover new ones,
> old friends and ones they never knew they had.
> And may your peace, a peace that embraces *Ruth*,
> be their peace on that day
> and in all the days that lie ahead.
> In the name of Jesus the peacemaker, we pray.
> Amen.

Death of a Pet

Molly, a widow, was talking to me after the Sunday service about Andy. "He was such a good friend to me, always there when I needed him," she recalled. "He never let me down. You know, David, every day I miss him so very much." If you had been eavesdropping on the conversation and didn't know Molly, you would have been forgiven for thinking that she was talking about her late husband and not her Cocker Spaniel who had many of the faithful qualities that were noticeably absent in Arnold!

It has been my experience that the death of a family pet can cause more grief than the death of a husband or wife, especially where the relationship with the spouse was not a good one. A conversation like this one with Molly is a reminder that as pastoral caregivers and worship leaders we are called to use the same skills in being with those whose pets are dying or have died, as with their human counterparts.

There is a reluctance to formalize the burial of a well-loved dog or cat or bird, yet there is something inherently right in offering to God our thanks for the life of a pet shared over a number of years. Last summer, my wife and I watched our neighbour's grandchildren trundling what we thought was a toy animal around the backyard in a child's four-wheeled cart. We found out later that it was the body of a pet cat. It was being shown the places it liked best, where it had played and where it had chased butterflies and hunted birds over many years. A hole was dug and the cat buried following the last garden tour.

For the grandchildren, it was not only a chance to say goodbye to an old friend, but an opportunity to see what happens when a living creature dies and to ask the good but simple questions that only a child will ask: "Mom, will Rover go to a doggy heaven?" and "Will he meet up with grandpa who you said is there?" and "Mom, I don't want you to die. Will you?"

The burial of a pet is the time for some simple yet heartfelt sentiments to be expressed, and the grieving process to be started. The worship leader can be the one to make this to happen.

CHAPTER 9

Suicide

One of the most troubling situations that may be encountered is when the family member who has died took her own life. In my experience these have usually been young people, but increasingly these days older people in terrible pain and distress seek to bring their life to an end. This death is of another dimension from that of a death from cancer, stroke, or accident and affects family members and friends in a profound way and may affect the pastoral caregiver significantly as well.

As a pastoral caregiver it would be most useful if you recognized the special understanding required in handling suicide deaths and prepared for this situation by attending a course such as those offered by the Living Works organization. The following comment from the Suicide Prevention Resource Center is helpful in understanding the background to suicide:

> Those who take their own lives are often suffering from some form of mental illness. Those who end their lives do not act out of moral weakness or a character flaw, as some used to think. They are nearly always suffering from intense psychological pain from which they cannot find relief. In 90 percent of suicides, this pain may be associated with a brain illness, such as depression, schizophrenia, and bipolar disorder, and is often complicated by alcohol or other drug abuse.[1]

The illness may have existed for some time or it may have come about recently. These people are often not able to make rational choices, the way most people are able to do. There are effective treatments for these brain illnesses, but too often people suffering with this psychological pain are not able to (or choose not to) find access to those treatments. In some instances, even when treatment is given, it is not enough to prevent the suicide.

In a proportion of cases, suicidal acts are responses, sometimes impulsive responses, to difficult life situations, however temporary those situations may be. Even very close family members and friends may not have had sufficient awareness of the issues to understand the true severity of the crisis.[2]

One service I was asked to conduct was for a young man who moved to a major city far from home. Abe had lost his job, had no friends, and was in severe financial difficulties. He could see no way out of his stressful situation and took his own life. His supportive family would have been more than willing to help him out if they had known the dire straits he was in, but in his disturbed state he kept his difficulties to himself and could see no way out of them.

Some suicidal individuals go to great lengths to hide evidence of their self-destructive plans, and some show their intent in various ways. However, the signs of self-destruction are difficult to recognize for a variety of reasons. So when you get the comment, "What could I have done to prevent this?" which is usually articulated by at least one family member, it is probably fair to respond, "Not very much," and give the reasons—as explained above—why it is very hard to determine whether the family member has been planning to take his own life or not.

Appropriate Language

It is helpful to get the language right when in conversation with the family and when preparing and giving the meditation.

> Although common English usage includes the phrases "committed suicide," "successful suicide," and "failed attempt," these should be avoided because of their connotations. For instance, the verb "committed" is usually associated with sins or crimes. It is more helpful to understand the phenomenon of suicide as the worst possible outcome of mental health or behavioural health problems as they are manifested in individuals, families, and communities. Along the same lines, a suicide should never be viewed as a success, nor should a non-fatal suicide attempt be seen as a failure. Such phrases as "died by suicide," "took his life," "ended her life," or "attempted suicide" are more accurate and less offensive."[3]

Note: there will sometimes be pressure on the worship leader not to mention the word "suicide" or even not to say that the person has, "taken her own life." This pressure is to be avoided. If there is an obituary in the paper the euphemism "died suddenly" is often used, but in most cases the word is usually out and friends and family members are aware that this is not a sudden death due to illness. The net result of not mentioning the word "suicide" or not indicating that the person has taken his or her own life is to bring an air of unreality to the service or celebration. The worship leader who is asked to cover up a suicide would do well to refuse and to let the family find someone else to take the service.

Those in Pain

There is currently much controversy over the legal right of a person to end his own life because he is in unrelieved pain. That is when healthy living is no longer possible and troubled existence is the reality. In this situation, the pastoral caregiver is in an excellent place as an unbiased observer to enable the person who is in pain and his family members to express their feelings to one another and to bring as much comfort as possible to both the one in pain and his loved ones.

The Meditation

There is a need to avoid anything in the meditation that could encourage vulnerable persons in the congregation to model the suicidal behaviour. This will be especially important in the case of a funeral for a young person. Consequently, it is important not to glamorize the current state of "peace" the deceased may have found through death. It is useful to remember that there may be persons who are dealing with psychological pain or suicidal thoughts and the idea of finding peace or escape through death may make the idea of suicide attractive to them. In the same way there should be no sense in which suicide should be shown in such a light as to appear as a reasonable response to particularly distressful life circumstances.

Instead, make a clear distinction, and even separation, between the positive accomplishments and qualities of the deceased and his or her final act. Make the observation that although the deceased is no longer suffering or in turmoil, we would rather she or he had lived, and lived in a society that understood those who suffer from mental or behavioural health problems and supported those who seek help for those problems without a trace of stigma or prejudice.[4]

Make specific suggestions that will unite the community around the purpose of caring for one another more effectively. Also, ask the young people to look around and notice adults on whom they can call for help in this or other times of crisis, such as teachers, counsellors, youth leaders, and sports coaches. Consider pointing out specific adults who are known to be particularly caring and approachable. Note the desire of these adults to talk and listen to anyone who is feeling down or depressed or having thoughts of death or suicide. In the course of this discussion, endeavour to normalize the value of seeking professional help for emotional problems in the same way one would seek professional help for physical problems.

The worship leader has a unique opportunity in the meditation to speak to other young persons about the value of life and the burden that is laid on those who are family members and close friends of the person who has taken her own life.

---

[1] After a Suicide (Suicide Prevention Resource Center, 2004). Reproduced with permission.

[2] Ibid.

[3] Ibid.

[4] Ibid.

CHAPTER 10

Death of a Child

The death of a child is the most difficult of all bereavement situations. It is of a whole other dimension compared with the losses of other family members and friends. There is not only the loss of a so well-loved member of the family circle, but also the loss of all that the child might have done and become, all the experiences of life with its joys and sorrows that are no longer possible. The desolation and feelings of loss are often overwhelming to the surviving moms and dads.

You may have to talk with parents who have lost a baby in a crib death, who have lost a boy or girl through an accident at home or through illness, or parents who have lost a teenager in a car crash. It will be some of the most difficult pastoral work that you will ever do.

You will have to be ready for a whole range of feelings experienced by the parent or parents. For some, it will be sheer disbelief that the child is gone forever, even if her death was expected. For other moms and dads there will be guilt feelings over actions taken or not taken that could have resulted in her life being saved. A sense of guilt is not all bad since for some parents it provides a reason for their loss and therefore gives them a sense of control over it.

For some, there will be a sense of the unfairness that their son or daughter has died while other children of their friends or family members are still happy and healthy; for others it will be anger, even anger at God for what has happened and a consequent loss of faith. As one bereaved parent said to me, "If God can allow my son to be run over by a car, what is the good of worshipping God?"

It is not just the parents that will have been affected. There may be brothers and sisters and loving grandparents who will be suffering in different ways through the loss. What can you do as a pastoral caregiver to help the family?

For a start, you are a safe person to whom they can turn to express their deepest feelings in absolute confidence. You are there for them no matter what happens, and this will be strength at a time of great vulnerability and fear, for they can speak to you of everything that is on their mind. This is the most valuable gift you bring to the pastoral conversation—the ability to hear what is on the mind of the parent or parents. You will listen attentively and you will not put limits on the time you are available to them.

When working in a pastoral care role, it is useful to note the different gender response where there has been a miscarriage or where a baby has died shortly after birth. The mother has had an intimate relationship with the child since conception; she knows the baby's ways and personality, and the loss is of a person, a small and not yet developed person, but a person none the less. For the father, the loss is still huge, but will not be so personal or devastating. There is the sense of the loss of all that the child might have become, but the idea that "We can have another child" can come creeping in. There is a danger that if another child is conceived shortly after the death of a baby, the child will be seen as "replacement" and treated as the deceased child would have been, rather than as a unique little one in his or her own right.

A word of caution! If in your conversation with a parent or parents you are encountering extreme feelings of depression or sadness that have not been shared with others, and especially if you hear of a desire by one parent to take his or her own life, then you should encourage the bereaved person to see a doctor. The key here is serious intent. One person may say, "I feel so miserable, I wish I could end it all," without any intent to follow through, but if the bereaved person reveals a thought-out plan to take his or her own life, then you must inform the appropriate authorities. In a situation of extreme depression or emotional turmoil, it is important that the pastoral caregiver is aware of her own limitations and refers the person promptly.

In spite of your listening and presence with the family, it will not be possible for you to feel fully the pain of the parents. This can only be done by persons who have gone through the same experience. The Compassionate Friends (TCF) is one of several organizations that enable bereaved parents to help other bereaved parents. The empathy generated in such groups is health bringing to parents who have the feeling that in their loss they are alone, the only ones to have had a child die. They say, "Who else can understand the terrible feelings of loss and pain that we have suffered?" When they hear the words "I can!" and listen to the account of how *another* beloved child enjoyed life, and then died or was killed, and the devastation that has followed for a family like their own, there is a unique compassion that flows. There is a fellow feeling that heals and sustains.

In these groups, the names of the deceased children are used frequently, and stories of their lives remembered and recounted. Many parents will find this to be in sharp contrast to the family circle where family members will avoid mentioning the name of the child or the telling of activities and funny stories for fear of stirring up repressed emotions. It is a reminder to you, the pastoral caregiver, to speak of the boy or girl who has died by name and not to be afraid of retelling stories that you remember from your own experience or that of your faith community.

As with other self-help groups, it is not the expert in their midst who is looked up to as the source of all wisdom, but people like themselves who speak directly from their own experience of loss. The parents helped in this way will find that in time they will be able to help others who are in the hard place of bereavement.

Two key factors in the success of these groups are that members are able to talk in complete confidence and that it is initially complete strangers who are encountered. There is no need for polite introductory chit chat or catching up with family news. The grieving parent is able to get down to what is on his mind—the death of his well-loved child.

In some groups, the self-help process is supplemented by lectures, videos, and question and answer sessions, but the core activity is the sharing of experience from parent to parent. These groups are not perfect; for example, parents might encounter dominant personalities who tell them exactly what they *should* do. However, generally these groups will be sources of healing and understanding.

One of the actions you can take as someone new to the area is to compile a list of appropriate self-help groups in your neighbourhood so you are ready to refer when the time comes. It is also useful to ask around about counsellors who are prepared to work with bereaved parents on a one-on-one basis. If you are asking around, it is worthwhile to determine those counsellors whose clients have had helpful outcomes and those whose clients have been less satisfied.

Now all this is great if you live in an area where there is a chapter of a TCF or a Sudden Infant Death Syndrome (SIDS) group, where the parents of children who have died are able to get together and talk of their loss. What happens if you are a pastoral caregiver in a rural area and there is no self-help group around? The same principle applies. Find someone who has gone through the experience as the grieving parent and encourage them to share on a one-on-one or parent-with-parent basis. Social workers who have this as their working area and a family doctor may be sources of information about those who have lost a child and may welcome the chance to help their patients or clients in this way.

If you discover there is an unmet need in your area for a self-help group for the death of an unborn baby, a crib death, the death of a child or teenager, you could be the one to organize an initial meeting.

If you find yourself challenged by pastoral care in this area or by the needs of dying or bereaved persons, then you may respond to the challenge as a call to undergo some additional training. Organizations that can help you with this training include the Canadian Association for Spiritual Care and The Association for Clinical Pastoral Education (USA).

Where the child has been in school, there will be a need of the classmates of the child who has died to have counselling available, and most school districts or areas provide this. The administrator of the school district should be contacted if this service is not available.

As you talk to the parents about the loss of their school-age child, it will be prudent for you to be thinking about the school-age children who are coming to the service—what their needs will be, what scripture passages and other readings will speak to them, and how the vocabulary will have to be pitched at a lower grade level than usual. You may want to ask if another child or parent or teacher could be called to speak about the child who has died. Even a few carefully chosen words from individuals close to the child who has died will have a major impact for good.

CHAPTER 11

Children and Their Grief

As the worship leader in the pastoral care role, you will often become aware of and know the children who are affected by the dying and death of a parent.

If a parent is dying and the child wants to see him, then the child should be given the opportunity and the time she needs to be with the parent. If the parent is connected up to equipment that makes breathing easier or reduces pain, then one of the nursing staff should be encouraged to tell the child in simple language what is going on.

If the child doesn't want to come to the hospital, then it is fine to leave him at home with a compassionate friend. Undue persuasion will be counter-productive.

It is necessary to include the child in the grief process. Children experience stress and deep sorrow if they are excluded or ignored after the death of a cherished family member. Where it is the child's mom or dad who has died, the surviving partner is often the focus of much attention from family members or friends. There will be friends and family dropping by who are usually seldom there, the TV may be turned off, the usual games not possible, and the iPad hidden away. The result of this new pattern of activity in the home is to disrupt the normal family routine established over the years, and it may be deeply troubling to the child.

What the child is wanting at this challenging time is consistent parental warmth and discipline, and when she receives this, she will respond positively to the new situation however challenging and disruptive it may be. If the surviving parent is not coping well with her own grief, then the child likely will not cope well with hers and may act out. What will help the child best is a surviving parent who is tuned in to her grief and responds directly to the expressed feelings and behaviours.

The death of a parent may be disturbing from a number of points of view. The stress may be financial as well as emotional, and there may be thoughts of moving away from the neighbourhood. The role of the pastoral caregiver can be to encourage the surviving parent to involve the child or children in the bereavement situation and to pay loving attention to them. There may well be questions about death and dying, and the parent will do well to answer them directly and honestly without giving any more information than is required.

This is a time when, in children's story terms, the "Snow White" approach, where the apparently dead princess is kissed and restored to life, is not helpful. Better the "Old Yeller" story where the well-loved dog, after its fight with the wolf, has to be shot, where death is seen as final and irreversible, the way things are in the real world.

And games are important, for the world of children is a world of play. When children are playing, one often assumes that they are okay, that they aren't "getting it," or that they don't understand. Adults also err by not allowing children to play at times of stress and death. For example, a parent might scold a child by saying, "How can you be out playing when grandma has just died?" However, play is how children work out what they are feeling. Children will also "dose" grief; that is, they will focus on the grief for a small amount of time, then continue with their normal activities and return to the grief later. So the pastoral caregiver can have a role in encouraging the child to play, for while playing, she may work out some of her grief feelings. The pastoral caregiver may also encourage the parent to let the child have fun in her usual playful ways.

When adults are caught up in their grieving, it may be difficult for them to be aware of the needs of the children who also are grieving, so the pastoral caregiver has a role in giving neighbours and friends of the bereaved parent permission to pay careful attention to children. This opportunity to have children's grieving needs on a par with those of the adults is something the children may initially seem to want to avoid, yet many of them will at heart long to be included. There are conflicting emotions at work here. While some will long to be hugged and cuddled, others will want to feel free to cry or to express anger. Some will want to run away and hide, while others will want to appear to be "strong." So the pastoral caregiver should encourage friends and family members to take notice of the children and allow them to express their own feelings—in their own time and in their own way. One thing is for sure, children are remarkable in sharing their feelings when given space, acceptance, and safety.

When it comes to planning a service, it is good for the pastoral caregiver to include children and to listen carefully to their questions, their comments, and their memories about the person who has died. It will be helpful to include them in the service. If possible, it will be helpful to involve them in the ritual—lighting candles, telling stories that relate to them, using their ideas, and giving them a special place. Always give them the opportunity to attend the service.

CHAPTER 12

Speaking about the Deceased

Worship Leader's Meditation

When the worship leader returns home from visiting the family, he will take time to be quiet and pray and will read through the material he gathered at his meeting with the family a couple of times. He will then determine what makes up the core values of the person who has died and what theme emerges from stories family members told around the room. It is helpful to leave this information to settle overnight before writing the meditation.

As a result of talking with the family, there are two situations in which the worship leader may find herself. She may be responsible for crafting the meditation to include information about the life of the person who has died, or there may be a eulogist who is responsible for this, and so her meditation will focus on the way chosen scripture resonates with the life of the deceased.

These days, since there is often a eulogist, I arrange two parts as the worship leader. In the first part of the meditation, it is good to centre on the fact of the death of the person and our need to say "goodbye" to her. The first part of the meditation also provides an opportunity to introduce the theme and leads to the eulogy. Here is an example:

Readings: Luke 11:34–36 and Romans 8 (selected verses)

We are privileged people, for we meet to celebrate Connie, one who was gracious and caring, whose long and good life was a light to many, an inspiration to those who knew her, one whose love touched each friend and family member.

As you know, Connie died quickly and though for her it was a blessing that she was spared the struggle of poor health, for us it is tough because we did not have the time we wanted to visit her, and to linger thoughtfully over our goodbyes and express them directly to her. There is much thanks and many good memories that we would have liked to share if only we had had the opportunity, and we are aware that we are going to miss her so much in the weeks ahead.

"If then your whole body is full of light…it will be as full of light as when a lamp gives you light with its rays" (Luke 11:36) wrote Luke in his gospel, and we are going to hear now of that loving light. We will hear from Joe, her son, and Phyllis, her daughter, who have experienced that light because of their closeness to Connie, but also as family members who reflect that light.

The second part of the meditation includes a word of thanks to the person/ persons who have given the eulogy, addresses the loss that has been suffered, and acknowledges the need of those gathered to deal in a positive way with the grief they feel. There is a call to congregational members to support the grieving family. Then follows a reference to the faith life and practice of the person who has died, leading to the note of resurrection hope of the life that will begin when this one ends. The meditation ends with an assurance that the love and peace of God will be the ultimate destiny of the deceased.

Joe, Phyllis, you have given your last and best gift to us and to your mother, the gift of loving memories. What you have done is so difficult, but we are deeply grateful. You were so good to your mother in those last few days and so caring. The two of you, with your sister Bridget and brother Ralph, were there when your mother needed you; you could not have done more. Your children and members of the wider family circle are in the thoughts and prayers of everyone here, as are those who cannot be with us today, but are with us in spirit. It is because you loved Connie so much that you miss her so much and feel her loss so acutely, and I challenge you to put into words your deepest feelings about Connie and to share them with a good friend or minister, someone you can trust.

We have heard how Connie was the most positive and practically helpful person to be with. She looked for the best in everyone she met and because she looked for the best, she usually found it. Connie was both delightful and enlightening and the source of her radiance is not hard to find as she was a person of faith, a living faith with an active edge—shopping and caring for a neighbour who had tripped on the ice, providing a loving home for grandchild Susan when her mom had to go into hospital for a short stay. (You might add: "You have your own stories, shout them out!") She was reluctant to talk about the Jesus whose way she followed, but she was absolutely sure that God had work for her to do and was absolutely ready to do it. It was the way of Jesus that illuminated her path, the compassionate and just way. "What can separate us from that loving light?" Paul might almost have written. (See the passages from Romans 8 on page 265.)

I am convinced that Connie could face the end of her life with such grace, with such an uplifted spirit because she knew beyond any doubt that death was a stopping-off place before she reached an existence where the infirmities of this life are over forever. You know as I know that because of her faith the prospect of death left her unafraid.

We who are left on the earth side of death rejoice that Connie has entered into the peace of God that passes all understanding, the peace that is ahead for us when this life draws to a close for us. We are sad, we are very sad that her light will not lighten our lives again, but we are challenged to let our light shine in our particular corner of the world with that same faithful intensity that embraced God's servant, Connie. Amen.

In this situation, there were family eulogies, but where there are not, the worship leader has the responsibility to include a sketch of the person who has died. It will be good if she is able to retell some family stories to make clear what he was like. Where the worship leader has had a personal or faith community relationship with the person who has died, it is helpful to include some of her own stories. The stories of the life and work of the person in the faith community fit naturally in the second part of the meditation.

Eulogies, Tributes, and Talks

The word "eulogy" is not one we use much in everyday life. It comes from the Greek, meaning "good words." When it is used in the context of a funeral or life celebration, these good words are often spoken by a family member or close friend of the family about the person who has died.

The person who is giving the eulogy is in a tough spot, for she has to forgo her time of grieving in the service and speak of her loved one. I often say that the words that we hear are "grace to us," that is, they are a freely offered and wonderful gift. They do not have to be polished or clever or intellectually profound, but they do have to come from the heart, and if they do, they will be received and treasured and will be the means through which others in the congregation are encouraged to tell their own stories and remember with their own joy and tears the person who has died.

I like to think of the eulogy in terms of art. It is not an entirely accurate picture of the life of the person who has died, with all the details carefully filled in, but a quick study, a sketch, an impression of the person as he was seen by the one chosen to give the eulogy. The great eulogist can be compared to an insightful impressionist painter, a Renoir or a Degas.

In contemporary services, it is commonplace for family members or good friends to be asked to talk about the person who has died. There is value in having a close family member or good friend do this as they speak from personal knowledge, and there is an authentic ring to their words. They will be able to share a wealth of stories that quite naturally point to the core values, priorities, and loves of their beloved one.

There are some challenges. The close bond of family will mean that there will be an emotional content to the talk that may get in the way of a straightforward delivery. A son or daughter may be overcome with emotion when speaking of their mother or father and have to stop talking during the eulogy or in the worst case, be so distraught that they are unable to continue. The worship leader needs to be ready for this.

Usually, the family member will know if she will be able to speak. If she is hesitant or feels that she will dread the event, support her feeling that this task is not for her. Give her the alternative of writing a script that another brother or sister might read or that you as worship leader might read. Better still, have a member of the wider family circle speak for all and have the close family members collaborate as the talk is put together.

If the speaker has not spoken at the service of a close relative before, the worship leader might want to say something like "Francis, you do not need to feel you have to speak at your mother's service and that is quite okay. (*Give him time to respond!*) It will be wonderful if you are able to do this because I know you were so close to her, and your words will be a very special gift to us all. You may find that you get choked up with emotion as you speak. Don't worry. Simply stop, get yourself together, and then go on. Everyone will understand if you have to stop. If you find that you are unable to continue, then have a script available, and one of your sisters will carry on from where you left off or I can read it for you."

Often, you will be asked about a suitable length of time for the talk or talks. I would encourage the eulogy not to exceed 12 minutes in total. This would allow for three family members or friends to speak for four minutes each. The problem is that as worship leader you have no control over the length of the talks. I have had family members promise to limit their talk to three minutes, then speak for an average of 15 minutes each. The worship leader might say something like "There is so much to say about your dad so I know you will find it difficult to keep your three talks to 12 minutes, but *you* know what it is to listen to a long speech or sermon. Better have the people wanting more than have them restless in their seats."

You could encourage the family to e-mail their scripts to you well ahead of the service. If, after reading the content, it is apparent that they will run over the allotted time, you could point out the time overrun, suggest that some of the material be left out, and even suggest the areas where changes might be made. Sometimes, the worship leader will have been a good friend of the deceased and can speak from his time with her, incorporating his thoughts with those of the family in different places in the service. For example, during the final section about the hope of a life after this one ends, it might be appropriate to speak of the life of the person in the faith community—the areas she served including some stories of her faithful service.

If this concern about time limits seems a problem to the family it may be appropriate to have an open mike and allow anyone who wishes to speak without limit. In this case, it is good to warn the congregation with something like "We will be having an open mike, and anyone here is free to share their stories about Frank. We realize that for some of you, sitting for a long time will be tiring, so feel free to get up and walk around and help yourself to a cup of coffee." As an alternative, the worship leader may schedule a formal break in the proceedings and invite the congregation to stretch their legs and have the musician play when it is time to return.

At the end of the day, the length of time that chosen family members and friends take with their memories and eulogies is beyond your control. All you can do is ensure that the congregation has the opportunity between speakers to stretch, take a drink of water, and if necessary leave the service.

How to Write a Eulogy

Many of the comments outlined above will apply to the task of writing a eulogy, but also you will have your own experience with the deceased. Before anything else, write down on a single sheet of paper your thoughts and some stories that come immediately to mind. Don't dwell on what you are doing; just let the memories flow. Then take a look at what you have written and see if a theme comes to mind. It could be that Frank was a gardener or a loving grandparent or that a feature of his life was welcoming strangers, or that Louise was a fisher or a quilter and a feature of her life was helping those who were starting off in new ventures.

You don't have to discover a theme, but remember that this is not a biography but an impressionist sketch, and a strong theme may provide the framework that enables the eulogy to come together.

Having done your own preliminary work, take it to the gathered family, thank them for their confidence in you as the eulogist, and share your first thoughts and theme and encourage them to do likewise. Remind them that it is the stories, not the facts, that will be remembered long after the service is over, and encourage them to share the stories that mean most to them and are most typical of the loved one who has died.

Your role in this situation will be less to ask direct questions and more to keep the conversation rolling and to interrupt when you need clarity or expansion on a topic that is central to the life that is being explored. "That story about Frank leaving his safe job in the bank for one as an accountant with a start up plastics company is a fascinating one. It seems like taking risks to have a satisfying life was one of the marks of his life. Are there any similar stories you remember?"

As you listen there will be some questions you will have in mind—some you will express aloud and others you will not, e.g., What was Frank's childhood like? Was it a joyful time or a struggle? And how did he relate to his mother and his father? Did he make friends easily, and does he still have the friends he made as a child or as a teen? What were his interests as a young person and where did he go to have fun?

How did Louise enjoy school, and what subjects and sports interested her most? Where did Louise meet her partner, and is there a story about their first meeting? What did Louise and her partner enjoy doing together, and where were they married? What was the work that Louise trained to do, and where did she work first? Was work more important than leisure activities or were social groups and outings more important than work?

What were Frank's leisure groups—bowling, hockey, the Royal Canadian Legion, softball, drama, painting? Did Frank take a leadership role in them? What jobs did Frank have in his working career, and how did he feel about his work? Did Frank enjoy leadership or did he prefer to have a defined and predictable role? How many children did Frank have, and how did he relate to them? Did he share equally the parenting role or was his partner the primary caregiver? What did the family enjoy doing together? (Family stories are always well received.)

Did Louise have just one partner in life or two or more? If more than one, how did they part? Death or divorce? How did she relate to her partners? Did Louise have a pet, and was the pet an important factor in her life?

Was Frank a churchgoer and if so, what part did he play in the local and area faith communities? (The worship leader will probably deal with this.)

What was Frank and Louise's state of health during their life and what part did it play in their life? Was keeping fit, running, or walking important to them? What was the cause of their death? How did they die? Easily and peacefully? Painfully? Fearfully?

If you are well prepared, you will have more material than you need, so the next task is to read through your notes a couple of times and evaluate what is most important and what fits in with the theme you have chosen. Highlight the stories and the phrases that will be heartfelt by the congregation and will cause them to say, "Yes, that was the Frank that I knew!"

When it comes to the framework of the eulogy, the introduction should set the scene for what follows.

A story that encapsulates the theme of the person's life is the best way and will immediately draw the attention of the gathered family and friends. Another way is to find a short phrase that briefly and succinctly sums up the life. The following is how I summed up my mother's life: "Mom enjoyed life and loved her home. She was a happy person whose happiness was infectious. She was a hospitable person whose hospitality was a byword…"

As you begin to write the main part of the eulogy, remember it is you who are speaking first and foremost from your own experience, so don't be afraid to use "I" statements, e.g., "I first met John when we were in the Cub Scouts; I remember that the Cub leader despaired of us ever mastering the reef knot."

If you have a good story from the family to use, then give the name of the family member who told it to you, e.g., "Ian, Frank's youngest son, tells of how…" and make sure that you have the story right by getting the family member to check it prior to the service. As you are writing, keep asking yourself, "Is this important to the chosen theme, and does what I have written reflect the values of Frank's life?" If the person who has died had a poem or passage of scripture that was important to him or a phrase that he had in a prominent place in his kitchen or work room, then consider using that as a part of the eulogy. You do not have to be grammatically correct in every detail; use the words that come from your heart rather than the ones that sound impressive, but make sure if you use slang terms or swear words that you keep them relevant and to a minimum. One other concern: off-colour jokes are not acceptable at a funeral.

There are three ways commonly used to end the eulogy, all of which speak of how the person who has died will be missed and how they will be remembered. Probably the best way is to use a story that summarizes the theme you have chosen to describe the person's life and leave it at that, although these stories are hard to come by!

The second way is to find some good words to sum up the life of the person and affirm how much they will be remembered, e.g., "Frank taught us so much about the giving of talent and ability to help others. His influence will live on among us for the rest of our lives. We will miss him so much."

The third way is to speak to Frank as if he were present in the hall or sanctuary with the guests or congregants, e.g., "Frank, you have taught us through your life about how to use our God-given talents. We will try to follow your example. We will miss you so much."

Remember that the key to writing eulogies is to use stories, but also to keep to what is essential and to write from the heart! When you have finished writing, show the finished draft to a family member and get her to check it through. If you have any doubts about the facts or the stories, check them out with the person who gave you the material.

Combined Family Eulogy

Some of the best eulogies I have heard have been those written when the family members got together before the service and, over hot chocolate or a bottle of wine, worked on a combined family eulogy. This avoids four or five members taking time at the service by recalling the same stories or recounting the same family events.

This process requires a "captain" for the eulogy team and a fair degree of co-operation among the participating members. It will be effective, not just because duplication is avoided, but also because one story from one family member sparks memory of another story and another situation. It is important for the team captain to have an idea of the time allocated by the worship leader for the family eulogy, and if this limit is to be exceeded, to give notice of the total time to the worship leader.

Eulogy Delivery

It is one thing to write a faithful eulogy, but until the "good words" are delivered, it isn't a eulogy! If you are the sort of person who is able to speak with a minimum of notes, then assemble the notes, find a quiet place, and deliver the eulogy—to the mirror, to the cat, or to a family picture. Speak slowly and as clearly as you are able, and then try it out on your spouse or find a good friend or trusted family member and deliver the eulogy to them, asking the questions "Was I too fast or too slow or just right?" and "What did you understand from the words I spoke as the central theme of Louise's life?"

If you are in any doubt about your ability to remember what you want to say, then deliver the eulogy from a full set of notes. If you are new to eulogy delivery, ask to have a voice rehearsal in the hall or sanctuary ahead of the service or celebration. Make sure that you have the sound system switched on, but remember that a room full of people will deaden the sound, and you may have to speak louder.

Before the service, test out the mike, and if it is not working, check with the worship leader or the sound technician to get it operational. Ask someone at the back of the room to check the sound level and to tell you if your voice appears to be too loud or too soft.

CHAPTER 13

Before the Service

Pre-funeral Gathering (Visitation)

A gathering before the funeral or life celebration, either at the funeral home or church, is often suggested by the funeral director and has more than one purpose. Traditionally, it was an opportunity to visit with or see the body of the deceased and to understand that the person you knew well, laughed with, ate food with, played hockey with, shared friendship with, is indeed dead. The presence of the body is a reality check. There is value in doing this, but if the body lying in the casket does have significant differences from the person when they were alive—clothing, hairstyle, or skin tone—the last impression may be one that people wish they had not seen.

This gathering time is an occasion to visit with close family members and give condolences, share stories, and exchange good memories. Increasingly today, there is an urn or a closed casket present, in which case, the nature of the gathering changes. There is still the opportunity for folk to realize that their loved one or friend has gone forever and a time to offer sympathy to close family members, but with food and drink provided it becomes an occasion for reunion, especially for those from out of town.

In the Roman Catholic tradition, public prayers are offered for the person who has died and for the family and other mourners, and though this is a practice found in other denominations, it does not happen often. What does happen in certain parts of Canada is that the casket is brought from the funeral home to the local church. Before the public gathering, family members meet, often only with their priest or minister, to view the body of their loved one, and prayers are offered by the minister or priest.

As the worship leader, you may be asked whether the public gathering is needed, and you need to be ready with your reply.

In some parts of Canada, it is tradition. A funeral is not a funeral unless
there is a gathering before the service—an informal way for community and
church members to connect, tell stories, and share both laughter and tears.

In our increasingly urban society, there is neither the time nor the inclination
of many families for a pre-funeral gathering. Certainly the family will want
to see the body of their loved one if they have not done so before, but they
can do this privately in the funeral home with or without their minister present. A public gathering is seen as an additional end-of-life cost with nothing
achieved that cannot be achieved at a reception directly after the service.

A Collage or a Video
The old saying "a picture is worth a thousand words" has some truth to it.
There has long been a tradition of having a collage of family pictures at the
back of the sanctuary or in the refreshment hall. The congregants love to
look at the family pictures. To see the snapshots of the deceased person on
the beach or at a family gathering is usually to see them enjoying themselves,
relaxed and having fun. We are able to identify with these situations. So why
not go one step further and have a video playing at the same time as the
eulogies are being delivered? Modern digital technology makes it possible to
use the screen on which the hymn words and prayers are displayed to project
still or moving pictures while the eulogies are in progress.

Skype or Streamed in Real Time
There was a time when the only people who could be present for a service
were those in the congregation, but times have changed. At a recent service
in our church not only were congregants in our town present, but also grandchildren in Australia and India were watching the service on Skype. Laptop
computers were set up in the sanctuary, and the grandchildren were able to
be a part of the service although they were thousands of miles away.

Current technology allows the services to be broadcast online and viewed in
real time through streaming video, and though it is yesterday's technology,
it is also easy to record the service on a CD, burn copies, and send them to
family members unable to be present.

The role of the worship leader is to bring these possibilities to the attention
of the family and to be sure which ones are available to them. Always make

sure that the transmission is tested by a competent technician or family member before the service begins and that the technician monitors transmission during the service time.

Physical Objects and Pets

"When you think of Dad, what first comes to mind?" The response to this question will often be an article of clothing or an object that speaks of the leisure interests of the one who has died, e.g., "When I think of Dad, I think of him wearing that dreadful old hat, working in the garden with a spade that has half the handle missing" or "When I think of Mom, I think of her picking those wild daisies at the cottage wearing that pepper spray can to keep the bears away." Iconic physical items worn and carried have a place alongside the photographs of Mom/Dad on the communion table or at least at the front of the sanctuary. If Dad was never happier than when he was canoeing, why not have his canoe brought in and placed at the front of the sanctuary? The image of the physical object will be remembered long after the most eloquent words spoken have been lost from memory.

In these days a laptop computer or cellphone may be the items to have at the front of the sanctuary. If the cellphone is called at a predetermined time, it will never be forgotten!

For the service leader, there may be a need to raise the issue of what is acceptable in the sanctuary and what is not. The girlie calendar that Dad always kept behind the workshop door would not be acceptable, neither would the apron with the words "What happens in Vegas stays in Vegas" that Mom got on a "Red Hats" trip to Sin City! Having said this, the worship leader should go the extra mile to accommodate the wishes of the family.

One of the tasks that the family usually takes care of when they arrive at the church on the day of the service is to set up the table with flowers, a photograph of the loved one who has died, and the iconic object or objects. It is good to fill in the before-the-service time in this practical way. One of the problems is that the candles and cross may get obscured or moved somewhere else. It is the worship leader's task to make sure they have their traditional and prominent place on the communion table. If space is an issue, the worship leader will be able to find a table that can be set up adjoining the communion table on which family photos and objects may be placed.

Both my partner, Kathy, and I have had requests from dog owners to have well-loved pets present during the service/celebration and have made that possible. If the dog is well behaved, why not? The son of a person who had died brought his father's cherished mongrel to the front of the church for the time he gave the eulogy. The dog stood at the side of the lectern as good as gold while the son spoke and trotted back to the front pew when the speaking time was over. On another occasion, the person who had died was instrumental in starting a pet visitation program in a local old folks' home.

To make sure that those with allergies to dogs are alerted, it would be wise to have a notice about dogs being in the sanctuary both in the newspaper notice and in a prominent posting on the door of the church.

Fraternal Organizations

If the person who has died has been a member of a fraternal organization, that group may feel that it is appropriate to hold their own service at the same time as the celebration/service you are responsible for. One of the office holders may contact you or a family member and say, "We usually have a short service before or after the family service." The more assertive leaders will put the request across in a way that leaves you feeling there is no way you can refuse. The family members may decide to give their assent or are quite within their rights to say, "No, we don't want that, but we will be happy if the group comes to the service with their customary uniform or dress." They may wish to invite the group to act as honorary pallbearers. If the approach is made directly to you, the worship leader, you should discuss the request with the family member who is your contact person.

If the family members are happy with the organization having their own service, it should preferably be carried out before the family service. Ask the group contact person how long the service will last, and discourage any service that exceeds 10 minutes. There may be resistance to this, but if so, offer to work with the group to edit the service for length. Discourage a eulogy as you have no control over the length of this tribute to the deceased. Some speakers can speak wonderfully and concisely, but others may go on and on and say very little.

If there is a time during the evening before the service when the family is receiving friends at the funeral home or in the church, suggest that the fraternal organization service be held then.

Checklists

As we have seen, a whole lot of preparatory work has been done ahead of the day of the celebration or funeral. The worship leader has a range of practical tasks not only to make sure that she is able to offer a worthy service, but also to make sure that those who come to the service are welcomed and treated well. There are variations of the practical work that has to be done by the worship leader, depending on whether the service is in her church or held at another location. The amount of work will also be less if the funeral home is involved and especially if the funeral home's chapel is used for the service.

I have detailed the specific tasks in appendix 1, pages 253–259:

- Worship Leader's Checklist (own church)
- Usher's/Funeral Helper's Checklist
- Worship Leader's Checklist (other location)

CHAPTER 14

What Makes for a Good Funeral?

As a member of the congregation at a funeral or celebration service, have you ever come out at the end of the service and shared with the person next to you, "Wow, that was a good funeral"? Most people have made this sort of comment at one time or another without usually analyzing what it was that worked for them in the service or in the time afterwards. It is useful, then, to give some pointers to the elements that make for a good funeral, not so much as a means of providing a step-by-step guide, but as a foundation on which a worthy thanksgiving and celebration experience may be created.

As has been mentioned in earlier chapters, a primary element will be the pastoral relationship between the worship leader and the person who is dying and his family. The nature of his death, how the person died, will also have a bearing on the service, and this in turn will lead to a consideration of the readings and liturgy that will form a part of it.

Thanksgiving for this unique life will form an important aspect of the service—you only live and die once! And whether the person who has died was a member of the local faith community will be significant as will his membership of political, sports, and social groups, and the other communities of which he was a part.

The music that is a crucial part of the service will determine its tone and mood, but there will remain a need to speak of the loss that has been suffered by family and friends and how the presence of the person who has died is to be found or recognized in the social hall or sanctuary.

A good funeral or celebration is a tough experience to prepare for, but is well worth the effort.

Pastoral Relationship

What makes for a good funeral, a good ending? It starts with your first contact with the family when you are invited as a leader of a faith community to minister to the person who is dying. If you are the minister or the pastor of a congregation to which the dying person belongs, then your contact with the church member may have been of long standing, and you may have got to know her in the days when she was active in the local church and town. This relationship means that you bring shared experiences, joys, and challenges to the bedside of the person who is dying. Maybe you knew her as a member of your Bible study group or as a fundraiser for a new hymn book. If the church member is close and known, she will have an enhanced level of trust and confidence in your ability to accompany her on the last stage of her life's journey.

A problem arises when the church member has become a close friend of the worship leader or minister.

In my first pastoral charge in Saskatchewan, I was befriended by an elderly woman who saw at once that I had no conception of how cold it might become when the prairie winter set in, and one afternoon when I came in shivering from the bitter cold, she told me in no uncertain terms that I needed a coat. "I have a spare one of Joe's. Here it is; make sure you wear it!" she said as I prepared to leave the house.

Our family was an ocean away from parents and grandparents, and Ethel became family to us and to our children. Eighteen months passed, and Ethel and Joe went into a care home. Shortly after Ethel died, I was asked to conduct the funeral. It was incredibly difficult. Here I was, the minister and worship leader, when what I needed to be was in a pew as one of the mourners. I got through the service, but there were several pauses as I stopped to fight back my emotions.

Everything you do that comes within the meaning of that term "pastoral care" with the person who has died will impact the preparation of the service and the Spirit that is within the service on the day of celebration or funeral

The Way He Died

"About that day or hour no one knows" (Mark 13:32) is true of the "last times," but also true of the way and place we die. For some, death is natural and gentle after a long and happy life, a peaceful last breath with family all around, but for some, death is tortured and horrible. We don't know when or how we will die, and it is just as well!

A good funeral is where those preparing for it will have responded to these two factors in a compassionate and pastoral way.

If the death is of an old person at a time when his body and mind were beginning to fail him, then there will be relief that Jack did not have to struggle on and receive increasing levels of care. But it is good to be aware that there will be family members who will still miss his presence, and it is necessary to speak to their loss and to review his life, giving thanks for all that has been accomplished in it.

If the death is sudden—accidental or as a result of the person taking his own life—then the priority in the service will be to deal compassionately and sensitively with those who have suffered the death of a loved one. Jill's family will be emotionally in turmoil at the sudden loss, and the readings, the prayers, and the meditation must address the situation. This is not the time to voice rationalizations such as "Everything happens for a reason, and one day we will understand" or "Well, you had Jill for 17 years at least, and that is a blessing." The good funeral in this situation will confront the enormity of the loss and appreciate that the emotions are overwhelming as in "Why Jill? Why now?" There will be a time of thanksgiving for Jill's life during the service, and this is an essential part of it, but it is secondary to the concern for the unbearable heartbreak of family and friends.

Scripture and Secular Readings

Some worship leaders use the same scripture passages for every funeral they conduct. So one hears Psalm 23 or John 14 (1–6 and 27) forced into reflecting the lives and death situations of Jack and Jill and all the others in between. A good funeral has scriptures that are relevant to the person who has died.

For Jack who died at a good age, peacefully, with his family around him, "Everything has its time" (Ecclesiastes 3:1–8) would be appropriate, and for Jill's suicide, "Out of the depths" (Psalm 130) will strike a chord with the struggling and loss-stricken family.

Finding the scripture or scriptures that fit the family situation is an art. It is advisable not to go to the pre-service meeting with the family with any fixed idea about scripture selections. It is best to wait until the family conversation is over, read your notes over very slowly, prayerfully, and carefully, and then search and determine which scripture passage seems appropriate. It is useful to tell the family members that this is the process you will be following.

Sometimes, the decision is easy. If the person who has died is a healer or a teacher, then there are many scripture passages that will speak directly to the deceased. You can choose from the gospel passages. But even here you have to go carefully. It may be that the person who has died was a teacher, but she had a deep love for her partner or pet or for a voluntary enterprise in which she was involved so that 1 Corinthians 13, the "Hymn of Love," would be a more appropriate choice.

In appendix 2, page 260, I have detailed key scriptures, but the list is by no means comprehensive, and you may have to dig deep into your scripture knowledge to find a suitable passage. Internet searches will be useful if you cannot find the scripture that fits the person or situation, or word searches using a good analytical concordance.

Don't be afraid to use books that share other people's celebrations or funeral meditations as a source of scripture or as a framework for the meditation. You will be able to modify them to your own needs. The use of extracts from books or poems that resonate with the person, his life, his loves, his faith life, or his work life is to be encouraged. The scriptures were written 2,000 plus years ago and speak to their time, but we need in today's services spiritual and secular writings that speak to our time. For example, there is little in the gospels that relates to the challenges and joys of living in community, but in the book *Community and Growth* by Jean Vanier (a saint of our time), there is a treasure trove of insights and experience that can be used to focus and reflect on the role of the deceased in community. My partner, Kathy, was conducting a funeral for a devoted dog owner and found a poem that spoke perfectly of the love of a dog owner for her pet and best friend.

Some liturgists discourage the use of secular readings in the same place in the service order as sacred readings, feeling this to be unworthy, but I believe that readings that have the divine spirit within them are fully acceptable and can be used with the same authority as the Hebrew and Christian scriptures.

A good funeral service or celebration will align the scriptures and secular readings with the person who has died. There will be a resonance between personality and the sacred—and not so sacred—word.

Thanksgiving

You live once and die once (unless reincarnation is a part of your theological understanding), and you have only one chance to give thanks for the life of the person whose service you are conducting. The thanksgiving you offer should be careful, compassionate, balanced, and true. This is easy to say, but not so easy to achieve!

There is an opportunity to give thanks for the person's life, especially her life in the family circle, before she dies. If you are the person providing pastoral care to the dying family member, then it is appropriate that as a part of the goodbye process you remind family members how much the act of thanksgiving will be appreciated by their loved one. If you are offering a prayer at the bedside, then thanksgiving will form an important part of the prayer. You will thank God for the many gifts given and received within the family circle, for those who give care at the hospital or hospice facility, and for the hope of a life that continues on after this earthly life is over.

In the family discussion prior to the service, an important question is "What do you think we should give thanks (to God) for in Jill's life?" Remember, you may need to probe a little in order to get a balanced set of viewpoints. Sometimes "the elephant in the room" is never mentioned, and it is important to have it expressed, even if its existence is not voiced during the service. An addiction to drugs or to alcohol may radically affect a person's life, and if this is widely known to family members and friends, your avoidance of it will bring a sense of unreality to the service. It is possible to use a euphemism, such as "Jack's struggle with his demons," but it is far better to be straightforward and talk about "Jack's struggle with drink." This is the true situation, and people in the congregation know all about it, so why disguise the true situation?

Where a person has taken her own life, the same principles apply. Again, if this sudden death is generally known to be a suicide, it is healthier to be direct about it and use the word "suicide." (See chapter 9, page 81.)

Thanksgivings can be part of the opening prayer as a general thanks to God for Jack's life, but clearly they form a major part of the eulogy and the worship leader's meditation. Try as hard as you can to put the thanksgivings in perspective and before you write or type your script, sort out what are the *big* thanksgivings and the *small* thanksgivings and give them appropriate weight in what you say. If you have a prayer of thanksgiving toward the end of the service, pick four or five of the major thanksgivings and offer these to God, leaving space for the members of the congregation to add their thanksgivings silently or aloud. (See "Prayer of Thanksgiving" on page 155.)

A good funeral service will allow time and space for offering thanks to God for the life of the person who has died.

Faith of the Deceased

One of the reasons that funerals have been replaced by secular celebrations of life is that in the past, the faith status of the person who has died was ignored. The "one size fits all" service was offered, and those who were active members of a faith community and those who had not darkened the doorway of a church in years were accorded the same liturgy. No wonder that when it became socially acceptable for persons to stipulate that they didn't want a religious service, the alternative of a secular celebration of life took hold.

During the conversation with the family, it will be easy to determine how much the faith of the person who has died meant to her and to the family. Was Jill a member of the church? Was Jill a church board member or Sunday school teacher? Was she a leader in the church? Was Jill a member of the women's group? Did Jill go to worship on Sunday morning? These questions and others like them will establish how Jill related to the faith community, and this will have an effect on the celebration or funeral service.

If Jill is a solid church member, it would be appropriate for members of the congregation to participate in the service by reading scripture or offering prayer. The use of a creed that outlines the belief pattern of the church might also be appropriate as might the celebration of Holy Communion. If there is a discussion as to where the service should be held, Jill's membership or involvement in the local church should be an indicator that the right place for the service should be the sanctuary where she worshipped.

A good funeral will take account of how the person who died related to the local church.

Needs of the Faith Community

Faith community members may have been among the visitors spending time with the one dying, and the pastoral care team may have visited on behalf of the church. The dying person may have (with permission) been prayed for during the worship service. In this situation, the local faith community will want to mourn the loss of one of their own. If the funeral is in the sanctuary where the deceased worshipped and there is participation in the service by those whom she knew, then there is a sense that this is *their* service as well as that of the family. If the hymns chosen are funeral hymns beloved by the church or hymns or songs of praise that everyone knows, this will help to give the local faith community partnership in the service. The worship leader will speak of the deceased during her meditation and refer to her service in the church with some stories, but it might be helpful if the board chair or another church member speaks of the deceased's faith life and service as a part of the congregation.

Members of the congregation will usher the friends and family members to their seats and be responsible for making sure that everyone signs the guest book.

One of the most important services that can be offered to the family is the church hall for a reception after the service, a place where family and friends can meet, eat, drink, and share stories and memories. Church members who help in these "small" ways will feel that they have given one last gift to their departed church member. For an active church member it would be appropriate if one of the destinations of memorial gifts was to the faith community.

A good funeral will be one where the faith community plays a significant role in the whole bereavement event, including the service. Her death is a *community of faith loss* as well as a loss to her own family members.

There is a postscript to this section, for this is an opportunity for the faith community to show their welcoming nature to those who are outside their boundaries or on the fringe. If the grieving family and friends are treated with compassion and sensitivity, then the message will come through that this is what the church is about and this is what God is about. A good funeral is often the door through which persons who would not normally consider a life of faith come to see its value and purpose.

Needs of Those with No Faith Community

Over the last 20 to 30 years, there has been an increasing number of families that have no links to a local faith community. We have dealt with this in an earlier section of this book; see pages 13–16. The key to a successful celebration of life for a family with no significant faith is to establish this fact early and to be clear that you have no desire to convert them. Invite family members to check through the service and meditation to make sure that there is nothing there that is not in accord with their beliefs. Mind you, this does not stop you from praying for the family every step along the way!

Gospel Hope

Hope is the common denominator present for a whole range of deaths for which pastoral care is given and funeral and celebration of life services are prepared. The note of hope will be clearly sounded even where a tragic death occurs and where grieving is most acute. In the midst of life there *is* death, but in the midst of any death there is *a profound and timeless hope* rooted in the resurrection of Jesus.

And this is not hope against hope. It is hope based on solid Bible foundations (see chapter 2 "Biblical Roots," page 20). Where the person has no Christian faith, it is good to make clear that the person who has died will live on in the memory of his loved ones and will by his living have contributed to the communities of which he was a part and the experience of humanity in his particular area of living.

A good funeral will be shot through with hope. However, a good funeral will also give a hopeful account of the person who has no faith or little faith and the person who would claim to be a spiritual person though not in any way religious.

Good Music

In many non-Westernized cultures, music at a funeral is accompanied with dancing. Often, the music has the rhythm one can swing and sway to; it is heartfelt and speaks to the emotional side of loss. North American and European cultures are usually more restrained in their grieving, and their music is restrained as well. People often stick with what they know, and what Westerners know is not sung with a whole lot of enthusiasm.

Music can reflect the different stages of the funeral and the character of the person who has died. If the person has come to the end after a life full of love shared in the family and a job that was rewarding, there is a whole lot to give thanks for, and the thanksgiving may be reflected in the songs, the hymns, and the music before and after the service. Thanksgiving music is upbeat, loud, buoyant, and joyful, and (dare we say it) perhaps some clapping and moving to the beat might be encouraged.

Look in the subject index of your hymn book or song book and choose something that is appropriate and, above all, well known to the congregation, e.g., "Now Thank We All Our God," "Praise the Lord with the Sound of Trumpet," and "We Give Our Thanks." If you have a music director who knows her stuff, consult her about a suitable song or hymn, consider the possibilities, and don't feel you have to go along with every suggestion. Talk over the different selections, but remember, you are the worship leader and the final decision is yours.

Sometimes, it is possible to combine an upbeat hymn of thankfulness with a key area of the person's life, e.g., for one who was a lover of nature, you might choose "All Things Bright and Beautiful." For a fisher, you might select "Jesus, You Have Come to the Lakeshore" or "Jesus Calls Us." Sometimes, you have to search diligently for the right piece of music. Sometimes, the family will know all the favourite songs and hymns of the person who has died, and one or two may be selected. Time for reflection and prayer may be needed before the final selection is made.

How Many Hymns?

For most services, two or three hymns are sufficient, and while the first one will usually be a hymn of praise, the second hymn may be one that speaks to the feelings of those who are at the service: the sense of loss that is being experienced or the sense of unfilled potential. Good hymns in this category are hard to come by. "Strength to the Troubled Heart," "Lord of All Love," and "Grief of Ending, Wordless Sorrow" are great hymns but rarely sung, and because they are rarely sung are rarely used. For that second hymn or song you may have to substitute a well-known song of faith or new life, such as, "Will Your Anchor Hold" or "In The Bulb There Is a Flower."

If the cause of the death is a suicide or an accident, then find a song or hymn that meets the emotional needs of those who are present. Perhaps a song or hymn that speaks of peace, such as "I've Got Peace Like a River," "Come and Find a Quiet Centre," "Comfort, Comfort Now My People," "Make Me a Channel of Your Peace," "Peace for the Children" (for which you might add a verse, "Peace for her/his mom and dad"), and "I Have Called You by Your Name."

The final hymn will have within it the gospel note of hope. Whether death came in a natural and peaceful way, or after a time of sustained struggle, or as a result of violence or accident, there is joy that the person who has died has gone from death to new life. This is a hymn or song to be sung with faith and enthusiasm, and even some non-church people will sing out a little louder, so if the family has one to suggest and it is known, this is the time to use it. Some songs that have the note of hope within them include "Joyful, Joyful, We Adore You," "Great Is Thy Faithfulness," "Thine Is The Glory," "Jesus Came Bringing Us Hope," "I See a New Heaven," "Blessed Assurance," and "Rejoice, The Lord Is King."

The songs or hymns used in the service must be covered by a licence held by the church, and a royalty paid if no licence is in operation.

Where the person who has died was a solid faithful church member, then he will have had favourite songs and hymns and likely many members will know what they were. Include as many favourites as you can and don't be afraid to add a couple to the usual two or three. It is worth checking with the church secretary to see if the deceased person left instructions about the service and in particular the hymns she wanted for her funeral.

Challenging Requests
Occasionally, you will be asked to include secular songs that might present challenges on several levels.

Sometimes, it will be difficult to obtain the words or music of a selected song, although the Internet is making it much easier to discover both. Watch out for copyright issues!

Another issue is that when considering popular songs, the lyrics might be inappropriate and sometimes downright obscene. However, often a secular song can be right on target even though the Holy Name or Holy Way are not mentioned, in which case, don't hesitate to use it. So what are the criteria here? My sense is that you would not normally let language be used in the service that is not used in the neighbourhood daily newspaper or on mainstream radio stations. This would include words used by you as worship leader, any person giving a eulogy, and the lyrics in any of the songs. The same goes for the images in video content. If your judgment is challenged by others on this issue, point out that there will be different people at the service, some of whom might be made uncomfortable if a series of four-letter words feature in a song or reading. They will remember the inappropriate language and not the essential content of the song or service. My practice has been to gently steer the family away from the inappropriate songs, have them suggest alternatives, and have the less offensive ones played as part of the music to which the family comes in or goes out of the sanctuary.

I also believe there are exceptions to this clean language policy and in my own experience have led a service where the favourite song of a young man who had died in a vehicle accident included some raunchy language. It was played at the end of the service. I told the congregation, "This was Terry's favourite song. Some of you may find the language offensive, but it was special to him." I didn't get any complaints.

Moving Away from Golden Oldies

Most churches now have the ability to play CDs and some iPads through the sound system, and this gives the opportunity to include music that reflects the individual: her interests, challenges, and personality. Rather than have an old faithful choir member give a rendering of "Amazing Grace," have the technician play "Lady Madonna" for the single mother who had a hard life and died far too early, or better still, include a clip of this song being performed live. Rather than a solo of "In the Garden" for the exile from Scotland who never forgot the country of his birth, have a recording of "My Love Is Like a Red, Red Rose," the Robert Burns classic. And for the youngster who died accidentally, "Somewhere over the Rainbow" sung by Eva Cassidy could fit the bill or a track from the youngster's favourite group.

To counter feelings of loneliness, you might play "You'll Never Walk Alone." For a veteran, you might select Vera Lynn's "We'll Meet Again," or for almost anyone, The Rankin Family's "We Rise Again." A key here is to have an office administrator or techie in the congregation who can embed YouTube and video clips in the PowerPoint order. The use of a secular song that fits the person who has died and that the congregation knows can be power-fully beneficial to those who are grieving and those who are celebrating a life recently ended. You may not know the popular songs very well, but don't be afraid to ask around.

A useful exercise here is to consider your own funeral and the hymns and songs you would like to be included during the service and before and after. Then consider the reasons that you have included these pieces of music. If you have the opportunity, talk to a colleague or fellow worship leader and share your decisions around music.

A good funeral will have music that touches the heart and lifts the soul, and it doesn't have to include even one of the golden oldies.

Speaking to the Loss

Death is the ultimate in loss for there are no second chances, no going back and putting things right. I can think of only one funeral I have conducted where there was joy in the place of loss. For the rest, loss was a reality, and the degree of loss experienced was proportionate to the love experienced within the bonds of friendship or love given and received within the family circle.

As a worship leader one of the factors you will be assessing will be the degree of loss that has been experienced. Clearly if it is a baby or a child who has died, the loss will be huge, as will be the case where there is accidental death. However, when a mother dies at 95, peacefully in her sleep, the loss will be balanced with a sense that a full life has been completed, and when a father of 85 years dies after a year's wheezing struggle with lung cancer, the loss will be tempered with relief that suffering is over.

In your conversation with the family, you will likely determine the degree of loss that is being experienced, and you will note the family members who are able to deal easily with the loss and those for whom the loss is causing anxiety and stress. We mentioned the pastoral role earlier, but there is also a chance in the funeral service to squarely face the emotions that are being experienced.

One of the first emotions you will face is the sense of loneliness that is being experienced by close family members and the following Howard Thurman passage speaks directly to the difficulty of being on your own.

We share with you the agony of your grief,
The anguish of your heart finds echo in our own.
We cannot enter all you feel
Nor bear with you the burden of your pain;
We can only offer what our love does give;
The strength of caring,
The warmth of those who seek to understand,
The silent, storm-tossed barrenness of so great a loss.
This we do in quiet ways,
That on your lonely path
You may not walk alone.[1]

In the meditation, one of the most valuable statements you can make is to mention the close family members by name and then to verbalize the sense of loss that is being felt by them. They will not respond aloud, but will affirm the feelings of loss in the silence of their hearts. It is helpful to speak of the danger of putting a hard shell over unresolved grief.

In one of the *Ladies No. 1 Detective Agency* books by Alexander McCall Smith, the wise key character, Precious Rambotswe, gives some advice to her hero, Clovis Andersen, whose wife has recently died: "'It is good to talk about late people, Rra,' she said quietly. 'It is what they want us to do. Late people would be happy if they knew that we were talking about them.'"[2]

As you put your meditation together, there are a variety of factors at play: the relationship that mourners had with the deceased, their personalities including their emotional makeup, other losses they have faced, and current areas of stress. Further, their reactions to loss will be in proportion to how they are facing the fact of their own death and whether there is any risk in it coming soon.

If there is the slightest evidence of difficulty in dealing with serious loss, it is good to suggest that the individual consult a bereavement counsellor, minister, or other professional. As worship leader in the pastoral role, you will be on the lookout for tried and tested counsellors ahead of need. It is a fact that if love for the deceased has been strong, then grief will be in direct proportion to that love. A good funeral service will take account of the grief being experienced—and to be experienced—by congregational members, and through readings and the content of the meditation will engage that grief.

Loved One's Presence

Half a century ago, most funerals were earth burials, and the body of the person who had died would be brought into the church or chapel. There would be an opportunity for family members to see the earthly remains of their loved one at a private or open viewing before the service (see chapter 13 "Before the Service," page 101). There would be a last look before the service began, the deceased person would be present during the service, and then the body would be taken out for burial at the end of the service. There is value in having the body of the person present because family members, young and old, know that this is June or Jim (Grandpa or Nana), and he is dead—no doubt about it.

Today, an increasing number of persons are being cremated. How do you create the same sense of presence? One way is to ensure that the urn with the cremated remains of the deceased is present, can be seen by everyone, and is accompanied by a large photograph of the deceased, which is also visible to all. [Ahead of time you might invite people to write letters to the deceased and have those letters interred with the remains or cremated with them.]

Will the Service Be Worthy?

If you have worked carefully and attentively with the family and liaised in a friendly way with the funeral home, the faith community, and its music director, it only remains to prepare the service and to offer it prayerfully to God. It will not be perfect, but it will be worthy. The account of Betty's funeral that follows is an example of how a good funeral might look and the reasons for it being good. It felt right to me.

Betty's Funeral

There was nothing special about Betty's life. She had trained as a nurse's aide, married, and had two children. The marriage didn't work out, and she had become the sole provider for her son and daughter, had cared for them wisely, and nurtured them into jobs and families of their own. Just as a comfortable retirement was within her reach, Betty had contracted a fast-moving cancer and had died within two months of her first symptoms.

I was asked to conduct the service by one of the local funeral directors and met with the family and her best friend a couple of days after her death. As we talked, it became clear that Betty was one of those people loved within her family circle and liked by everyone she came in contact with. Apart from choosing the hymn "How Great Thou Art," the rest of the service was left to me, but her best friend agreed to give a eulogy at the service, which was held in the local funeral home.

One of her fellow workers called me (without prompting) at home and gave a glowing testimony of Betty's above-and-beyond help to the residents of the care home where she worked. What became clear from the discussions with the family and from my conversation with her friend and her colleague was that Betty was one of those rare saints, not nauseatingly nice but fun and compassionate at home and at work. Everyone liked her. It was a funeral that I looked forward to leading.

As people gathered, I could see on the faces and hear in the conversations the sense of loss that friends and work colleagues were feeling. Right at the start of the service I felt what can only be described as The Holy amongst us. The familiar scripture at the beginning of the service, "Blessed are those who mourn, for they will be comforted," (Matthew 5:4) was spoken directly to the congregation and was needed by them. The note of hope sounded in the passage from John's gospel: "Jesus said to her, 'I am the resurrection and the life. Those who believe in me, even though they die, will live, and everyone who lives and believes in me will never die'" (John 11:25–26). The note of hope of a life that begins after this one ends was heard in a fresh way, and I sensed that hardly anyone in that congregation believed that Betty's existence was over. She would live on, how and where weren't the important things—as an angel or as a spirit—it didn't really matter. She would live on; she was living on!

The opening prayer alerted us to the presence of The Holy with us and with Betty, and the singing of the first hymn, "Joyful, Joyful, We Adore You" was enthusiastic—and I hadn't seen them as a singing crowd! A reading of Psalm 23 followed— the heartfelt poetry of a writer who speaks of God's comfort. One of the gospel passages of Jesus the healer tied in with Betty's work, and the reading from John's gospel about Mary in the garden encountering Jesus spoke clearly of the joyous certainty of the life that begins when this one ends.

Then Jody, her best friend, gave a eulogy that spoke with sincerity and with humour of Betty's compassion, her loving role as a mother, and her ability to have a good time. I followed this with a reflection on the John 20 passage (see page 264), and then offered a prayer of thanksgiving for Betty's life with time for each congregational member to silently voice their own thanks. We joined in the Lord's Prayer. The words didn't mean a lot, but the act of saying the prayer brought us together. I followed this with an invitation for all to come with us to the cemetery for the service of committal, and we finished with the hymn "How Great Thou Art," followed by a commissioning to members of the congregation to remember Betty, to express their deep feelings at her loss, and to believe the promise of new life. A blessing completed the liturgy in the chapel.

The service content was in itself nothing unusual, but the whole bereavement experience, the time of preparation with family and friends, the prayers and readings, the eulogy, and the meditation together transcended the separate parts and made for a "holy whole." When the earthly remains of Betty were lowered into the grave and I said, "Into God's keeping and into God's unfailing love we commit our sister…" we felt that Betty, who was lovingly remembered, was with the loving and Holy One now.

Betty's funeral was a good funeral.

Could it have been a better funeral? It could. There was no opportunity for people to share their memories at a meal or story-sharing time around the table after the service, and no visitation before the service. There was little opportunity for friends who didn't go to the committal to express their sympathy or tell of their love of Betty to the family members. I had encouraged this to be a part of the celebration, and it was not done. And further, Betty was a person of faith but not a formal Christian faith and had no connection with a local church. If she had been, this would have been reflected by the participation of the congregation before and during the service and the response of the congregation at the funeral itself.

---

[1] From *Meditations of the Heart* by Thurman, Howard. Reproduced with permission of BEACON PRESS. Republished in a book via Copyright Clearance Center.

[2] Excerpted from *The Limpopo Academy of Private Detection* by Alexander McCall Smith. Copyright © 2012 Alexander McCall Smith. Reprinted by permission of Knopf Canada. Reprinted by permission of Birlinn (UK) and Random House LLC (USA).

CHAPTER 15

Post-funeral Pastoral Care

The person who cares for the family of the deceased pastorally before the funeral continues in this role after the funeral is over. So as the family is going down to the refreshment hall, the worship leader should monitor the emotional state of close family members. If they are upset, the worship leader will encourage the family members to take some time for themselves in a room away from the refreshment area and others who have attended the service. They may want time for themselves to grieve with one another or they may need the worship leader in her pastoral role to be with them with words and hugs. To care for the family members is the primary role of the worship leader following the service or celebration.

The worship leader should contact the family within the first two to three days (or within the first week at the latest) and offer to visit at the family home or the homes of family members who are having trouble with their grief. If there are difficulties with grief work or if there are special needs, for example, if there are grieving children, referral should be made to the local bereavement group or to a grief counsellor, psychologist, or psychiatrist.

It is crucial that the worship leader knows her limits and is ready to refer as is appropriate. She should also know the bereavement resources available in the local community for grieving family members, and stock necessary pamphlets and brochures.

Post-funeral Grief Work

As an intern chaplain in an acute care hospital, I was visiting one afternoon with a man in his mid-sixties who was about to have an operation. We began with casual conversation about the weather and last night's hockey game, and then Bert told me that the date was close to the anniversary of the death of

122

his mother. Assuming this was a recent event I expressed my sympathy and gave Bert, who was an only child, the opportunity to talk about the feelings around his loss. He told me the story of how he knew that his dying mom wanted him to come and see her, but he kept on putting off the visit because he was far away in a steady job and he was afraid to lose it. He began to weep as he went on to recount how his mother died before he set out to see her and then, to cap it all, he arrived home too late to attend the funeral. As he cried I sat with him and he said, "You are the first person I have ever talked to about this." I asked him, "Well, when did your mother die?" He said, "Thirty-five years ago."

If grief work is not done following the death of a loved one, the feelings around the loss will persist until they are dealt with. Often, the temptation of the worship leader is to make a quick post-funeral phone call to the person who has been bereaved and unless there is a major concern expressed, assume that the family member is getting over her loss and leave her alone, but as with the man I encountered on the hospital ward this may not be the case.

The Meaning of Grief
Grief is the normal and natural response to loss, and the emotional intensity of the grief is in direct proportion to the closeness and depth of loving relationships experienced between the person who has died and the family members or friends. The worship leader in a pastoral role needs to be aware of the radical change that has taken place in the life situation of the person who has been bereaved and be ready to go with them as they set out on this untried but potentially fulfilling path.

Most likely the bereaved person will not be "herself" and will suffer a range of physical and mental states very different from normal; she may be much more irritable than normal, or feel more tired, or have an upset digestive system. One of the roles of the caregiver is to reassure the person grieving that these very different sensations are a part of the normal experience of grief and she is not out of her mind as she may be imagining.

There will also be a range of feelings that will relate to the person who has died—his age and the circumstances of his death; whether he was expected to die; whether his death came suddenly or was an accident. There may be relief that the loved one is no longer suffering, and there may be anger, even anger directed at God, that the loved one has left so quickly. There could be denial that he has died: "I keep on expecting that he will come through the door at the end of the day like he always did." There may be profound sadness in the loss coupled with perceived guilt about how the medical treatment was handled, and there may be guilt experienced because conflicts or differences that cast a shadow between the deceased and the surviving family member or members will now never be resolved.

Added to the anger and sadness and guilt may come bargaining attempts. In one pastoral charge, I worked with a non-churchgoing family whose son was permanently disabled in a car crash. In the early days, when it was not certain whether or not he would be fully restored to health, the family members came to church Sunday by Sunday. Their reasoning was an unspoken bargain that if they worshipped faithfully, God would reward them with improved health for their son, but when it was obvious that the young man's disability was permanent, they stopped attending worship.

Listening and Not Listening

As well as the feelings of the person who has been bereaved, there will also be the feelings of friends to take into account. The pastoral caregiver may account for the absence of family members and friends by explaining that some will feel out of place in this post-bereavement situation and some will have grief issues of their own, which have come to the surface and which they are finding difficult to face.

A good friend will give very little advice and will simply listen and be with be the bereaved person in his support and encouragement for the journey forward, while the well-meaning but not so helpful friend will offer much advice. I've heard advice like "My grandmother said that everyone who has lost a partner should be getting back to normal in six months, max!" or "Try golf, a cooking class, some new activity, and you will forget all about your loss." In this situation it is often the friend's own needs that are brought to the fore, and she may become frustrated if some "progress" is not being made because it restricts her ability to do what *she* wants. For the bereaved person, it is important not to let anyone dictate her grieving path. It is her grief, and she is entitled to it, and each grieving person needs to be ready to say a firm "No" when well-meaning friends try to persuade her to make commitments she is not ready to make and go places she is not ready to go. The pastoral caregiver will be able to affirm the bereaved person as she goes her own way and makes her own choices for good or ill.

Stages of Grief

Grief takes its own time, and the length of time varies widely from person to person. Rather than seeing grief as a progression from one carefully defined stage to another, it is more helpful for the pastoral caregiver to see it as a series of waves, a sea of ups and downs where the two good steps forward are often matched with one step back. It will be easy for the grieving person to become downhearted by a short-term lack of progress so that he feels stuck in a rut. The worship leader in the pastoral care role will be aware of this and will applaud him when the grieving process is going well and progress is being made, but will also be there when the bereaved person is depressed and lonely and says, "I'll never get back to normal." The way back from a major loss requires a large measure of willpower, and the pastoral caregiver can enable this to take root and grow. Rabbi Earl Grollman puts the situation clearly and succinctly: "Grief is a process. Recovering is your choice."[1]

It takes much patience and endurance to stay with the person who is down-hearted and depressed, and the pastoral caregiver needs to monitor her own mental and spiritual health and be ready to take a break if she is feeling overly frustrated or downhearted.

Practical Actions

If the bereaved person asks the pastoral caregiver, "What practical actions can I take to speed my progress through this time of grief?" then it is good to have a few practical suggestions ready. Perhaps the most important pre-liminary comment is to assure the bereaved person not to expect too much progress too soon, to reassure her that being stuck in her grief progression is perfectly normal, and point out the positive changes that have been made. It is also useful to suggest some practical actions that could make a difference.

One useful action is for the bereaved person to face the feelings that are most difficult to put into words and to share them in confidence with one other person, such as a best friend, a minister, or a well-loved family member. It is difficult to underestimate the value of this confidential, one-on-one sharing, and the pastoral caregiver may be the person to encourage the sharing or be the listener. The role of the confidant is not so much to give an opinion, but to listen deeply to the expressed feelings and to reflect back quietly and compassionately what is being said.

It may also be helpful for the grieving person to put his deepest feeling down on paper or to start a grief journal. Putting pen to paper or entrusting these feelings to a computer file will enable him to see they are real and may enable him to see that progress is being made. If there is unfinished business between the grieving person and the person who has died, it could be helpful to write a letter stating directly how he is feeling—to express anger, to state where he made mistakes (or where he thought *she* did), and to ask for understanding or forgiveness. This is a tough thing to do as I know from my own experience, but it can helpfully remove some of those road blocks to grieving. If this letter can be shared with another person, so much the better. The letter might also include the things the bereaved person always wanted to say to his loved one but never quite got around to putting into words.

Another practical suggestion from the pastoral caregiver can be to speak about the need to resume the activities that gave the bereaved one satisfaction before the bereavement happened. So skating or card playing may be resumed, a fraternal organization rejoined, or meeting for coffee with a cherished group of friends may become a part of her weekly routine once more. It will also be helpful to resume the fitness routine neglected in the process of bereavement. If the bereaved person is healthy physically, she will likely feel better mentally as well. Some like to exercise alone, while many others will benefit from having others around to encourage and spur on. The community of a friendly gym can be a positive and strong support, as can a positive and good-humoured walking partner.

Faith Community and Spiritual Care

It will be a natural function of the worship leader in a pastoral role to remind the bereaved person of the concern of the faith community for her at this time and to encourage her to attend services and social events. Worshipping for the first time will be a challenge, but likely there will be people who will show their love and concern in different ways and will go out of their way to welcome her. If the bereaved person has no formal faith and does not belong to a faith community, the pastoral caregiver may want to explore the spiritual practices of prayer and meditation that have been helpful to her in the past and could be especially meaningful to her now. As in the time before the loved one died, it may be helpful for the pastoral caregiver to ask if a prayer would be helpful and to offer some carefully chosen words at the end of the time spent together.

Local Support Groups

The pastoral caregiver will be familiar with the support sessions and bereavement groups offered in the local community and will be able to encourage the bereaved person to contact the group coordinator. It may be that the bereaved person feels uncomfortable or worried about going to the chosen group for the first time and it would be useful for him to speak to the group leader. The leader could put him in touch with a member who could meet him at a mutually agreed place and help him go through the door for the first time.

Grief and Clinical Depression

The difference between grief and depression is sometimes hard to determine, but if the pastoral caregiver encounters the bereaved one in a withdrawn state, or if she is finding life hugely meaningless or talking of suicide, then clearly action should be taken. The pastoral caregiver would do well to suggest that she needs to see a doctor or a grief counsellor, help her choose the professional, and if needed, go with her to the first appointment. It may also be advisable to talk to a trusted family member about what is happening.

Alcohol and Drugs

The person who has been bereaved may feel that alcohol or prescription and other drugs will mask the pain and shock of loss. The problem is that drink and drugs hide the true feelings and only provide temporary relief to the grief that is being felt. The pastoral caregiver should be on the look out for the beginning signs of drug and alcohol addiction and steer the person who has suffered loss toward an acceptable local source of treatment.

Signs of a New Direction

The pastoral caregiver will stay with the grieving one as he encounters the many new and unforeseen life experiences that occur as his old life pattern ends and a new pattern of life begins. During this period, the bereaved person will have been exposed to many challenges—personal, relational, financial, and spiritual. A few will have been defeating and devastating, but many will have been a source of unexpected joy and growth. One of the caregiver's roles is to celebrate the successes along the way.

So when the person who has been bereaved is able to talk about his loved one who has died with love and with joy and not with constricting emotion, he is making progress. And when he is able to make fresh friendships without worrying about what his former loved one would think, he is forging a new life that will be fulfilling and happy.

It is good to keep in mind that grieving is never finished and however successful the process might appear, there will be occasions when the feelings of loss and loneliness will sweep over the bereaved one again.

Marking the Anniversary

For most people who have been bereaved, the date of the anniversary of the death of their loved one will be significant. It will be a day that will bring back memories of the death experience and the feelings of all that has been missing since the loss. Often the advent of the anniversary and the day itself will intensify the feelings of grief already present. From the viewpoint of the worship leader, it will be good to call the person who has been bereaved at the beginning of the bereavement week and offer to come for a visit.

The pastoral caregiver should also be aware of other special dates like birthdays that the bereaved person shared with her loved one. The emotional effect of these may seem out of proportion to the caregiver, but talking about them and their significance ahead of the day may be the best way to deflect an emotional storm.

---

[1] From Rabbi Earl A. Grollman, DHL, DD *Living With Loss; Healing With Hope* audio visual tape, with permission from Global Distributions Networks, Inc.

CHAPTER 16

Other Cultures, Other Faiths

As a pastoral caregiver or worship leader there is a call to be sensitive to the needs of families of cultures different from your own or of mixed cultural traditions. How can we accommodate practices from different countries of origin, from the cultural or religious background of significant members of the family, and from the predominant faith practices of the local community? We live in a world where the cultural barriers are constantly crossed and where intermarriage is common.

Aboriginal Persons

In Canada, the first people to inhabit the land were tribes and groups of Aboriginal people and peoples who developed their own spirituality, long before the white Caucasian immigrants brought their European Christian ways to the continent. I am indebted to the Reverend Maggie McLeod, Executive Minister, Aboriginal Ministries Circle, The United Church of Canada, for her insights into the challenging situation that Aboriginal groups face in response to the religions of the first European newcomers to the North American continent. Maggie writes:

> The United Church's A New Creed expresses how "God has created and is creating." The Aboriginal view of Creator also affirms that all life, past and present, is to be acknowledged with gratitude and celebrated. The phrase used by many First Nations peoples, "All My Relations," is wisdom that captures humanity's relationship to Creator God and creation—the earth, its creatures, the water, the plants, and indeed the cosmos are all interconnected to the circle of life. Aboriginal community embraces death as part of the circle of life. We are born, we grow into childhood, and we travel into youth and

young adulthood; then, the last years of the four cycles are Elder years. All stages of life have a season and a purpose, similar to that which is expressed in Ecclesiastes 3:1: "There is a season, and a time for every matter under heaven."

Many Aboriginal communities, both rural and urban, are experiencing a spiritual and cultural renaissance. After hundreds of years of living with the impact of a colonization imbued with cultural and spiritual superiority, Aboriginal peoples are reclaiming their culture, language, identity, and spirituality. Restoration to Creator's wholeness is a complex journey. First Nation communities are at various stages of this healing journey. While some Aboriginal communities have reclaimed traditional burial ceremonies and customs and are working alongside Christian communities of faith to meet the needs of grieving families, there are other communities that are very much rooted in the Christian context and believe that the two cannot be combined.

The legacy of colonization and governmental policies has resulted in devastating losses for Aboriginal community. While many layers of grief exist, so does a pervasive resiliency. Aboriginal people are a story-telling people. In fact, the sharing of story is in itself an act of healing and honouring of life. It is important for the community to gather at a time of loss, to share what they have by way of story, food, song, prayer, and ceremony. The minister will gain valuable guidance by listening carefully to the needs of family and community in a time of loss and bereavement.

How does this work itself out in practice? Can non-Aboriginal people get fresh insights into the funeral or celebration of life from considering the Aboriginal way? We take a look at a funeral or life celebration in the First Nations communities of Goodfish Lake–Saddle Lake Pastoral Charge in north-east Alberta with the help of the Reverend Robert Wright, the United Church minister of those pastoral charges. He writes:

Often the body of the person who has died will be brought from the funeral home to the cultural centre a few days before the service. Usually for two evenings there are services where friends and family are able to view the body and offer prayers led by lay persons as well as clergy. There will be refreshments, songs, and stories shared at this time.

The service, the celebration of the person's life, often lasts all day and is in the cultural centre as there is more room than at the church— and the funeral is recognized as a community event, not just for one denomination. The minister of the pastoral charge joins the day's events together as celebrant and pastoral caregiver, but the Elders, priest, and pastors of other denominations and traditions have a part in the proceedings if they are available and feel comfortable in [participating].

It begins mid-morning with gospel singing and the drummers drumming, and this is followed by a prayer offered by one of the Elders in the Cree language. After a welcome from the family, the Chief and Band Council bring greetings to the gathered congregation. This welcome is followed by the singing of a hymn, often "How Great Thou Art."

The minister then offers a prayer along with words of hope and comfort, including an adapted contemporary prayer (from *Celebrate God's Presence*), which includes elements of thanksgiving for the life of the person who has died and compassion for family members. This is followed by the Lord's Prayer and the United Church's A New Creed or other creedal statement.

Then there are usually four traditionally used scripture readings from the Bible and teachings of the Elders, read if possible by family members and friends spanning the generations. The readings are followed by one or more planned eulogies or tributes to the person who has died. After this, there is often a PowerPoint presentation with pictures of the person's life, backed by favourite secular and sacred songs, and then friends who are moved to do so have the opportunity to speak of the deceased. This time of sharing may include a singing of the traditional Cree song "Love One Another" (Sakihitotan) and favourite gospel songs, including "Peace in the Valley," "Where the Roses Never Fade," "I'll Fly Away," and of course, "Amazing Grace."

The minister gives a meditation reflecting on the life of the deceased person in the light of one or more of the scriptures and the teaching of the Elders. This is followed by a closing prayer and congregational members joining hands for the singing of the last hymn, usually "Bind Us Together." Following the commissioning and blessing, there is a time to greet and bring words of condolence to the family.

The final service act is a farewell to the person who has died. One by one, family members and friends file past the coffin and offer their farewell, "We never say goodbye," in prayer, or in a few words, or by the symbolic leaving of a small gift—some sweetgrass, tobacco, or a crucifix for example. The drummers drum, alternating with gospel singers at this time.

The coffin is then closed and sometimes taken by horse and wagon to the cemetery for the committal service. A feast follows with lots of good food and talk about the person who has died, with laughter enjoyed as well as tears, and many stories told and retold.

Non-Aboriginal people often come away from the day of celebration surprised by the flexibility of the service. Nothing is carved in stone here! The order of prayers, tributes, and hymns is open to change by the presiding minister in consultation with family, leader of worship, and other clergy. Neither are there time constraints. The elements of the day, especially the eulogies and tributes, take whatever time is needed for the persons who are speaking—another half hour, another hour more than was expected is okay. I remember on one occasion being taken on one side by the manager of a crematorium and reprimanded for going five minutes over my allotted half hour and then being told that if it happened again, I would be banned from taking services there. This is the exact opposite of the situation at the Goodfish Lake–Saddle Lake Pastoral Charge where, when celebrating a life, time is the servant, not the master!

In this situation the cultural identity of the deceased is honoured with drumming, sage, or sweetgrass, depending on cultural concerns and the participation of the tribal Elders in the service.

Newcomers from Africa and Asia

For many years, it was European immigrants who made up the largest groups of newcomers to the North American continent, but this situation has changed and continues to change. There are many today who come from Africa and from South-East Asia and China. These newcomers often had different ways of observing the rites of mourning and burial in their home countries; some they have brought with them, and some not. As pastoral caregivers and as those who lead worship at funerals and life celebrations, we are able to learn from ritual practices of another country.

Here is an example from the Methodist Church, Ghana, where a compassionate social network that includes church members is responsible for the care of the loved one and close family members of the person who has died. Even a spouse who has no significant family members is not left alone.

When a member dies, it is the church that takes the primary role in organizing the care of the family and the preparation and delivery of the service. Following the long-time Methodist practice of dividing the membership into "classes," each with its leader, it is the class leader whom the family contacts first when a loved one dies. The class leader in turn contacts the members of the member's class and the minister of the congregation. Some of these class members accompany their leader and the minister to the family home where the family is comforted and an informal worship service is offered with prayers, scripture readings, and familiar songs.

In many churches, there is a funeral committee of a few members who are jointly responsible for planning and delivering the services in consultation with the minister and family. Often the whole faith community is involved in the funeral. There is usually a service held soon after the death of the church member and though the congregants' clothes would be in the mourning colours of red and black, the music would be upbeat and free and the celebration punctuated by many amens and alleluias. The service is informal enough that the order can be interrupted and a tribute to the deceased offered or a song of praise suggested and sung. The service is followed by the interment, and about a week later, there is another service, this time focusing on thanksgiving for the person's life. Again, the feeling is upbeat and joyful, and the service is punctuated by song and memories—the mood this time matched by the colourful clothes of the participants, often whites and blues. Neighbouring congregations join in the service and meal that follows.

Clearly, in the Methodist Church, Ghana, the expectation is that the church will take a lead in the care of the family of the person who has died and in the leadership of the funeral services. Though in a Western context the family has a more prominent part to play, perhaps we might explore how church members generally might play a more significant role.

The liturgy in the Methodist Church, Ghana, is similar to the liturgy that Methodist missionaries brought to that country. In much the same way, the liturgies in India, Korea, and China, for example, in many cases still bear a close relationship to the liturgies of the mother churches—Anglican, Presbyterian, or Roman Catholic—of missionaries who introduced Christianity to those countries. When the second or third generation of Christians arrive in North America or Europe as immigrants and establish their own churches, the liturgies they use, including the hymns they sing, are often derived from the liturgies the missionaries introduced. They are familiar and comfortable.

What happens when we are faced with the need to honour two very different faiths when a person dies?

Christian and Buddhist

My first experience of being called on to work in a partially non-Western cultural context was when I was asked to work with a Buddhist priest to create a memorial service for a member of my congregation whose roots were in both the Christian and the Buddhist faiths.

We started from the premise that both faith traditions would be honoured in the ceremony and that symbols essential to the two faith groups would be given equal place in the United Church sanctuary. On the table at the front of the sanctuary we placed both a shrine, at which incense was burned, and the cross, which was normally at the centre of the communion table. The Buddhist priest and I found that there was a natural progression in the services of both faiths that enabled us to alternate sections of Christian and Buddhist liturgy. Before each section, we explained the meaning of the liturgy in the faith context to the congregation and then offered the words.

It was a positive experience for both the Christian and Buddhist faith groups, and I enjoyed working with the priest. Pastoral care to the family was also shared between us.

CHAPTER 17

The Funeral
or Life Celebration Service

A frequently asked question during the conversation with the family before the death of a loved one or when the worship leader meets with the family after the loved one has died is "What will the service be like?" This is often followed by the comment "I hope it won't be too long!" Both question and comment are important.

It is useful to explain to the family what is the basis for the service and what it will be like. For a wedding there is usually a rehearsal, and the key members of the wedding party are walked through the ceremony. Do they remember their role: where they will stand and what they will say? Not exactly, but after the rehearsal they will be more familiar with the ceremony and their part in it and will be much more comfortable on the day as a result. A rehearsed funeral is a rare event, but as the worship leader you are in a position to make clear what will happen on the day—before, during, and after the service—and thereby reduce the anxiety level of the family members, close friends, and participants.

You are able to do this by first of all telling the family of the compassionate and loving God that is at the heart of everything: "In life, in death, in life beyond death, God (compassionate and loving) is with us" (A New Creed). You are able then to make clear the three foundational blocks on which the service is based: the need to give thanks for the person's life; the need to acknowledge and speak to the loss that is felt within the family circle, among close friends, and in the communities of which he was a member; and the need to speak of the hope of the life that goes on for the departed loved one and for those who have come to remember him, in spite of this loss.

You will go through the gathering for the service, the service itself, the committal service (if there is one), and finally what happens after the service is over—the meeting with friends and the reception. It will be helpful if, when you meet with the family, you have copies of either a service that you have recently conducted or a simple outline of a service that enables the family members to see how the liturgy will flow.

Service Choices

There are four basic choices that are possible for the family:

- a service in the church sanctuary or funeral home chapel
- a service in the church sanctuary or funeral home chapel followed by a committal service in a cemetery or other dedicated place
- a graveside service at the cemetery or other dedicated place
- a service in the home, garden, community hall, or other meaningful place

If the family has a connection with the local church or if the loved one who has died was a church member or an adherent, the local church will be the natural place for the service. Not only will the family find a welcome and a friendly place for the service, but holding it in the church will meet the need of the faith community to participate in remembering the loss of one of their own. They will work this out by participating in the service—offering prayers or reading scripture, through music or choral singing, by decorating the sanctuary—and by providing food for the family guests. The loved one who has died will have entered the Christian church through baptism, have been a member of a Sunday school, and have been confirmed and married within the faith community. It is fitting then that she should leave this earth surrounded by her faith friends and to the accompaniment of the songs, the sacred words, and the gospel hope that were an essential part of her faith.

When the worship leader encounters family resistance to a service being held in church, it is appropriate that she should say to the family of the deceased, "You know, Alice was much loved within the St. Andrew's faith family as well as yours. I think this is the place for her funeral."

Until recently, it would have been assumed that the celebration/funeral would be followed directly by a service of committal, where the final burial happens or where the cremated remains are located in a specific place. This can no longer be taken for granted. A trend recognized by clergy and funeral directors alike is for the family to wish to delay the committal.

There are times when this is entirely reasonable, e.g., the interment is arranged in another part of the country where the spouse or family member of the deceased is buried, or it may be that the weather is dreadful and it makes sense to wait until spring. What makes no sense is for the loved one's last earthly remains to be kept on a shelf in the living room or left gathering dust in a cupboard in the guest bedroom. The result of a postponement of burial is often an extension to the grieving process. Almost without exception funeral directors will rightly encourage the final deposition of the cremated remains directly following the funeral service, and as a worship leader you would do well to affirm this practice for the sake of the mental and spiritual health of the family.

There will sometimes be a request by family members for a graveside service. The request is usually for a shorter, simpler service and is made because the family is small or non-existent and few persons are expected to be present. The request is also made because it costs a lot less to have a service outside the church or funeral home.

Where the request is made because the loved one who has died "requested it," and there is a significant number of family and friends, it is helpful if you as worship leader face the family members with the reality that the graveside will not be a convenient place for the service. Older people will find it harder to walk to the service site and to stand during the liturgy; those hard of hearing will need to get close to the worship leader; and the service will be a trial to all if the weather is poor.

I was pressed to conduct a graveside service for a well-known community leader in mid-December. The family told me that it was a private service, but word leaked out, and a good number of friends and persons who had been helped by the person who had died came to the service—which was held in a snowstorm. We were cold and uncomfortable and for the sake of those who were old and infirm, I cut the service length to a bare minimum. No one came away from the service feeling good, and the life of one who had served his fellow men and women faithfully was not worthily celebrated.

There is a place for the graveside service, but the worship leader should articulate the challenges clearly to family members if it seems an inappropriate way to celebrate the life of their loved one. Where the request is made for cost reasons, both the church and the funeral home have the option of reducing the fees or waiving them altogether.

The funeral/celebration of life does not have to be held in a sacred place. If the person who has died is a member of a church, this is the natural place for a final Christian rite of passage to be held, but where there is no church connection, other locations may be considered. If there is a small family group, the home of the deceased is a suitable location with all the mementoes and pictures that are familiar to family members surrounding them. I have celebrated more than one life in a living room, and my wife held a most meaningful service in the garden beloved by the person who had died.

Where there is a need to provide a larger space for friends and family, a community or Legion hall may be appropriate, or for the golf enthusiast a club dining room that overlooks the 18th hole. In these situations, it is necessary to balance the appropriate location with the needs of the congregation to hear well, to have a clear view of those who are leading the service, and to have suitable music and visual aids to worship without distraction.

Typical Service Order

Opening music and video
Call to worship and welcome
Scripture sentences
Preface (why we are here)
Song or hymn of praise (well-known)
Opening prayer
Prayer of confession (optional)
Secular reading
Hebrew or Christian scripture readings
Song or hymn (appropriate to the deceased's life or sense of loss)
Meditation (part 1)
Eulogies
Meditation (part 2)
Prayer of thanksgiving and the Lord's Prayer (sung or said)
Announcements (the place and time of interment and refreshments)
Commendation
Closing song or hymn (upbeat, hopeful, and well-known)
Commissioning
Blessing
Close of service (optional hymn or song)
Fellowship and refreshment time

Service Content

Beginning

Traditionally, the service begins with the congregation rising. The worship leader will give the invitation "Please stand if you are able." If there is a coffin, it will be carried or wheeled in with the worship leader leading the procession. As the worship leader slowly moves to the front of the sanctuary she speaks some sentences of scripture. More often today, the coffin or urn will be in place in the sanctuary already and the worship leader will offer some of the following scripture sentences after the words, "Let us worship God."

Hebrew and Christian Scriptures
For everything there is a season,
and a time for every matter under heaven:
a time to be born, and a time to die;
a time to plant, and a time to pluck up what is planted;
a time to break down, and a time to build up;
a time to weep, and a time to laugh;
a time to mourn, and a time to dance...
For everything there is a season:
a time to be born, and a time to die.(repeated)
(Ecclesiastes 3:1, 2, 4)

God is our refuge and strength, a very present help in trouble.
(Psalm 46:1)

Cast your burden on the Lord,
and [God] will sustain you.
(Psalm 55:22)

Jesus said... "I am the resurrection and the life.
Those who believe in me, even though they die,
will live, and everyone who lives and believes in me
will never die."
(John 11:25)

Blessed are those who mourn, for they will be comforted.
(Matthew 5:4)

The eternal God is your dwelling place,
and underneath are the everlasting arms.

(Deuteronomy 33:27, Revised
Standard Version)

We believe that Jesus died and rose again, even so, through Jesus, God
will bring with him those who have died.... Then we who are alive,
who are left, will be caught up in the clouds together with them to
meet the Lord in the air; and so we will be with the Lord forever.

(1 Thessalonians 4:14, 17)

For a Child

"Truly I tell you, whoever does not receive the kingdom of God as
a little child will never enter it."
And he took them up in his arms, laid his hands on them,
and blessed them.

(Mark 10:15–16)

As a mother comforts her child,
so I will comfort you [says the Lord.]
As a father has compassion for his children,
so the Lord has compassion for those who fear [God].

(Isaiah 66:13; Psalm 103:13)

Other Sentence

Say not in grief, "He/she is no more,"
but live in thankfulness she/he was.

(Hebrew proverb)

For Someone Who Led a Tough Life and Came through Stronger

For every hill I've had to climb, for every stone that bruised my feet,
for all the blood and sweat and grime, for blinding storms
and searing heat, my heart sings out a thankful song;
these were the things that made me strong.
For all the heartache and the tears, for all the anguish and the pain,
and for the hopes that lived in vain, I do give thanks.
For this I know, these were the things that made me grow.

Anon.

Welcome

The worship leader gives her name and on behalf of the faith community welcomes friends and family to the service, e.g., "I am David Sparks, minister of St. Andrew's Church, and I'm glad to welcome you, the friends and family members of Ruth, to this memorial service. It is good to be with you at this time." If the service is to proceed with the hymns, prayers, and other elements unannounced, this is the time to mention it.

Preface

Worship leader: Why have we come to this service? (*The following selections answer this question. Choose one that fits your context.*)

We have come to this service to celebrate the life of (*name*), whose life has ended.

It is good to be here!

We have come to join with others who knew *him/her* and loved *him/her*, to share our memories, and to tell our stories.

It is good to be here!

We have come to tell of all we have lost in (*name*)'s passing, to put our grief into words, and to follow words with actions.

It is good to be here!

We have come as family and friends to remember the effect of (*name*)'s life on each of our lives and to give (God) thanks.

It is good to be here!

(Optional) We have come as those who believe that death is not the final end that it seems to be and to rejoice in the hope of a life that begins when this one ends.

It is good to be here!

(*Add your own reasons why it is good to be here!*)

Greeting

Grace to you and comfort
in the name of God our Maker
who knows the count of the hairs on our heads
and the days of our lives;
in the name of Jesus, our brother and friend,
who has journeyed on all our roads with us,
and in the warm embrace of the Spirit of Life
whose care surrounds us always.

Bob Root[1]

Invitation to Worship

It is one of the most difficult things we are asked to do today:
to say goodbye to someone whom we love,
someone who may have always been there,
someone without whom we can hardly imagine our lives.
But that is what we have gathered here today to do:
to celebrate the life of (*name*),
to give thanks for all that has been good and loving,
to ask forgiveness for anything that was not as we might have hoped it
would be,
to bring ourselves and all that we feel
into God's presence,
that God will bless us and keep us close.

Bob Root

Sisters and brothers,
we have come together today because
(*name*) has died.
We come to commend *him/her* into God's care with gratitude,
and seek God's grace to comfort us
at this time of loss and change.
We gather this morning to worship God:
God, whom we know through the living of our lives,
God who is beyond all that we can ever know.
We gather this morning to worship God:
who brings the day to birth
and calls the sunset to its close
to make way for another day;

who makes life stir within us;
and welcomes us in loving arms when life here is over.
We gather this morning with thanksgiving for the life of (*name*),
who has lived among us
and is now with God.
Come, and let us worship God.

Bob Root

Grace to you and comfort
from God whose love created us,
from God known in Jesus Christ,
who lived our life, felt our pain, knows our hearts,
and from God the Spirit whose compassionate embrace
gives us courage to carry on when life is dark and bleak.
My friends, we have gathered here today because (*name*) has died.
(*At the end of a lengthy and devastating illness, which has turned the world upside down.*)
(*Name*)'s body has finished its work in our midst and *she/he* is at rest, at peace.
We have come, family and friends,
to give thanks to God for the joy of sharing life with *her/him,*
to offer to (*name family members*) our heartfelt sympathy at this loss,
and to support one another at this important time.
It is holy ground on which we stand.
And so, first of all, I want to light a candle as a reminder
of the brightness that (*name*)'s living has brought to each person who knew *her/him.*
Let us come now and place ourselves in God's care, for we know that in life, in death, and in life beyond death, God is with us. We are not alone.
In this strong faith, we are together.

Bob Root

Greeting for a Christmas Funeral

Grace to you and comfort,
in the name of the babe born in the manger on Christmas Day,
in the name of the Creator who set the stars in place,
in the name of the Spirit of Love who dwells deep within each of us.

Bob Root

Season of Easter
We have come together to worship God, and to give God thanks and
praise for the life of (*name*) who has died.
We have come together to remember (*name*),
to share our memories of *her/him,*
and to celebrate the life of one who has been good for us.
We are here as a pledge of our support for the (*name*) family.
We are here to recognize the limits and fragility
of this human life of ours,
and we come in this season of Easter to hear God's Word of hope as we
walk through the valley of shadows, and to rejoice in the risen
Jesus Christ who is proof positive that death lies totally defeated.
Thanks be to God!

In the name of Jesus Christ we gather this day.
We gather to gratefully remember (*name*)
who is gone from among us.
We gather to thank God for *his/her* life in family,
in friendship, and in community;
we gather to express our loss and to proclaim
our resurrection hope,
and our trust in the Living God.

Difficult Circumstances
Friends, we gather in the protective shelter
of God's healing love.
Here we are free to pour out our grief,
release our anger, face our emptiness,
and know God cares.
We gather to comfort and to support one another
in this time of (*grievous*) loss,
(*especially remembering…*).
We gather to hear God's eternal Word of hope
that can rid us of despair and
can move us to offer heartfelt praise to God.[2]

Friends, we gather to grieve our loss
and to comfort one another in our sorrow.
We gather to give thanks for the life of (*name*),
and to surround this (*family/these loved ones*)
with our support, strength, and encouragement.[3]

We have come to worship God and to remember (*first and last names*).
His/her life among us is over, but *his/her* life embraced by God's love
has only just begun.
(*Name*) was a significant person in our lives:
one we knew, one with whom we shared,
one whose love and concern has strengthened us.
We will miss *him/her* more than we can say.
And we meet in the knowledge that the death of another person
stirs deep feelings within us:
feelings of joy but also feelings of loss and sorrow,
feelings of fear but also feelings of huge hope.
(*What would have been the feelings stirred by the death of this person?*
Feelings of guilt, feelings of regret for what might have been?)
We rejoice that we are able to remember and give thanks today.
We rejoice that we are able to share stories
and express our feelings today,
and to do so in the name and in the way of Jesus, God's chosen one;
Jesus, who died and has risen. Amen.

For a Youth
Grace and comfort to you
from our loving God,
from our brother Jesus,
and in the warm embrace of the Spirit of Life,
who calls us into being
and walks with us on our journey
in good times and bad
and who welcomes us with great tenderness and compassion when life
comes to an end.

My friends, we have come here *this morning*
because a terrible thing has happened.
(*Name*) has died, and we can hardly believe it.
Life snuffed out like the flame of a candle,
in the twinkling of an eye,
without warning, without preparation,
without time to say "Goodbye,"
or all the thousand-and-one other things
we wish we were able to say to *him/her*.
(*Name*) died living fully the days that were given to *him/her*,
a youth full of promise and hope.
And so we come today,
and people have come for days,
in wonder and disbelief,
to share our tears and draw strength from one another,
to share our delights and gratitude for knowing *him/her*,
and to ask for resources stronger than our own
to deal with this tragedy,
for our strength is gone.
In the welcome and the safety of this place,
let us gather now.

                                        Bob Root

For Use in a Hall or Garden

In this place of friendship/in this place of peace,
we gather to remember (*name*), our friend and family member.
In our time together,
we will cherish *his/her* memory,
give thanks for *his/her* (*long*) life,
comfort *his/her* loved ones,
become aware of our limited lifespan,
(rejoice in the hope of a life that begins when this one ends),
and renew our determination to make the most of each day
that lies ahead of us.

You may write your own answer to the question "Why are we here?" and formulate it in the Preface, for example:

> We are here:
> together, to remember and give thanks for *Ruth*'s life,
> to show our support for *Ruth*'s family,
> to remember those in *Ruth*'s communities (*name them*)
> who are grieving,
> to show our support to those in *Ruth*'s church who are missing her,
> to give God thanks for *her* support of us in some very different ways.
> We are here to support each other in our common grief,
> and to recall our own feelings about death,
> to be sent out with hope and determination,
> (*where it's an accidental or sudden death*) to express our disbelief that
> death has happened,
> to receive hope for relief in the sadness we feel,
> (*at death of a child*) to share our supreme sadness that this life
> with all its potential is over so soon,
> to comfort the distressed parents,
> to share our love with her friends.

Opening Words

My name is (*name*).
I (*am a representative of the Christian faith,*
and) work with *The United Church of Canada,*
and welcome you as we gather today
to mourn the death and
to celebrate the life of (*name*).
We are here to say thank you for the many ways
that (*name*)'s life touched you and others,
and we gather to gain life insights from *her/him,*
and to commend *him/her* to the Mystery at the heart of life.

It is never easy to be faced with the reality of death.
Many different feelings will be stirring within you,
feelings of loss that (*name*) will no longer be part
of your everyday life,
and feelings of thankfulness for good times shared.

There will also be feelings of grief over the remembered loss of family
members, friends, and other loved ones.
(*follow with a time of reflection*)

Today we will reflect on
all that (*name*) accomplished
and the goals *she/he* achieved.
We will celebrate the depth of love
and friendship *she/he* showed in *her/his* life.
We will recall our individual memories of (*name*)
and the times we spent together.

We also gather as a community,
united by our common love for (*name*)
and by the Spirit of love that is ever with us
in whatever way we name that spirit,
"Creator," or "God," or "Higher Power,"
the Spirit of love that is there to empower us and strengthen us,
to comfort and to challenge us,
to offer healing to us, and to offer peace on the journey of grief.
We gather to remember that the Spirit fills us with hope,
hope of a life that begins when this one ends.
We gather to remember that by trusting a presence
greater than ourselves,
we can find hope, peace, and love.

Cynthia Breadner
(as inspired by Fred Joblin)[4]

Invitation to Worship
Grace to you and comfort
from our Maker, from whose loving arms we come,
and into whose loving arms we return
when life on earth has come to an end,
in the name of our brother Jesus,
who walks with us as friend and companion throughout our journey,
and in the kindness of the Spirit of Life,
whose presence gives us strength to live day by day.
My friends, we have gathered here this afternoon
because (*name*) has died.
At the end of a long, rich, full, well-lived life,

in the natural rhythm and cycle of the seasons,
(*name*) has inherited the promise of the faith in which *she/he*
lived and died and which held *him/her* firmly.
We have come, family and friends, to honour *him/her,*
for *she/he* has earned our praise,
to support one another, for this loss is significant,
and to ask God's blessing on all our living.
Come and let us worship God.

Bob Root

Opening Prayers

Our opening prayer is a way of expressing our belief that:

The loving and compassionate God has a place in all we do
at this service.
We can direct our thanks to God, entrust God with our concerns and
anxieties.
We can take heart that in the silence and darkness of bereavement that
we experience, the risen spirit of Jesus Christ will be the hope of renewed
relationship and light to us.
We can comfort one another.

> Creator, Spirit of life, you have shared with us
> the life of (*name*), and it is with grateful hearts
> we give thanks for all the goodness in *her/him,*
> which now lives and grows in us and others.
> As now we honour (*name*)'s life and say "goodbye,"
> we seek to find comfort in our loneliness,
> allow forgiveness where it may be needed,
> and gain courage to face the future unafraid.
>
> Strengthen and draw us closer to one another.
> Enable us to serve, and give to us that sense of peace and joy
> that comes from knowing we are connected in life
> and beyond this life. Amen.

Cynthia Breadner (as inspired by
Fred Joblin)

Opening Prayer: Death as Part of Life

O God, Creator of all life,
help us to accept death as a part of life,
trusting in your goodness and great love
for every one of us.
We feel now the pain of parting with the one we love,
but we rejoice that *we/so many* were privileged
to experience life with *her/him.*
We entrust (*name*) to you in death,
as in life you entrusted *her/him* to us.
We pray in sincerity and hope. Amen.

William Kervin[5]

O God, you brought us to life, and you remind us that death is
a natural part of life.
We come this (*morning/afternoon*) to celebrate the life of (*name*) whom
we have known and loved, a friend and family member who has died.
We give you thanks for the whole range of human experience that was
his/hers: the wonder, the joys, and the challenges.
Bless us in these moments of remembering
that we may share the good stories of her life,
and comfort (*name*)'s family in this time of loss,
and comfort one another.
We pray in the name of the compassionate one, Jesus Christ. Amen.

God of all, you formed us in our mother's womb and brought us
to know life and love here on earth. The hairs on our heads are all
numbered, and you know their count. Each part of our living is in the
embrace of your care. And so, dear God, you know the sorrow in our
hearts as we gather in this place, brought together by (*name*)'s death.
You know also, dear God, how grateful we are for the days that we
have shared.

Enfold us now into your tenderness, that in this time together, we
might find healing and comfort, and offer you our praise. In Jesus'
name we pray. Amen.

Bob Root

Connection with God in Life and in Death

There is no end to your compassion, Loving God.
It has touched us throughout the journey of life,
in help when we needed it most,
and hope when we reached life's lowest ebb.
It was there at the end of (*name*)'s life and felt through the
presence of *his/her* family members and friends.
It is here this morning as we express our thanks to you,
and go about our remembering and telling our stories.
It will be there for us in the days
ahead as we face our loss and go about our grief work.
As (*name*) knows your eternal embrace, so give us that same wonderful
hope that when our finite time merges into your time of infinite love,
you will be there for us. Amen.

Timeless God

God of all time, God of our time,
we come before you in hope this (*morning/afternoon*).
Grant us joy in our remembering
and thankfulness for a life now complete.
Grant us openness as we express our loss
and comfort when we feel alone.
(*Name*) knows your peace now,
and the testing times of this life are over.
(*Name*) is embraced by your love now,
and your love will never let *her/him* go.
Eternal God, your hope is sure. Amen.

Death of a Cancer Sufferer

So many good and productive years lay before (*name*),
so many days to enjoy with family and friends,
so many days to share laughter and to give help,
so many days to make the world (*or local community name*) a kinder
and more compassionate place.
It is because (*name*) died far too early that we feel *his/her* loss so acutely
and recognize how much we will miss *her/his* influence for good.
Be with us, compassionate God, and for the sake of (*name*), who died,
renew us as people of justice, kindness, and caring,
your chosen people. Amen.

Death Due to an Accident

We come to this service scarcely able to believe that
(*name*) has gone from his family and friendship circle.
His/her absence is difficult to believe possible, difficult to take in.
We need your presence, O Most Loving God, to bring the reality of
(*name*)'s death home to us, to enable us to comfort one another,
and to assure us that in your loving presence *she/he*
is safe and happy and at peace.
Reassure us in this time together that there is no fear of ours that
is not known to you and no anxiety that is beyond our scope
to handle.
We meet in the name of Jesus, your chosen one, who died suddenly,
tragically, so much before his time. Amen.

For a Child

Loving God, your embrace (*holy hug*) supports us in life,
your Spirit watches over us in death.
We bless you for the joy shown by Jesus in little children,
and the assurance that of such is the kingdom of heaven.
In our sorrow, make us strong to commit ourselves
and those we love, to your unfailing care.
In our perplexity, help us to trust when we cannot understand.
In our loneliness, may we remember (*name*) in love,
trusting *her/him* to your gentle embrace and keeping. Amen.[6]

Loving God,
this family, these friends, loved (*name*) so much.
This family, these friends, miss (*name*) so much.
We are glad you stand with them and support them
at this time of loss.
Your love is infinite and compassionate;
in your love this little one is safe and always will be.
Your peace is limitless and certain;
in your peace, this family, these friends
may know a place of refuge, a place from which to venture out.
As you have blessed (*name*) so bless *his/her* loved ones
in the name of Jesus, who blessed the little children. Amen.

Loving God,
your eternal hug (*holy hug*) is for (*name*) who has died.
We have so many good memories of all *she/he* was to *his/her* parents
and to us *her/his* family and friends;
memories to bring us to tears, memories to make us laugh out loud,
memories of the times *she/he* played with us, memories of the time *she/he* helped us and brought a smile to our faces.
We have been blessed by *her/his* presence among us,
and we remember how Jesus blessed the little children
who came to him and accepted them.
We know, Loving God, how you have welcomed (*name*), and we ask
that we might show our thankfulness for *her/his* life by sharing our
stories and supporting the children we know and those we don't know
whose needs are great.
We pray in the name of Jesus, who cared for boys and girls. Amen.

Prayer of Confession and Words of Assurance

When there are expressed feelings of guilt around the death of a loved one,
a simple prayer of confession may be helpful to the grieving process. The
words of assurance bring a sense of forgiveness and peace.

Eternal God,
In life and in death you are there for us,
we can count on you.
In our looking back you go with us,
and as we remember today you are our guide.
We are troubled in our remembering
by words unsaid and deeds not done.
We are troubled in our remembering
by opportunities missed and trust broken.
We are troubled in our remembering
by links of love ignored and faith forgotten.
In your compassion, grant us forgiveness.
In your mercy, grant us peace.
(*time of silent confession*)

Words of Assurance
One: Loving God,
you give us the opportunity
to put the past in the past.
You encourage us to make a fresh start.
Your pardon is for us and with us today.
We have nothing to fear.
All: Thanks be to God! Amen.

(*Select appropriate sections of this prayer.*)
Merciful, understanding God,
you know us through and through;
you are aware of our sense of unworthiness, and we
remember deeds and words that hurt, that caused anger,
bitterness, and resentment.
(*time of silence*)

Your word is **pardon,** that sense that we may know release
from the tyranny of past words and actions.
You are aware of our sense of loneliness;
we have feelings that no one else can know and share;
we experience anxiety and fear.
(*time of silence*)

Your word is **presence,** the presence of caring people,
known and loved;
the presence of your strengthening, hopeful Spirit.
We have a strong sense of things left undone.
We are aware of all that could have been said or shared
or achieved.
(*time of silence*)

Your word is **freedom**; you allow us to break free
from the guilt that binds us, balancing our regret for
all we would like to change in the past with
memories of good times shared together.

You, Loving God, are aware of the situations where we
have put ourselves first and others last,
where we have been unfaithful to you, to your faith community,
and to our family members and to our friends.
(*time of silence*)

Your word is **grace,** free, unmerited love,
symbolized by the cross of Jesus,
a love that covers all our sins, a love without any limits at all. Amen.

Assurance of Pardon
Know, believe, and accept the graceful forgiveness of God.
You are God's chosen ones. Accept God's peace. Amen.

A Blessing after the Meditation
May you be blessed in your grieving.
May you find the peace that passes understanding.
May you know healing in your heart.
And may you keep (name)'s love ever close,
that you might share it with everyone you meet. Amen.

Bob Root

Prayer of Thanksgiving
During the service we will have offered thanks for the life of the person who
has died through eulogies and the meditation. These thanksgivings will echo
the feelings of the family members and friends of the deceased and will have
stimulated them to remember other events and situations for which they are
thankful. In thanksgiving prayers we direct our thanks to the God who has
given us life in all its wonder, its variety, and its beauty.

In the following prayers of thanks there is time and space allowed for our
own thanks to be offered to the Holy One. There is also a time for the thanks
of the faith community to be offered. There is no sense here that the rough
side of life is to be ignored or glossed over, but this shadow side is to be balanced by the immense and graceful gift that is our brief space of living on
this earth and all that may be accomplished during this time.

General Thanksgiving
(*Sections may be selected.*)
Eternal God,
Source of life,
beyond knowledge and thought,
mysterious and profound;
we give thanks
because we have seen you
in (*name*), who has died.

We give thanks for your life in *her/him*
with all its achievements, all its struggles,
and for your love,
given and received by (*name*)
among family and friends.
We give thanks to you, our God, for (*name*)'s life.
(*Include here three or four short specific thanksgivings, e.g.,*
His love of his children and grandchildren
His concern for refugees,
His delight in gardening
His enjoyment of soft ice cream.)
And, in a few moments of silence,
bring our own special memories and thanksgivings before you.
(*time of reflection*)
And, in a few moments of silence, we bring the memories
of this *faith community/church* before you.
(*time of reflection*)
It is because of our good and varied memories
that our sorrow, now, is real
and our loss great.
Through one who enriched us by *her/his* presence...

As we honour (*name*),
we commit ourselves to live in *her/his* way,
with generosity, with caring, with concern for each other,
and a song in our hearts
to make life not only bearable,
but also joyful and fulfilling
for all who struggle and are afraid.

As we honour (*name*),
we pray for ourselves,
because death disturbs us deeply
and raises unanswerable questions for us.
But we pray we may not be embittered by (*name*)'s death,
nor by the way in which it came,
that it may not cause us to think less of life but more;
that it may not turn us on ourselves in self-pity,
but will make us more eager to comfort others
in any sorrow of theirs.

Loving God,
give us all we need
for courage and strength today,
all we need for hope and peace today.
Be with us
here and everywhere;
be present for us
now and always,
Fulfiller of our past,
Strength of our present,
and Promise of our future,
through your Chosen One, Jesus Christ. Amen.

Alan Gaunt (adapted)[7]

God of the living, God of those who have died,
we come before you with thankfulness today.
We thank you for (*name*)'s life,
all the joy and achievement,
all the struggle and tough times.
The good memories shine out and invite us to
laughter and to share our own stories.
The broken dreams and the suffering
call us to remember
and to see the same patterns in our own life's journey.
We thank you for
(*Include three or four short, specific thanksgivings, e.g.,*

Her love of her nephews and nieces
Her concern for those who have no permanent home
Her delight in painting
Her enjoyment of the lakeside cottage.)
In moments of silence we will offer our thanks and our
memories of (*name*) to you in prayer.
(*time of silent reflection*)
In moments of silence, we offer the thanks of this faith community
for all (*name*) gave in worship, service, and caring here.
(*time of silent reflection*)
It is because of our cherished memories
that we feel keenly the loss of (*name*)
and bring before you *her/his* family members.
(*list names and relationships*)
We bring before you all who will miss (*name*) so much.
In their remembering, bless them,
in their loss, be patiently with them,
in their grieving, comfort them,
in their new beginnings, stand with them,
and commission us as your helpers to
work with all those who mourn.

And grant us peace as we consider the limits
that are a reality of all our lives,
the limits that opportunity places on us,
the limits that our health imposes on us,
the limits that our limited lifespan brings home to us.

God of the living, God of those who have died,
in life and in death we are yours,
your love will never leave us. Amen.

We give you thanks, loving God, for your presence at every twist and
turn of life and we thank you for your presence with us when the
rhythm of our limited time merges with the beat of your eternal time.
You have been with us as we have today remembered (*name, our friend
and family member*).
We thank you for the length and breadth and depth of (*name*)'s life, all
of its challenges and all of its moments of wonder and fulfillment.

Each one of us here has memories that come to mind, and we bring them before you in moments of silence.

(*time of silent reflection*)

Many of the events we have remembered we will share over the coming days:

(*Here follow some memories of the deceased. They can be enhanced by showing video clips or still photos of the person in life situations, e.g.,*)

Memories of (*name*) in *his workshop.*

Memories of (*name*) as *she made jam for her neighbours.*

Memories of (*name*) laughing and playing with *his grandchildren.*

Memories of (*name*) in *the garden she loved so much.*

These memories warm our hearts, but they also deepen the sense of loss we feel at this service.

We thank you for them and we pray especially for (*name*)'s family as they come to terms with life without their loved one.

Your love, O God, is with them all the time.

Your Spirit will be experienced in a loyal companion when they feel alone.

Your Spirit will be experienced as a sense of hope when they are down or depressed.

Your Spirit will be experienced as a way forward when the future seems uncertain and bleak.

Your Spirit will be experienced in joy and laughter as memories are shared.

Hold (*name*)'s family members in your embrace and bless them, loving God, and reassure us as we are aware through (*name*)'s death of our own limited lifespan.

Renew in us the certainty of your love, the love that will not let us go. Enable us to fully live each day with the care-fulness, adventure, and justice to which you call us, and enable us to see those who have suffered loss and stand with them shoulder to shoulder.

Our prayers of thanks we offer in the name of Jesus, risen and at work through today's disciples. Amen.

Thanks in the Testing

Eternal God, with your whole church we rejoice
that nothing in life or death,
in this present age or in all the ages to come,
can separate us from your love
revealed in Jesus.
We hold on to that when as today we are tested by the loss of (*name*),
our good friend and family member;
tested when as a faith community we realize we have lost one of our
own;
tested by the reality that we won't see *him/her* again;
tested by the simple fact that we will miss *him/her* so much;
tested by thoughts of service and caring that might have been;
tested by the reality that we, too, will die.
And as we remember that the love of Jesus was shown
in down-to-earth practical ways—unselfishness,
compassion, healing, noticing, peace-bringing, and
trusting friendship—so we remember those aspects of (*name*)'s life
that resonated with God's chosen one.
In moments of silence we bring before you, Most Holy One,
our thanksgiving.
(*time of silent reflection*)
In moments of silence, we remember (*name*)'s worship and service in
this *church/faith community.*
(*time of silent reflection*)
As we remember (*name*) with thanksgiving and joy, so we are glad that
for *him/her* all the hard times of sickness and struggle are over and
done with and *he/she* is reunited with those who loved *her/him* and is a
part of that community who praise the Holy One without end.
Encourage and strengthen us through our sense of loss, O God.
Be with us as we remember and give thanks in the days that lie ahead.
May the Christian love that (*name*) knew and shared
firmly guide and challenge our way of living,
and may the risen hope of Jesus lead us on through death,
to your closer presence.
Amen.

Exceptional Loss

We didn't want to be here, God of love;
we did not want to hear the cherished memories of (*name*)'s life
or be aware of the huge loss that has been experienced.
We didn't want to be reminded of our own limited lifespan.
We didn't want to listen to the words of scripture that speak of eternal
life, not at this time, not in this place.
But in spite of our wish to be anywhere but here,
we came and we are glad.
We are glad that we have been here to share in worship and to be with
(*name*)'s family, to comfort one another.
We are glad that we have been able to recall our own special memories
of (*name*).
We bring some of those memories silently before you, loving God;
we bring them with our deep thankfulness.
(*time of silent reflection*)
We are glad that we have been able to link our memories with those
of others, remembering (*name*)'s love *of the outdoors, her/his* creative
approach to *cooking*, the joy that was hers/his when *the grandchildren
came to stay...(include remembered joys of the person who has died).*
And as our memory is deeply stirred, so the extent of this so sudden
and tragic loss experienced by (*name*)'s family and close friends comes
home to us. We stand ready to be a strong support to them in the
weeks and months ahead, a practical help in getting through the issues
that have to be faced when a loved one dies, but also as those who are
simply there for them, to share conversation and to listen when grief,
in one of its many disguises, makes its presence felt.
And we are glad, but also disturbed and challenged, as the significance
of our limited lifespan comes home to us. We realize that we are called
to listen to the sacred words that speak of a life that begins when this
one ends and use them to enliven our daily work and activities.
Thanksgiving is sometimes the natural and easy way to go;
sometimes it results in unforeseen challenges and requests.
We offer our thanksgivings to you, loving God,
and ask that you use our talents and skills at this time of loss to help
(*name*)'s family and as we encounter others who have experienced loss.
We offer our prayer hopefully for in Jesus Christ you have opened up
for us the full dimension of compassion. We pray in his name. Amen.

Exceptional Loss and Unresolved Feelings
The death of (*name*) has been hard on all of us.

We have been angry about the way *she/he* died. We have been angry because there might have been more done to prevent (*name*)'s death. *We have been angry that those who were responsible have not been held to account.*

We have even been angry at you, God; we have felt *that you remained unmoved by this tragedy/ could have stepped in and stopped this terrible event (or other feelings).*

So we give thanks for this service for it has given us an opportunity to see (*name*)'s death in other ways.

We thank you that we have been able to look at the wonderful times and achievements of (*name*)'s short but full life. (*Include details.*)

We thank you for the certainty of your presence with (*name*)'s family and for those who have been there to comfort, to support, and to be the incarnation of your compassionate presence at this dark time. We remember them; we pray for them.

(*time of silence*)

We ask that you will help us to value those qualities that you have endowed us with, and to value each day we have to use them.

We pray in the name of Jesus Christ, whose inspiring, courageous, and justice-seeking life was ended way before its time. Amen.

Death of Young Person at New Year
Compassionate God,

we are at a time when words seem so inadequate and our emotions threaten to overwhelm us.

Help us to trust in your consoling love and a mercy that never fails.

Embrace us with gentle understanding.
Uphold each of us in everlasting care.
When tears overflow, may they cleanse our souls.
When sadness weighs us down, lift us up with holy power.
When anger dominates the very core of our being,
grant us the breathing space to find hope.

Blessed God, we pray for (*name*)'s family and for the circle of friends who were family to *him/her.*

We offer to you *his/her* (*hockey/soccer/softball team*), who have been devastated by *his/her* loss, and we pray for the many people of this locality (*name of city or town*) who are still in shock.

O God, at this time of end-of-year celebrations, give cool and wise heads to young persons; when temptation and pressure persuade, may each look for alternatives that are safe and fun.

Embrace each of us with your strong arms of mercy—blanket us with peace and sustain us with your ever-present love at this time of sorrow, O Holy One.

For we pray in the name of Jesus, a young man killed in the prime of life. Amen.

Laura Turnbull (adapted)[8]

Commendation/Committal

Where the church service is complete or where the interment or scattering of ashes will be at some date yet to be determined, it is the usual practice to commit the loved one who has died to God. If there is a casket or urn present, the worship leader places his hand on the casket or urn and says words such as these:

Eternal God, for whom time is nothing,
Compassionate One, who received our loved ones when their lives were complete and will in turn receive us,
we praise you and we bless you that you bring (*name*),
our friend and family member, into your eternal presence.
We rejoice that for (*name*) all sickness and infirmity is over and done with, struggle is forgotten, and death itself is past.
We rejoice that *she/he* is secure within your divine love in a way beyond our imagining.
Bless us as you have blessed (*name*), and be with us when we feel lonely and afraid.
Fill our hearts with good memories of *her/him* as we return to our homes.
We pray in the name of the risen Jesus, defeater of death. Amen.

Eternal God,
We entrust (*name*) to the memories of each person
present in this place and to the memories of many
who could not be here today.
We entrust (*name*) to your unfailing love.
We entrust (*name*) to your abiding compassion.

Into the hands of a loving spirit,
we commend (*name*).
We celebrate our belief that (*name*) is now at peace
and experiencing, in joyful spirit,
the beauty of life beyond this life.

Cynthia Breadner (inspired by
Fred Joblin)

(*Name*), go forth from this world
knowing that you are loved beyond the telling of it,
that you will be missed beyond the knowing of it,
that love never ends,
that you will be remembered and cherished,
and that one day,
we will be together again.
Now may you rest in the peace
that is prepared for you
in the wonderful presence of God.

Bob Root

Eternal God,
we entrust (*name*) to your unbounded love,
we entrust (*name*) to your unbounded care.
We have lost (*name*) from our midst, but we know
that *he/she* is at one with that great cloud of witnesses
that no one can number.

Be with us as we remember (*name*) fondly
and work through our grief.
Be with us as we share stories and
celebrate *his/her* time with us.

Be with us as we feel our own length of years
and strive to make the most of each hour of each day.

We put our trust in the risen Jesus Christ,
who leads us on through death to eternal joy.

And the grace of Christ who leads us,
the love of God that sustains us,
and the fellowship of the Holy Spirit
that works through us.
Be with you and with those you love,
now and always.
Amen.

May God in kindness bless our loss.
May God in wisdom receive our thanks.
May God in hopefulness bring us to a new tomorrow.
Thank you, God, for who you are to us,
and who you will continue to be.
Go in peace.
Until we meet again,
may you be held in the palm of God's hand,
this day,
this night,
and forevermore. Amen.

Bob Root

(*Name*), go forth from this world
knowing that you have been loved,
that you will be missed,
that love never ends,
that you will be remembered,
and that one day,
we will be together again.

Bob Root

Commissioning

The committal can lead directly to the commissioning (see examples above) or the commissioning may be separate. The congregation is invited to stand.

> Take courage.
> Be confident and strong.
> Go where you must go, do what you must do.
> Shed tears, endure sorrow, live with loneliness,
> but rejoice in memory.
> Comfort each other, but put your hope in the Risen Christ,
> who leads us on through death to resurrection and to eternal joy.
>
> Alan Gaunt (adapted)

Following the singing of "She Flies On" (*Voices United* 380), you might use the following commissioning and benediction:

> *On a journey just begun, she flies on.*
> *And in the passage of her flight,*
> *her song rings out through the night,*
> *full of laughter, full of light, she flies on.*[9]
> Enriched by our relationship with (*name*),
> strengthened by the comfort of God,
> companioned by the friendship of Christ,
> let us leave this time and place of worship
> with the blessing and peace and love
> that is God's gift to us
> this day, this night, and for evermore.
>
> Bob Root

Sending Forth

> God goes with us,
> rejoicing in our memories,
> feeling our grief,
> shedding our tears,
> (entering our loneliness),
> bringing us closer together,
> restoring us to life,
> setting hope clearly in front of us.
> The source of courage and peace,
> God goes with us, God will never leave us.

(The following prayer is based on A Song of Faith, a United Church affirmation of faith.)

Divine creation does not cease
    until all things have found wholeness, union, and integration
    with the common ground of all being.
As children of the Timeless One,
    our time-bound lives will find completion
    in the all-embracing Creator.
In the meantime, we embrace the present,
    embodying hope, loving our enemies,
    and caring for the earth.
Go into the world with a daring and tender love.
The world is waiting,
go in peace, and all that you do, do it by the power of love. Amen.

Cynthia Breadner (as inspired
by Fred Joblin)

The words of our commissioning are words to ponder:
Live simply,
love generously,
serve faithfully,
pray daily,
and leave the rest to God.

Blessing/Benediction/Offering of God's Peace

The last liturgical action in the service is for the worship leader to offer a blessing. The function of the blessing is to remind the congregation that the Holy One is at the heart of all that has been done and for each person to feel that, as they go from the service, the Spirit of God goes with them and will go with them in the coming days.

And now may the God who keeps our going out and our coming in,
from this time forth and forevermore,
hold you tenderly,
wipe your tears,
enable hope to be reborn in you,
and heal your hearts,
with the blessing of love, this day and forevermore.

Bob Root

The grace of Christ attend you,
the love of God surround you,
the Holy Spirit keep you.

Go from here in the way of the Compassionate One,
the God of Loving kindness,
the Christ who served continually,
the Spirit who is within each caring act.

May the blessing of God go with you,
the compassion of Jesus enthuse you,
and the Holy Spirit call you to action.

May the road rise to meet you,
May the wind be always at your back,
May the sun shine warm upon your face,
May the rains fall soft upon your fields,
And until we meet again,
May God hold you in the palm of God's hand.

Traditional Gaelic blessing

Peace to you all.
Peace to each one of you.
Peace when loss is defeating.
Peace when loneliness aches.
Peace when the future is uncertain.
Peace when the circle is broken.
God's peace that is foundational.
God's peace that is unending.
God's peace, a peace overflowing with love.
The peace that passes all understanding.
Go in peace! Amen.

A Commissioning and Benediction
Today—it's the only one we have,
and it is God's gift to us.
So as we leave this time and place of worship,
may we go with ears open to hear God's Word to us,
in all the places our feet take us,
in all the people that we meet on the road,
in all that we do in God's world.

Bob Root

Benediction
And now let us leave this time together,
firmly anchored in the love of God that will not let us go,
linked arm in arms in strong and secure friendships,
trusting in the promise of healing,
and grateful for the gift of life to hold us, enrich us, and keep us
this day, this night, and always.

Bob Root

Service Ending

The blessing is the formal end of the service. If the interment is to follow the service directly, the worship leader will go in front of the casket as it is moved down the aisle with the family behind it. If there are cremated remains, then a family member may carry the urn with the worship leader leading.

For many services the urn will be left in place on the communion table and the worship leader asks the congregation to stand and leads the family out of the sanctuary.

In some funeral homes, the practice is for the congregational members to file out past the casket or urn as an act of respect to the deceased. Some will touch the casket, and some will offer a silent prayer as they pass.

It is good if a well-known and upbeat song or hymn is sung as the family members leave.

Service of Committal

The funeral director and worship leader will lead the family and friends to the graveside. If the remains of the loved one are in a casket, they will be carried by pallbearers chosen by the family and under the direction of a member of the funeral home staff. The urn may be carried by a family member. The arrangement of the family around the grave will be the responsibility of the worship leader if no funeral home staff member is present. Because the service is carried out in the open air and sound does not carry well, it is essential for the worship leader to "shepherd" the family members and friends close together. The worship leader should take note of the age and physical abilities of elderly family members prior to the service, and folding chairs should be brought to the graveside even if the elderly congregants initially decline to use them.

If the weather forecast threatens rain, then umbrellas should be brought by the family members, and the worship leader should bring her own. This umbrella should be held by another during the service. If the weather on the day of the service turns very cold or if there is heavy rain, the worship leader may suggest to the family that the service be completed in the sanctuary or other place. She will point out the dangers to the health of the living and that these outweigh the need to be present at the final service for those who have died.

Call to Worship

Scripture sentences different from those above may be used. The worship leader may want to think about the state of mind of the mourners before choosing specific passages. Some selections follow.

> You are indeed my rock and fortress [O God];
> for your name's sake lead me and guide me.
> (Psalm 31:3)

> Peace I leave with you; my peace I give you.
> I do not give to you as the world gives.
> Do not let your hearts be troubled, and do not let them be afraid.
> (John 14:27)

Paul writes:
I consider that the sufferings of the present time are not worth
comparing with the glory about to be revealed to us....
Who will separate us from the love of Christ?...
For I am convinced that neither death, nor life, nor angels, nor rulers,
nor things present, nor things to come, nor powers, nor height, nor
depth, nor anything else in all creation, will be able to separate us from
the love of God in Christ Jesus our Lord.
(Romans 8:18, 35, 38, 39)

Thanks be to God, who gives us the victory
through our Lord Jesus Christ!
Therefore my beloved, be steadfast, immovable,
always excelling in the work of the Lord,
because you know that in the Lord your labour is not in vain.
(1 Corinthians 15:57, 58)

Graveside Preface

My friends, we gather in this place to honour the life of (*name*). We
come to remember (*name*)'s life and to acknowledge (*name*)'s death. A
cemetery is a wonderful place to learn about life. Here we remember
that the line between this world and the next is only a breath
away—not far at all. We cannot come here today and not know that
others have had broken hearts besides ourselves, and that, while our
experience of loss is uniquely ours, others, too, have known the pain
of physical separation. This family has stood in this place before to
honour loved ones. There are reminders all around us of our mortality.
But here in this place we find also the gentle spirits of those who have
gone before us, those folk who, by the strength given to them, lived
as fully and as richly as they were able and, having finished their work
among us, then returned to the welcoming arms of God. We are never
far from those we love, nor are they far from us.
Bob Root

Opening Prayer at Graveside
God, as we gather to give thanks
to you for sharing (*name*) with us,
as now we come to return (*name*)'s
earthly remains to their final resting place,
we ask for your comforting arms around us.
May we may know peace, healing, and hope today,
and in the days ahead.
Bless the ground that receives (*name*)
and bless those who have gathered to honour him.
We pray in Jesus' name. Amen.

Bob Root (adapted)

Committal
Prior to the committal, earth may be cast on the coffin or sand in the form of a cross on the urn. Then the worship leader will say the following.

Into God's keeping and into God's unfailing love we commend our *brother/sister* who has died.
(Funeral) We commit *her/his* body to the ground, earth to earth, ashes to ashes, dust to dust.
(Cremated remains) We commit *her/his* ashes to the *ground/place of burial*, earth to earth, dust to dust, trusting to God's great mercy by which we have been born again to a living hope through the resurrection of Jesus Christ from the dead.

or

In the strong hope of a life renewed beyond our understanding,
we commit (*name*)'s *body/these ashes* to the *ground/place of burial*,
thankful for all *his/her* life was to us,
deeply missing *his/her* presence with us,
believing *he/she* is in the company of all the saints,
confident *he/she* is embraced by God's love beyond all time.

As these words are being said, the casket or urn will be lowered into the ground or placed in the burial niche. The worship leader may invite family members to place flowers in the grave. At this time, family members and friends may reflect in silence on their loved one.

Worship leader then says, "Let us pray."

Prayer of Confidence and Assurance

Almighty God, you have bound together all your people in heaven and earth (on earth and beyond the limits of our existence) in one holy fellowship. Let not our thoughts linger here, but help us to believe that your servant's life has made a new beginning with your mercy and your love still around *him/her*. Strengthened by this assurance, may we return to the experience of life that awaits us in the world, resolved to be more faithful to you and more helpful to one another, for the sake of those no longer with us upon earth. Amen.

Alan Gaunt

or

This has been a hard day, loving God, for we have had to say farewell to (*name*), one so well loved. Accept our feelings of sadness and loss. But this has been a good day as we have remembered a life that has touched so many family members and friends with friendship and compassion, encouragement and love.
Accept our feelings of thanksgiving and joy.
(*Name*) has gone from us but *she/he* has not gone from you.
Your love that touched *her/him* in life has embraced *her/him* in death and will never let *her/him* go.
Believing this, we return to our homes with confidence for our faith has been strengthened and we have been inspired to serve our fellow men and women justly and compassionately.
We take all that was good and worthy in our beloved's life with us as we go.
In the name of the risen Jesus Christ, we pray. Amen.

Commissioning

(*Optional; see selection above.*)

Blessing

(See selection on previous pages.)

> Now may the loving kindness of the Holy One,
> the compassion of the Christ,
> and the enthusiasm/inspiration of the Holy Spirit
> be with you and with those you love,
> in time and beyond time. Amen.

Location of Committal

The location of the committal will be in a place authorized for human remains. For a body, there are specific areas—gardens of remembrance, cemeteries, columbaria—where the remains must by law be buried, but for cremated remains there are no regulations in most places except that they must not be scattered in a public area. What many people do not understand is that the cremated remains of a human body are not like dust, but consist of many small but highly visible skeletal fragments. If the person who died has requested that his ashes be scattered on the 11th green of his favourite golf course, it would be wise to check with the green keeper first! Common sense will guide most families. A request for the ashes of a loved one to be spread in the waters of the ocean, or a large lake, or a forest can usually be met with no problems. If, however, the request centres on a public park where the deceased was especially happy, his family should do well to think again.

An alternative here is for the largest part of the ashes to be located in a conventional garden of remembrance or niche and for a very small portion to be scattered according to the wishes of the person who has died. One challenge with random scattering is that there is no longer any place where family members may go to feel close to the last earthly remains of their loved one.

There are nowadays many innovative ways in which the remains or a proportion of the remains may be disposed of, e.g., blown glass containers, lockets, artworks, and even diamonds, and any funeral home will be ready to advise.

Graveside Service

It is assumed that this will be a simple service, combining major elements of the funeral service or life celebration with the interment, but with no music. With modern sound amplification equipment, however, it is possible to play hymns and songs and for singing to be a part of the service. If this is done, the use of well-known hymns or a soloist is recommended.

The service order will use the same liturgical elements as those in the funeral service or life celebration and the interment. The worship leader will lead the group from the cars to the graveside, going ahead of the casket or urn. When the casket or urn is in position beside the grave, she will gather the people together, and the service will begin.

- Scripture sentences (if not said on the way to the graveside)
- (Preface to the service)
- Opening prayer
- Readings: sacred and secular
- Meditation (may include short eulogy by a family member)
- Prayer of thanksgiving and the Lord's Prayer
- Words of committal
- Flowers/letters dropped in or on the grave by family members
- (Prayer of assurance)
- Commissioning and blessing
- Time for the family and friends to comfort each other and to pray around the graveside

Note: The meditation given by the worship leader will tend to be shorter and less formal than in the funeral home or church chapel. There should be an opportunity before, during, or after the meditation for family members to speak about their loved one. If the group is small, a general invitation may be given for people to offer "a few words about Dad/Grandpa/ John."

It is common practice for flowers to be dropped into the grave, but small and meaningful objects and personal notes may be dropped there as well. I know of a graveside service when a "Ticket to Heaven" was touchingly placed in the grave of a parent by one of her children.

If the weather is poor, then the service should be cut to a minimum or shelter sought. The eulogies can be spoken in the hall or home where the refreshments are offered. The health of the living should not be compromised by a long, uncomfortable service. Those who have died wouldn't want that!

Family-Led Burial of Ashes

There will be times when the family will choose to have an interment of ashes some time after the service with no clergy person or celebrant present. The question may well be asked of the worship leader who conducted the celebration or service, "How do we bury Dad? What do we say?"

The decision to inter the cremated remains of a loved one may be a signal that family members are ready to bring the time of grief to a close. Remind the family members that arrangements have to be made to open the grave. This can be done by contacting the cemetery office. It is useful to suggest that one family member coordinate the service, but participation of other family members, especially younger ones, would be welcomed.

A simple service such as the one that follows is usually sufficient. It is assumed that faith references will be appreciated. If not, some of the secular material may be incorporated.

> **Leader:** We have come to say a last "goodbye," to *Alex/Dad/Grandpa.* We are going to put this urn with *his* earthly remains into the ground in a moment, but we have also come to remember that *he* is surrounded by God's love now and always will be.

> **Family member:** This is a reading from the Bible (*or reading from another source*) that *Grandpa* always liked:

> For I am convinced that neither death, nor life, nor angels, nor rulers, nor things present, nor things to come, nor powers, nor height, nor depth, nor anything else in all creation will be able to separate us from the love of God in Christ Jesus our Lord.

> (Romans 8:38–39)

> Thanks be to God!

(Or read Psalm 23 or choose another reading, sacred or secular.)

Leader: We have some things to say about what we remember and will miss about *Grandpa*. Some of you have told me you want to speak, but others might have words they want to share, too.

Examples
Grandson: I will miss his fishing lessons.
Sister: I remember how when we were on the farm his job was to chop the firewood and gather up the hen's eggs. I will miss his big hugs
Brother: I won't miss his snoring in bed when we shared a room. I will miss his puns...well, maybe!
Wife: He was a good man, a good husband, and I'm already missing him a whole lot.

Committal

Leader: Into God's keeping for always, and into God's unfailing love forever, we commit these last earthly remains of (*name*), ashes to ashes, dust to dust. *He* is gone from us but *he* is with the Holy One, and so we let *him* go.

(*Two family members lower the urn into the grave.*)

Family Member: Let us pray. Loving God, we thank you that we have been able to gather as a family this *morning/afternoon* to remember our loved one and say "goodbye" to *him*.

We remember the ways in which *he* touched our lives with *wisdom*, with *practical help*, with *listening*, and with *laughter* (*insert the appropriate qualities*). In a few moments of quiet we will remember *Alex/husband/Grandpa* and some of those good times we shared with *him*, and some of the great family times. (*time of reflection*) *He* is gone from our family circle now, but we are sure *he* is with you, God of our time, God beyond time. We believe that *he* is fulfilled and happy and always will be, and that for *him* the good mysteries of what happens when we die have been revealed. We believe that your love, God, has hugged *him* tight and that your love will never let *him* go.

Be with us when we especially miss (*name*), our loved one, and be with us as we remember *him* and share our memories with each other.

We pray in Jesus' name. Amen.

The Lord's Prayer
(*optional*)

Placing of Flowers, Notes, and Mementos
Leader: This is your opportunity to place your flowers and other mementoes in memory of *Alex* on or in the grave. Come forward in your own time. (*Family members bring forward flowers and other items.*)

Leader: Let us all join hands.
Go with each one of us as we leave this place, gracious God.
In our remembering, bless us.
In our dealing with (*the loss of name*) (*our grieving*), comfort us.
As we share our feelings one with the other, strengthen us.
As we meet with you in prayer, bring us peace,
the peace that *Alex* knows—your peace, loving God,
that passes all understanding. Amen.

There follows a time of family hugs and greeting. There is time for personal reflection and prayer around the grave before all leave the cemetery.

Secular Celebrations
Whether or not this is a formal liturgy, it is necessary to have some words that speak of the significance of death and its natural order in the scheme of all living things.

Sentences
For everything there is a season,
and a time for every matter under heaven:
a time to be born, and a time to die.

(Ecclesiastes 3:1–2)

Say not in grief, "*He/she* is no more."
But live in thankfulness *she/he* was.

(Hebrew proverb)

Purpose of the Gathering of Family and Friends

The purpose of the gathering would be modified to reflect the non-religious content of the coming together of family and friends. Here is an example:

Opening Responsive Statement

We have come to this service to celebrate the life of (*name*), whose life has ended.

It is good to be here!

We have come to join with others who knew *him/her* and loved *him/her,* to share our memories, and to tell our stories.

It is good to be here!

We have come to tell of all we have lost in (*name*)'s passing, to put our grief into words, and to follow words with actions.

It is good to be here!

We have come as family and friends to remember the effect of (*name*)'s life on each of our lives.

It is good to be here!

Preface

(*Name*) was not religious, so today's celebration of life is steeped in a wider spiritual understanding, an understanding of how our existence is part of the evolution of all we know. By "spiritual" we mean that there was within *him/her* a deep awareness of what truly gives life meaning and purpose: showing love, being compassionate, giving to others, being welcoming as though everyone you meet is family, appreciating the gift of life, and giving back to others without expectation of return.

Cynthia Breadner (as inspired by
Fred Joblin)

We give thanks for (*name*),
whose life is over.
We have come to share our sense of loss
over our well-loved family member and friend.
His/her presence was there for us in times of testing,
and we are here for *his/her* loved ones as they feel their loss.
Her/his presence was there for us in times of joy,
and we are here for *his/her* loved ones as they celebrate *his/her* life.
The memories remain and will endure, and we are thankful.

Readings

There will be no opening prayer, but there could be readings. Mostly they would be secular, but again, some might be taken from the sacred writings of Christian, Hebrew, Buddhist, and other faith groups.

> Death is not the extinguishing of the light but the blowing out of the candle because the dawn has come.
>
> Rabindranath Tagore[10]

All shall be well, and all shall be well, and all manner of thing shall be well.

Julian of Norwich[11]

> Life is eternal and love is immortal,
> and death is only an horizon,
> and an horizon is nothing save the limit of our sight.
>
> William Penn[12]

High Flight

Oh! I have slipped the surly bonds of earth
And danced the skies on laughter-silvered wings;
Sunward I've climbed, and joined the tumbling mirth
of sun-split clouds—and done a hundred things
You have not dreamed of—wheeled and soared and
swung
High in the sunlit silence. Hov'ring there,
I've chased the shouting wind along, and flung
My eager craft through footless halls of air...
Up, up the long, delirious, burning blue
I've topped the wind-swept heights with easy grace.
Where never lark, or even eagle flew—
And, while with silent, lifting mind I've trod
The high untrespassed sanctity of space,
Put out my hand, and touched the face of God.

John Magee[13]

Death is not The End,
But the beginning
Of a metamorphosis.

For matter is never destroyed,
Only rearranged—
Often more perfectly.

Witness how,
in the moment of the caterpillar's death,
the beauty of the butterfly is born,
and, released from the prison of the cocoon,
it flies free.

Peter Tatchell[14]

Celebration of Life

We come to the celebration of life and the elements of thanksgiving and sense of loss that are usual parts of a Christian service. These elements will also be present here. What will not be present is the hope of resurrection found in all four Christian gospels and in the letters of Paul. What will be found is the sense that the deceased will live on in the memory of family members and friends. Read the following suggestion.

Safe where we cannot lie yet... (*see below, page 185*)

or

Afterglow

I'd like the memory of me to be a happy one.
I'd like to leave an afterglow of smiles when life is done.
I'd like to leave an echo whispering softly down the ways,
of happy times and laughing times and bright
and sunny days.
I'd like the tears of those who grieve to dry before the sun;
of happy memories that I leave when life is done.

Anon.

There will be a central emphasis on remembering the life in the celebration event that may not be prominent in a faith community service. But as the celebrant meets with the family it will be appropriate for him/her to carefully review the various aspects of the person's life as I have detailed in chapter 8 "Concerning the Family." All the areas detailed there will be covered: birthplace, early years, life in the family home or farm, work experience, friendship, marriage, children, family, and so on.

There are several different ways that the celebration of life may be handled, and all the elements detailed in chapter 8 "Concerning the Family," including the section describing the crafting of the meditation, will apply: the need to ask the appropriate friend or member of the family to give a eulogy and then the need to limit the time they speak; the wisdom (or not) of an open mike and an invitation to members of the gathered group to share a memory or story; the use of stories rather than facts because stories bring the person alive in a way that encourages family and friends to say to themselves, "Yes, Joan/Jim was like that"; and the place for photographs, video images, and physical objects relating to the person who has died.

Time of Giving Thanks

In the traditional church order a prayer of thanksgiving would follow. During this prayer aspects of the person who has died would be remembered, both aloud and silently, the sense of loss that those present are feeling to a greater or lesser extent would be brought out into the open, and the hope for a life that starts when this one ends would be advanced.

This last element of the celebration would not be mentioned in a non-religious situation, but thanks and the sense of loss could be usefully included in a secular celebration, plus the sense that the person who has died lives on in the memories of those who were near and dear to him.

If the person who has died has made a significant contribution to her profession or social group, her faith community or trade union, then she will live on through a group that has been enhanced, encouraged, renewed, or restored by her presence. This factor should be mentioned in the celebration time. So the celebrant might introduce this time as follows:

We have heard so many wonderful reasons to give thanks for Bill's life and some of his tough experiences as well. We want to give thanks for all of it—
the joy and the sorrow, the laughter and the pain.
(*Celebrant highlights some examples.*)
His lifelong appreciation of *country music,*
his skill in *wood turning and the beautiful furniture he made,*
his leadership in the *union movement,*
the love he shared with *wife, Norma,* and with the *children and grandchildren.*
In a couple of minutes of silence let us remember Bill
and all he meant to us…
(*time of silence*)

As an option this would be an appropriate time to ask people to share their own memories with individuals nearby.

We cherish the memories we have of *Bill* and we are aware of all that we have lost in *his* death. As we consider our own loss, so we are very well aware of all the close family have lost in *Bill's* death, and we remember them: *Norma,* in all you shared with *Bill* over the years; *Bill's son, Graham,* and daughters *Emily* and *April;* and the grandchildren whom *Bill* loved and played with so much. Sufficient to say that you are in the thoughts, not only of all of us here, but also of others who wish they could be with us today and are with us in spirit. It is hard to lose someone so caring and willing to challenge us to be the best we are able to be. I would remind you all that those deepest feelings of loss need bringing out into the open and sharing with a best friend or grief group or counsellor, for in the act of sharing, peace will come.

Bill has died, *Bill is* gone, but *he* is not forgotten. *He* will live on in the memories of each person here. The stories that we have and the stories that are our own will not die, but will be passed on and will delight generations yet to be. *Bill* has passed from our sight, but our memories remain, and we are thankful.

Conclusion

For the person who has died, there will be no committal to God's care, but for the environmentally concerned a commitment to Mother Earth is appropriate. Then the celebrant might say the following.

> I know that *Bill* would not want this to be a time when anyone felt left out and new friends were not made, so I will ask you to stand and greet those around you. Introduce yourself to those you don't know, sharing your own name.

This should not last more than two minutes, when the person presiding should ask the family and friends to sit down. Then the celebrant can give information about where refreshments will be served and some confident words to send the gathered group on their way with thanksgiving and hope in their hearts.

> We leave this time of celebration with thanks for every good memory that is ours with *Bill.*
> We will not forget *Bill,* nor will we forget *his* family in the days and weeks ahead.
> When we feel our loss, we will comfort one another.
> When we feel down, we will encourage one another
> When we feel afraid, we will receive strength from one another.
> And hope will go with us.

or

> In this place (*of worship or*) *of friendship,*
> **it has been good to be together.**
> To share our memories, the good ones and the hard ones,
> **it has been good to be together.**
> To meet old friends of *Bill,* to express our feelings at *his* death,
> and to comfort one another,
> **it has been good to be together.**
> To recognize the limit of our own lifespan and to face up to the mystery that lies ahead,
> **it has been good to be together.**
> In times of uncertainty and in the hope of renewed life day by day,
> **it has been good to be together.**

Secular Committal Service

The location of the committal or scattering of the last earthly remains of a loved one will affect the words said at the ceremony. The first situation to be considered is the committal of a body or cremated remains at a cemetery. The family member or celebrant gathers the friends and family members around the grave and begins the ceremony with a reading such as:

> Safe where we cannot lie yet,
> safe from the fret and fume;
> You and you,
> whom we will never forget.
>
> Christina Rossetti (adapted)[15]

Celebrant: It is good to be here as family and friends of *Fred*. We celebrate *his* life and we remember all *he* was to each one of us.

The celebrant will have spoken to family members to determine whether any of them wish to speak briefly about their loved one. If they do, this is a time to say what she/he meant to them. If no family member wishes to speak, the celebrant may talk briefly about things special to the person who has died, drawn from his conversations with the family.

We remember *his* love of the *grandchildren.*
We remember *his* life's work as a *teacher.*
We remember *his* enjoyment of *fishing.*
We remember *his* peaceful death.
And in moments of silence we will remember *Fred,*
the good times we spent together, the laughter we shared,
the tough times of ill health.
(*minute or two of silence*)

And now we commit the cremated remains of *Fred* to the (*good earth*).
(*Family members lower the urn into the grave.*)
Fred lives in the memory of *children* and *grandchildren.*
Fred lives in the stories of *colleagues* and *friends.*
Fred lives through his contribution to the profession of *teaching/ work in the union movement.*

Fred lives in *his* unique contribution to human experience.
We rejoice in the ways in which *he* has enriched our days,
each one of us in special ways.
Fred will not be forgotten.

---

[1] All prayers credited to Bob Root are used with kind permission of the author. They may be reproduced for funerals and celebrations of life only.

[2] Prayer from the *Book of Worship, United Church of Christ* ©1986 United Church of Christ. The Pilgrim Press. All rights reserved. Used by permission.

[3] *Celebrate God's Presence, A Book of Services for The United Church of Canada* (United Church Publishing House, 2000), p. 449. Copyright UCPH.

[4] All prayers credited to Cynthia Breadner (as inspired by Fred Joblin) are used with kind permission of the author. They may be reproduced for funerals and celebrations of life only.

[5] All prayers credited to William Kervin are used with kind permission of the author. They may be reproduced for funerals and celebrations of life only.

[6] *Celebrate God's Presence, A Book of Services for The United Church of Canada* (United Church Publishing House, 2000), p. 450. Copyright UCPH.

[7] Alan Gaunt © 1973 All prayers credited to Alan Gaunt have been adapted and/or used with kind permission of the author. They may be reproduced for funerals and celebrations of life only.

[8] All prayers credited to Laura Turnbull have been adapted and/or used with kind permission of the author. They may be reproduced for funerals and celebrations of life only.

[9] Our thanks for permission to quote from the song "She Flies On," words by Gordon Light © Common Cup Company.

[10] Rabindranath Tagore, 1861–1941. In the public domain.

[11] Julian of Norwich, 1342 ca.–1416. In the public domain.

[12] William Penn, 1644–1718. In the public domain.

[13] "High Flight" by John Magee. Copyright 2014 This England Publishing Limited. Used with permission.

[14] "Death Is Not the End but the Beginning" by Peter Tachell. Permission granted by author.

[15] "Is It Well with the Child?" Christina Rossetti, 1830–1894 (adapted). In the public domain.

CHAPTER 18

Meditations

Meditations 1, 2, and 3 are given in full. Toward the end of this chapter, I have also detailed some of the secular celebrations in full and one for a pet that has died. In other Meditations I have given Bible reading references and the meditation only. Where there are common readings, both secular and Bible readings, these are detailed in appendix 2 and referenced within the meditations.

Meditation 1   *Older Person (some faith)*

June was a supporter and worshipping member of the church, but took no leadership role. She had a straightforward Christian faith and a fulfilling life as a teacher. She travelled widely and had many good and close friends. The fact of an unexpected death and the surprise and unease of those who knew her suggested the following "The Paths that Lead to Peace" meditation. There was a eulogy given by Valerie, a close friend of June, that focused on June's teaching experiences and her travels. It included some touching and some funny stories.

Welcome

Scripture Sentences
The eternal God is your dwelling place,
and underneath are the everlasting arms.

(Deuteronomy 33:27, Revised
Standard Version)

Jesus said, "I am the resurrection and the life. Those who believe in me, even though they die, will live, and everyone who lives and believes in me will never die."

(John 11:25)

"Blessed are those who mourn, for they will be comforted."
(Matthew 5:4)

Call to Worship

We have come to this service to celebrate the life of *June* whose life has ended.
It is good to be here!
We have come to join with others who knew *her* and loved *her*, to share our memories, and to tell our stories.
It is good to be here!
We have come to tell of all we have lost in *June's* passing, to put our grief into words, and to follow words with actions.
It is good to be here!
We have come as family and friends to remember the effect of *June's* life on each of our lives and to give God thanks.
It is good to be here!
We have come as those who believe that death is not the final end that it seems to be and to rejoice in the hope of a life that begins when this one ends.
It is good to be here!

Opening Prayer

O God, you brought us to life and you remind us that death is a natural part of life.
We come this *morning/afternoon* to celebrate the life of *June,* whom we have known and loved, a friend and family member who has died.
We give you thanks for the whole range of human experience that was *hers*: the wonder, the joys, and the challenges.
Bless us in these moments of remembering that we may express our loss and comfort one another.
We pray in the name of the compassionate one, Jesus Christ. Amen.

Bible Reading
In God's House There Are Many Dwelling Places (see appendix 2, page 263)
John14:1–6, 8–14, 24, and 27

Meditation Part 1
We meet today in the name of the greatest peace-maker of all time, one the Bible tells us calmed the mentally ill, brought relief to the suffering, and a sense of forgiveness to the guilty. Jesus Christ was the great peace-bringer, and some of his last words recorded in John's gospel are these: "Peace I leave with you; my peace I give to you. I do not give to you as the world gives. Do not let your hearts be troubled, and do not let them be afraid" (John 14:27).

Peace, the deep peace that Jesus spoke of, is what we seek when we have so unexpectedly lost *June, loved and cherished as sister,* family member, and friend. For the death of a loved one is a peace-disturbing experience. It is a hard task to come to this place to say our last goodbye. Yet that is what we are called to do today, to say our goodbye to *June,* who has touched each person in this church, *June's* church, in different ways for good.

Our need is to come to terms with *her* loss gently and gradually, and to find and to feel that deep and lasting peace that Jesus spoke of—and it's not easy. And so, I want to touch briefly on some of the steps that we can tread along the path that leads to peace when someone close to you dies…

The first thing I want to suggest is that it is right to express in the most direct and forthright terms just how much you have lost in the death of this *sensitive, kindly, and thoughtful person who had a terrific sense of humour.* How much you have lost in the death of *June* whom you have known well, loved, and remember in your own way: with good memories of *her* church life here, memories of time shared with *her fraternal organization, memories of a caring neighbour, memories of holidays and leisure times shared, memories of a great baker, memories of her time at the seniors' home, and of course those special family memories. June* had a long life that was fully and well lived, and *her* passing leaves a gap that will be impossible to fill.

Friends and family members, your sense of loss needs to be brought out into the open, and your grief expressed before the road to peace is open. It's a good thing to share the feelings most difficult to share, most difficult to put into words—to share those things most difficult to say aloud, and to do this with a trusted friend or minister or counsellor. You will make a beginning when we share refreshments following the service, but this time is only a beginning, and I know you will go on remembering *June* in the years ahead.

We need to reflect on the loss that has been ours in *June's* death, and the next positive step is to think back over the memories of a unique lifetime. *Valerie,* who has been a good friend over the years, will give us a sense of how much *June* meant to so many.

(*The friend shares her memories of the one who has died.*)

Meditation Part 2

We have been fortunate indeed! I know *Valerie's* words will encourage you to share your own memories—to recall them and talk them over. You will have a chance to begin to do this at the reception after the service, for to put your remembering into words is a positive step along the path to peace.

You, family members, have lost so much in *June's* death, and we think especially of you, *Rachel,* in the death of a *sister* and of *Roger her brother* and *Dot her other sister,* who could not be with us today. We remember *sister-in-law Sharon, nephew Frank,* who is with us today, and other nephews and nieces. *June's* family members are in the thoughts and prayers of the congregation here this afternoon. And we think also of you who were good friends and strong sources of support to *June—Robert* and *Muriel* and *Laura, Tess,* and *Bill* to name just a few.

It is a simple thing to say, but true, that it is because you loved and cared for *June* so much, you will miss *her* so much! As you look back with joy, as you remember with feeling your family ties and friendships, so God's peace will be yours.

And peace comes as we acknowledge with joy that death is not an end, but a beginning. The passage of scripture that I read (from John 14) is often taken literally to mean that heaven is like a big house with many rooms. The more accurate intention of the evangelist was to indicate that there was room for all—no one would be excluded. He was making the point that in the mind of Jesus the end of life does not mean a final stop. He uses the symbolism of another dwelling place to make it clear that life goes on—where we cannot know, in what form we cannot be sure, but it goes on. *June* was a worshipper and member of the Christian faith community here and would have been aware that peace comes to us in the resurrection assurance, that eternal life is not a pious hope for a select and saintly few, but a reality that the Holy One has made possible for all. And it is this reality that *June* now knows. We rejoice that *her* time of infirmity is over, that *she* is reunited with those she loved and lost in this life, and is secured by the love of God whom she worshipped here.

"Who can separate us from the love of Christ?" writes the apostle Paul. "Can principalities or powers?" and we would say, "Can infirmity or old age?" "Can heights or depths?" writes Paul, and we would say, "Can the end of this earthly life?" Nothing in all creation can separate us from the love of God, which we know in Jesus the Christ. The most profound and real peace will come to us as we renew our faith in Jesus who knew fear and suffering in his lifetime, yet who gloriously lived beyond that death on a cross. In the name of Jesus and with faith in him, we can confidently affirm in his words to the disciples, the words that John shared:

> Do not worry about anything…. And the peace of God, which surpasses all understanding, will guard your hearts and your minds in Christ Jesus.
>
> (Philippians 4:6, 7)

Thanks be to God! Amen.

Prayer of Thanksgiving for *June's* Life

We give you thanks, loving God, for your presence at every twist and turn of life and we thank you for your presence with us when our limited time merges with your eternal time.

You have been with us as we have today remembered our friend *June*. We thank you for the length and bread and depth of *June's* life, all of its challenges and all of its moments of wonder and fulfillment. Each one of us here has memories that come to mind, and we bring them before you in moments of silence. (*time of silent reflection*)

Many of the events we have remembered we will share over the coming days:
Memories of June in her teaching years
Memories of June telling stories of her travels

Memories of June laughing and playing with her grandchildren
Memories of June in the garden she loved so much

These memories warm our hearts, but they also deepen the sense of loss we feel at this service.
We thank you, loving God, for them and we pray especially for *June's* family as they come to terms with life without their loved one.
Your love is with them all the time.
You will be experienced in a strong companion when they feel alone.
You will be experienced as a sense of hope when they are down or depressed.
You will be experienced as a way forward when the future seems uncertain, bleak.
You will be experienced in joy and laughter as memories are shared.
Hold *June's* family members securely and bless them, loving God; and bless and reassure us as we are aware through *June's* death of our own limited lifespan. Renew in us the certainty of your love, the love that will not let us go. Enable us to fully live each day with the care-fulness, adventure, and justice to which you call us, and enable us to see those who have suffered loss and stand with them.

Our prayers of thanks we offer in the name of Jesus risen and at work through today's disciples. Amen.

Commissioning
Share your memories;
remember the good times with *June.*
Share your loss;
there is a gap of friendship and love that cannot be filled.
Share your support for one another;
you will sustain and comfort each other.
Share your hope;
death is not the end, but a fresh beginning.

Blessing
And the blessing of God,
whose love is at the centre,
whose compassion is clear in Jesus,

whose Spirit defeats the power of death,
be with you now and in the time beyond time.
Amen.

Meditation 2 *Accidental Death of a Child*

Dean was only seven years old. He was an active and healthy boy, happy in his family and at school. His death was caused by a complication after a minor operation.

Welcome

Biblical Sentences

As a mother comforts her child,
so I will comfort you [says the Lord].
As a father has compassion for his children,
so the Lord has compassion for those who fear [the Lord].

(Isaiah 66:13; Psalm 103:13)

[Jesus said,] "Truly I tell you, whoever does not receive the kingdom of God as a little child will never enter it." And he took them up into his arms…and blessed them.

(Mark 10:15, 16)

Call to Worship

We have come to a place where sadness fills our hearts,
but we give thanks for *Dean* with stories and smiles.
We have come to a place where memories flood our minds,
but we are still as God's eternal peace holds us.
We have come to a place where we are able to comfort one another,
but we value the ways in which *Dean* touched each one of us and brought us joy.
We have come to a place where time and eternity merge into one,
and we rejoice that God's love is here, now and forever.

Opening Prayer

Loving God, this family, these friends loved *Dean* so much.
This family, these friends miss *Dean* so much.
We are glad you stand with them and support them
at this time of loss.
Your love is infinite and compassionate;
in your love this *young boy* is
safe and always will be.
Your peace is limitless and certain.
In your peace, this family, these friends
may know a place of refuge,
a place from which to venture out.
As you have blessed *Dean,* so bless *his* loved ones.
In the name of Jesus, who blessed the little child ren. Amen.

Scripture Readings

For all who are led by the Spirit of God are children of God. For you did not receive a spirit of slavery to fall back into fear, but you have received a spirit of adoption. When we cry, "Abba! Father!" it is that very Spirit bearing witness with our spirit that we are children of God, and if children, then heirs, heirs of God and joint heirs with Christ—if, in fact, we suffer with him so that we may also be glorified with him. I consider that the sufferings of this present time are not worth comparing with the glory about to be revealed to us.

(Romans 8:14–18)

Thus says the LORD:
In a time of favour I have answered you,
on a day of salvation I have helped you;
I have kept you and given you
as a covenant to the people,
to establish the land,
to apportion the desolate heritages....
But Zion said, "The LORD has forsaken me,
my Lord has forgotten me."
Can a woman forget her nursing child,
or show no compassion for the
child of her womb?

Even these may forget,
yet I will not forget you.
See, I have inscribed you on the palms of my hands;
your walls are continually before me.

(Isaiah 49:8, 14–16)

At that time the disciples came to Jesus and asked, "Who is the greatest in the kingdom of heaven?" He called a child, whom he put among them, and said, "Truly I tell you, unless you change and become like children, you will never enter the kingdom of heaven. Whoever becomes humble like this child is the greatest in the kingdom of heaven. Whoever welcomes one such child in my name welcomes me.

(Matthew 18:1–5)

Meditation

How do we get our minds around the fact that *Dean* has died, that we will not see *him* again, *playing in the street, laughing on the school bus, at the Recreation Centre?* It is so difficult to believe *he* has gone and so impossible to believe we will never hear *his* laughter, see *his* huge grin again. I believe that those of you who are *Dean's* friends from home and from school will find this especially difficult, and I want you to listen to what I am going to tell you.

The first thing is that you are not in any way responsible for *his* death. Nothing you said made any difference. The jokes you shared, the secrets you exchanged, the mean and bad things that you said, none of these made any difference, neither did the fights you had with *him. Dean* would have died anyway. He died because *he got really sick while he was in the hospital for an operation,* and no one could have done anything more to make *him* better.

And the second thing I want to say to you is that although you feel sad at *Dean* not being around, you probably also feel mad that *he* is no longer around to be your friend. It is okay to feel mad at *Dean because he is no longer around to play computer games with you, to go swimming, to be on the baseball team.*

Why not imagine *Dean* is in the same room with you? Tell him exactly how you feel; say your thoughts aloud to *him.* It seems a funny thing to do, but it will help. And take the time to tell your parents how you are feeling. They will listen very carefully to what you have to say and will be able to help. And you parents, you moms and dads, if you are unable to help your daughter or son, if you worry about them, I know you will be able to find someone who is skilled and trained and able to help them.

And you are probably wondering where *Dean* is now, now that *he* is dead. And the simple answer is that it is a mystery; no one really knows. Some people will tell you that *he* is an angel up in the sky, and some people will tell you that *he* is in "heaven," a sort of wonderful city up above the clouds. But the truth is that we can't be certain. *Dean* is not with us, we know that, but *Dean* is with God, we can be sure of that. The God we read about in the Bible has received *Dean* joyfully, and has hugged *him* like your mom or your dad hugs you—a big, big, hug, with lots of love in the middle of it! And that love of God will never let *Dean* go, not today, not tomorrow, not next week or month, or ever.

How can we be sure of that? Well, you know about Jesus, God's special and chosen person. Jesus knew that children were of first importance. When the friends of Jesus asked him who was the most important people in God's country, Jesus called a young person, probably the same age as many of you, and put her in the middle of the group. "Become not like a warrior, not like a pop star, not like a writer, not a like film star, but like a questioning, happy, enthusiastic girl or boy and you will have what it takes to be one of God's special people." That's what Jesus said. Well, he didn't quite say that, but that's the idea he was trying to get across.

It is God we thank for *Dean*'s life, and we have some people willing to talk about *Dean* for us now. (*Several eulogies follow.*)

Thank you all. You have informed us, you have made us laugh, you have touched us with your words, and we are deeply grateful to you. We have talked of how you friends of *Dean* will be missing *him* so much, but we want to say that we cannot come close to appreciating how much you, who are family members, will feel the loss of this *bright young guy*. First and foremost, *Adam* and *Jill,* our hearts go out to you in the loss of your *son.* We know how devastating the last few days have been and we do not have the words to come close to reflecting your grief, but we do feel for you and we are with you. We know that if you are overwhelmed by your intense feelings, you will search out and find the compassionate help you need.

To *Phyllis* and *John, Dean's Nana* and *Grandpa,* your loss is so great; you will miss your *grandchild* so much. Allow the grievous hurt to come and express it openly and directly to one another and to a best friend or counsellor who will listen deeply and understand. And that goes also to those of you who are fellow members of *Dean*'s family and to all of you who are their friends.

Dean is gone from among us, but in God's care *he* is safe and happy and complete. And it is God's peace we seek at this time and for all the days that lie ahead. Jesus once said, "Peace I leave with you; my peace I give to you. I do not give as the world gives. Do not let your hearts be troubled, and do not let them be afraid." We thank God for the short but wonderful life of *Dean*, but as we do this, we seek with confidence God's peace, the peace that goes beyond all human understanding. Amen.

Prayer of Thanksgiving for a Child
God, you are always with us,
when we are very young and when we are very old.
In all the ages and stages of life your love never leaves us.
And you were with *Dean* as *he* laughed and cried,
as *he* played and explored, as *he* hugged his *mom* and *dad,*
when *he* had fun with *his grandma* and *grandpa,*
as he watched TV and *used his iPod.*
We have our own special memories of *Dean.*
In moments of silence we remember......

Loving God,
receive these our memories, and memories that will be ours
in the coming days and bless them.
Be with *Adam* and *Jill, Dean's mom* and *dad.*
Give them courage and patience for the days ahead.
And be with *Phyllis* and *John, Dean's grandma* and *grandpa,*
who will miss *him* so much
Be with *Dean*'s school friends and members of *his Cub Scout group*
and *his* best friend, *Jason.* Help us to be your comforters, O God.
Enable us to put into words our feelings around *Dean*'s death
and share them with a trusted one.
We will miss *him* very much,
but *he* is safe with you, loving God.
He is happy with you, and we give thanks.

Dean is lost to us, but you have found *him* and will keep *him* always.
We believe that nothing will be able to separate *him* from your love,
not now, not ever.
We rejoice in the hope that one day we will all meet again.
We pray confidently in the name of Jesus, your beloved child. Amen.

Meditation 3   *Celebration of Life (non-religious)*

This is a non-religious event held in a hall. It centres on thanksgiving and
gifts. There is a meal, lots of food, and a variety of drinks. There is no speculation on a life that begins when this one ends.

Welcome

*(As each person arrives he/she is given a pebble. As the celebration begins a piece
of music that the one who has died loved is played.)*

We are the family and friends of *Pierre*. We have come together to celebrate
his life. We have come to acknowledge our loss, and we have come to encourage each other. Let us begin by celebrating the taken-for-granted fact of life,
which is the common miracle of each one of us.

Reading

*(A family member reads "The Cost" by Dorothy N. Monroe. See appendix 2,
page 267.)*

Stories

We celebrate life, but today we celebrate one particular life, *Pierre's* life.
And what does it mean to celebrate? The popular meaning of the word is
to have fun, and I believe there will be lots of good stories about *Pierre* and
much laughter—*he* was a fun sort of guy! But celebration at the end of a life
is much more than that. To celebrate at the end of a life means that we remember the whole of *his* life, and we are privileged that *his* daughter Joy will
recount some of the markers of that life as only a close family member is able
to do.

(Family memories from the loved one's birth to his death are shared.)

Thank you *Joy!* You have given us a gift that only a family member is able to do. And now *Pierre's best friend Jacob, who was with him when he was at the mill,* will speak of *Pierre's* work life and leisure activities.

(*Memories about the loved one's work and leisure time are shared.*)

Remembering is a vital task!

Meditation
(*The leader or another family member or friend reads "Remembering." See appendix 2, page 268.*)

I want you to spend a few moments bringing to mind your own memories; you may find it helpful to share them with those who are sitting around you.

(*Allow three to four minutes for sharing.*)

On the way in, you were given a pebble. I want you to think of these pebbles as representing our individual memories of *Pierre*. Put together, they represent our common memory, and that is what we are going to do now. On the table at the front of the hall you will see a square of pebbles placed there by family members. Just add yours to the pile and think of all the memories of people all over this country and from far beyond these shores who have a good remembrance of *Pierre*. And if you have a word or so to say about Pierre, the microphone is there to use.

(*Friends and family will come forward and place their pebbles on the growing pile. A few speak briefly about the loved one who has died. Some of these individuals will have been contacted ahead of the celebration.*)

A pyramid of pebbles—what a symbol of the many memories brought to your minds! The problem of remembering is that it brings home our sense of all we have lost in the life that is over: all its joys and all its sorrows. Especially we think of you who are close family (*mention these individuals by name*) and good friends. I want you to take a few moments of silence to bring your feelings of loss to mind, those areas of your life where *Pierre* was significant to you, those areas where he will be missed. And I want you to consider how you might help close family members and friends.

(*Leader reads "Meditations of the Heart" by Howard Thurman, see appendix 2, page 268.*)

Let us voice our thanksgivings and our hopes as we go from this community of family and friends.

We give thanks for *Pierre's* life with all its joys, all its achievements and its struggles, the dreams that came to life and the dreams that remained just dreams. We give thanks for the love *he* shared in the family circle. We give thanks for the encouragement *he* gave to *his* children, the fun *he* had with the *grandchildren*, and the enjoyment and care *he* shared among his friends. We give thanks for the work *he* did (*be specific*) and the fulfillment *he* found in that work. We give thanks for the ways in which *he* served the local community, and those people who will think kindly of *Pierre* and *his hidden kindness*.

We mourn *his* death, for we can't help thinking of all the good things that would have been possible had *he* lived. We will live with our feelings of loss, but we will move forward to new endeavours. We will find the peace we seek.

We believe *Pierre* is at peace, and as *he* is alive in our memory, alive in the communities *he* served well, so we know *Pierre* will never die!

We invite you to recover a pebble, take it with you, and hold on to your memories as you go from here.

(*A piece of music that the one who has died loved is played as people leave the gathering.*)

Meditation 4   *A Good and Faithful Person*
Fran was one of this world's good people. She was widowed early and had a hard life bringing up her two children. She was a church person, a worshipper rather than a leader of the faith community.

Welcome
(*Leader or selected congregant reads "A Statement about Death" by Geoffrey Lampe. See appendix 2, page 269.*)

Bible Readings
The Lord Is My shepherd (see appendix 2, page 260)

(Psalm 23)

The Road to Emmaus (see appendix 2, page 262)
(Luke 24:13–20, 28–35)

Meditation

It is a tough job to say goodbye to someone you love, someone who has been a good friend, someone who has been a special part of your life. We know from our own experience that even going to the airport with a family member or saying farewell to a friend who is moving to another part of the country are hard leave-takings. But what we are called to do today is so much more difficult. It is to say our final goodbye to *Fran,* family member, church member, and cherished friend. It's not easy, but we do so fully aware that the word "goodbye" is the short-form for "God be with you." God is with *Fran.* God is with us.

Alternative opening paragraph

Many of you will know the *For Better or for Worse* comic strip drawn by Lynn Johnston. In one particular episode, the character named Mike and his friend Weed are in the apartment they share when Mike gets a phone call from his sister. Mike turns to face Weed and with dismay on his face says, "My grandmother is in the hospital; it doesn't look good; she is going to die." And then, "Why is it that something that you have been expecting for a long time always comes as a surprise?" We know exactly what Mike means. We have seen *Fran*'s declining health—she has been going downhill for a while now—but *her* death still takes us by surprise, and that's why it hits us so hard.

Our reading from the New Testament is a traditional Christian story told by Luke. In it we encounter two companions who did not have the time to say their final goodbye to Jesus, their leader and friend. His death, which they knew was coming, has still hit them hard, taken them by surprise. They are walking along the highway and they are sharing their memories, reminiscing about their time with Jesus, talking about all the things that have happened. And as they walk along, the risen Jesus joins them, but they do not know that it is Jesus. And they tell this stranger about the many wonderful events of his life.

You know, that is one of the reasons we are here today—to remember the life of *Fran.* I will make a start in this service, but it is only a start, as you will carry on as you meet and visit with one another during the refreshment time following the service, and your remembering will continue in the days and the weeks ahead, just as our reading from Luke reminds us that there is nothing more helpful than a good remembrance.

And we do remember *Fran,* this well-loved and *loving woman, not tall in stature, but big of heart, and a caring person with a great sense of humour. She* was challenged by the far too early death of *her* beloved *husband,* but *she* met the challenge and made *her* way so well in *her* daily work. *Fran kept fit through swimming,* greatly enjoyed the time *she* spent *at the family cottage. She* had the great gift *of encouraging those close to her to see things from the other person's point of view. (Add a personal story here.)*

And *Fran* was above all a family person. I know that you *grandchildren* were a joy to *her* and that your *grandma* was not above spoiling you in the way that *grandparents* do, the way that *parents* know about, but turn a blind eye to.

And in later years, *Liz,* the two of you made a great team, helping and supporting one another, and not just looking after yourselves but also volunteering *at Maltby Residence—Jim was telling me that you specialized in manicuring the nails of the residents who found it difficult to do that anymore...and if you are a visitor to seniors' residences, you will know what an essential and necessary service this is and what an opportunity it presents for conversations.*

Although *Fran* lived a long and active life and far exceeded *her* threescore years and 10, *she* will be much missed by you, *her son, Jim,* with *Ruth;* by you, *Liz,* her sister and best friend; by *her grandchildren Conner* and *Amanda;* by special *niece Lina* and *nephew Fred,* and by many others of you.

It is tough to lose someone you love, someone who has been close and a part of your life for many years, but one of the best things you can do is to share your feelings around *Fran's* loss, especially the feelings that are most difficult to put into words. Share them with a good friend or someone you can trust completely, for in the sharing over time, peace will come...just like those two men in our reading. They are sharing their feelings with the stranger as they walk along; they invite him in for a meal and they talk out their good memories and their sense of loss some more. Then he gets up to go, and they recognize him as the risen Jesus, and suddenly he is gone from them. The Jesus they knew and loved is not dead but alive! The risen Jesus Christ is the symbol of hope for us all today. Death is not the dead end, far from it! Death is the gateway to the life that begins when this one ends.

This would be no surprise for *Fran*, no new concept. The hope of resurrection was something *she* would have appreciated from *her* many years of worshipping at this church, *her* church. *Fran* had Christian hope. "What can separate us from the love of Christ?" Paul asks. "Can heights or depths, can principalities or powers? Nothing in all creation can separate us from the love of God in Christ Jesus our Lord." Believe it, rejoice in it! God's servant *Fran* knows the truth of that now. *Her* life is over, and *she* knows God's peace, the peace that passes all human understanding. Thanks be to God! Amen.

Meditation 5   *A Young Woman (cancer)*
Rachel was a young wife and mother. Alongside her close family, there was a large community of friends grieving her loss.

Bible Readings
The Gift of Love (see appendix 2, page 265)
(1 Corinthians 13)

Now when Job's three friends heard of all these troubles that had come upon him, each of them set out from his home—Eliphaz the Temanite, Bildad the Shuhite, and Zophar the Naamathite. They met together to go and console and comfort him. When they saw him from a distance, they did not recognize him, and they raised their voices and wept aloud; they tore their robes and threw dust in the air upon their heads. They sat with him on the ground for seven days and seven nights, and no one spoke a word to him, for they saw that his suffering was very great.
(Job 2:11–13)

After this Job opened his mouth and cursed the day of his birth. Job said:
"Let the day perish in which I was born,
and the night that said,
'A man-child is conceived.'...

"Why is light given to one in misery,
and life to the bitter in soul,
who long for death, but it does not come,
and dig for it more than for hidden treasures;
who rejoice exceedingly,

and are glad when they find the grave?
Why is light given to one who cannot see the way,
whom God has fenced in?
For my sighing comes like my bread,
and my groanings are poured out like water.
Truly the thing that I fear comes upon me,
and what I dread befalls me.
I am not at ease, nor am I quiet;
I have no rest; but trouble comes."

(Job 3:1–3, 20–26)

Then Job answered:
"How long will you torment me,
and break me in pieces with words?
These ten times you have cast reproach upon me;
are you not ashamed to wrong me?...
For the hand of God has touched me!
Why do you, like God, pursue me,
never satisfied with my flesh?
O that my words were written down!...
For I know that my Redeemer lives,
and that at the last [God] will stand upon the earth;
and after my skin has been thus destroyed,
then in my flesh I shall see God."

(Job 19:1–3, 21*b*–23, 25–26)

Meditation

We do not want to come to this service this morning and say our farewell to
Rachel, for *her* life was far too short; there was so much more to accomplish.
But we do celebrate *her* life and we celebrate the love that was at the centre of
it—love so joyfully given to friends and shared within the family circle, with
husband, children, mother, sisters—love so happily received from so many of
you who are gathered here in church to remember *her* life, you who feel the
loss, the so painful loss, now *Rachel* is gone from among you. The apostle
Paul speaks of that love with all the eloquence at his command. He reminds
us that love is patient, love is kind; love does not rejoice in wrongdoing but

rejoices in the truth; love bears all things, believes all things, hopes all things, endures all things; love never ends. The Christian love that Paul speaks of never does end, and we are privileged that we will hear of *Rachel's loving life in a series of memories that the family has put together for us.*

(*A verbal collage of Rachel's life is given by a trusted family friend.*)

Thank you, *James,* and those of you who contributed to the family eulogy. Your words have been grace to us. No memories can say it all, no words can do justice to the full, glorious content of a life well lived, but these scenes from *Rachel's* life help us enormously. They prompt us to do our own re-membering, they help us in our grieving, and they remind us of the times when we laughed and cried with *Rachel* and the family....and they bring us back to love again. It is a hard reality but a true one, that because you family members loved *Rachel* so much, there will be no shortcut to peace for you. No one can take your grief away from you, but one fact is for sure, the thoughts and prayers of each person here and many who would dearly like to be here *this afternoon* are with you and will be with you in the coming days. We are here to pledge you our support.

We feel for you, *June;* how incredibly difficult it is for a mother to lose her child in her own lifetime. We are conscious of your great loss, too, *Di* and *Rosanne, Rachel's sisters,* and of your loss, *David, her brother. You and your partners* were so constantly and carefully with *your sister* when *she* needed you most. You did all you could for *her.*

I want to say a word to you, *Michael* and *Sharon* (*Rachel's children of six and eight years*). I know how much your *mom* loved you both; I know how much *your dad* loves you and gives you big hugs when you are at home. Well, God loves your *mom* very much and will care for *her* and love *her* forever and ever. Every time your *dad* hugs you, remember God is hugging your *mom* and loves *her* just like that!

Above all, we think of you, *Ted.* You have lost a *wife, a partner, and best friend,* one who has been your *soulmate* for so many years. We cannot begin to imagine how deep is your grief, but:

We are your companions along the way that is loss.
We feel for you, we are there for you.
We wish we could lift the weight of grief from you,
and though we cannot do that,
our support is constant,
our encouragement will not fail,
and when you have a need to talk,
anytime, anywhere, we will listen.[1]

A part of this sense of loss is the sheer unfairness of it all. If you, family members, are mad at the cancer that caused *Rachel's* death, if you are mad at God for seeming not to prevent it, then this is totally understandable. One of our readings is from the Book of Job. Job is a good man who gets a whole load of undeserved pain and punishment. Our Job reading presents a direct parallel to *Rachel's* early death. Why is it that bad things do happen to good people? Why can God not step in and change things for the better? Well, the ancient writer does not give any slick and easy answers. What Job looks for is a day when he can question God and God will give him clear answers, but that day never comes, and Job is invited to get along in a world where the situation is plainly unfair, and the good and caring people do get hurt, and hurt bad. At least Job has a whole lot of time to get his sense of the rottenness of it all off his chest, and he doesn't waste the opportunity! And it is a reminder to all of you who feel your loss acutely this afternoon, to share your deepest feelings with someone you trust. Share them with a best friend, or a minister, or a counsellor, and do not be afraid to join a group of people like you who have lost loved ones way before their due time.

It is only in finding the feelings you never knew you had, speaking aloud the words you never wanted to voice, sharing at the deepest of levels, that peace, the peace so earnestly looked for, will come.

There is celebration and there is loss here today, but there is one more essential task to be about, and it is the task of faith. *Rachel was a member of this church, attended Sunday school here, was brought up in a family where Christianity mattered....her children were baptized.* Doubtless *she* questioned, as Job in our reading questioned, the justice and fairness of life, but doubtless *she* knew the person of Jesus Christ as well. When the chips were down, God did not say too much to a troubled world, did not get into conversation with the leaders of the time. Instead, God chose Jesus, who called God "Abba, Dad," not to be a mighty ruler, not to be a clever politician, not to be as a mighty warrior, but in the form of a suffering servant, to stand fast against evil. And in his early thirties (would you believe) he ended up on a cross. And that same Jesus conquered death and is the risen symbol for us all.

It is not the nature of God to step in, to intervene and supernaturally save us, but God stands beside us feeling our pain and loss, and giving us in the risen Christ the sure hope that death does not have the last word. Death does not have the last word, but God's love does. God had the last word with Jesus, and God has the last word for *Rachel*. Like Job *she* knows that *her* Redeemer lives. *Her* struggle with cancer is over and done with; the suffering is past and forgotten. God's love is with *her,* and so *she* knows peace, the peace that passes all human understanding. And that peace will be ours.

Thanks be to our loving God! Amen.

Meditation 6   *Older Man of Faith (years of dementia)*
John was a family man and once a prominent leader in the local business community. He served in the local church, but then fell victim to a long and debilitating illness. In his last few years, he could not recognize his family. The focus here is giving thanks for a life, which is why the Letter to the Philippians was chosen.

Bible Readings
Paul's Prayer for the Philippians (see appendix 2, page 266)
(1 Philippians 1:3–11)

Jesus said to them, "I am the bread of life. Whoever comes to me will never be hungry, and whoever believes in me will never be thirsty. But I said to you that you have seen me and yet do not believe. Everything that [God] gives me will come to me, and anyone who comes to me I will never drive away; for I have come down from heaven, not to do my own will, but the will of [the One] who sent me. And this is the will of [the One] who sent me, that I should lose nothing of all that he has given me, but raise it up on the last day. This is indeed the will of [God], that all who see the Son and believe in him may have eternal life; and I will raise them up on the last day."
(John 6:35–40)

Meditation

"I thank God for you every time I think of you." This is the enthusiastic beginning to Paul's letter to the Philippians, and we who meet to remember *John* also give thanks. We give thanks for this *people-loving, family-loving, good-humoured, big-hearted man* and we give thanks for *his* life of care and service to others, a long life well lived.

"You are always in my heart," writes Paul, and those of you who are of *John's* family are truly heartfelt by those of us who gather to celebrate *his* life *this morning*. You have lost one who was well-loved within the family circle, *and although infirmity had diminished his quality of life*, his death will leave a space so difficult to fill. And so you come to say your last farewell to one who has touched your lives in so many different ways over the years. "I thank God for you every time I think of you," said Paul. It is our joyful task to remember *John,* and we are privileged that *son-in-law James, granddaughter Julie,* and *grandson Jason will remember him for us.*

(*Family members give their tributes.*)

Thank you. All your words have been graceful words for us.

We joyfully give thanks for the purposeful life of *John. In spite of John's poor quality of life at the end*, the act of celebrating and remembering brings home all you have lost in *his* passing, and this will be especially true for those of you who are *his* family members. We think above all of you, *Bet, his* well-loved *daughter,* but we know that *he* will be much missed, too, by *son-in-law James* and by his *grandchildren, Julie* with *Aaron* and *Jason* with *Jill,* and by the *great-grandchildren Defoe* and *Rob,* by *brother Bob* with *Chloe,* and by the wider family members, some of whom are here this morning and some of whom wish they could be and are with us in spirit. And we would remember another "family," *the Super Foods warehouse family,* so special and so close *over nearly half a century.* You, "family" members, will have your own very personal feelings at this time of *John's* passing, and I would encourage you to share those feelings with a best friend or trusted person, for as your grief work is carried out, so peace will come.

And remember that when Paul the apostle was giving thanks to God, it was prayerful thanks, and it was thanks to those who had helped him through their Christian life and work from the beginning until the present. "I pray your love will keep on growing more and more," writes the apostle, referring to the love shown within the budding Christian community at Philippi. *John was a church member, worshipping with our faith community and serving on the church council.* His faith was forged and sustained within the church, a faith in the God who has created us, a faith in the God who raised Jesus from the dead—Jesus who broke free from death.

John was someone who loved the outdoors (*include examples*) and *he* would agree with the writer who put the thought of rising from death another way. He described death as being like a door—a door to the outside—to a life after this. That's good symbolism for a way to make resurrection come alive for us—a word picture we can understand. And so we can have the most vital hope of all, the gospel hope of rising from death to life. John the evangelist records these words of Jesus: "I should lose nothing that I have been given, but God will raise me up on the last day."

We rejoice that for *John* the time of infirmity is over and done with, that *his* time of being a stranger to you is at an end. We rejoice that God has raised him up. We rejoice that *he* is reunited with *his* loved ones who went before and we rejoice that the loving God whom he worshipped and served has welcomed *him* into the eternal home, and that in that love of God *he* is safe and happy and knows the peace of God, that peace that goes beyond all we can speak of, or experience, or know.

Thanks be to God for the life of God's servant! Amen.

Meditation 7   *A Well-Loved Family Member*
In the reading from John's gospel, there are the contrasts of sorrow and joy that are found when we remember a close family member who has died. In the meditation, we remember *Kate,* a well-loved family member.

Secular and Bible Readings
"Gone Only from Our Sight" (see appendix 2, page 269)

Mary Magdalene Goes to the Tomb (see appendix 2, page 264)
(John 20:1–21)

Meditation

There is no doubt that Jesus had a normal family. We know who some of them were: Mary and Joseph, his parents, and James, his brother, who later became a leader of the early church; and we know from reading the gospel that they didn't always understand what their wandering, caring, prophetic family member, Jesus, was about. Don't we all have oddball characters in our families? But Jesus had another family, a disciple family, the 12 who were called by him—Peter, Andrew, James, John, and the others. In addition, there were those in the wider family circle, including several women of whom Mary Magdalene was one.

We heard in our Christian scripture reading how Mary Magdalene came to say her final goodbye to Jesus, her Lord, her good friend, the well-loved man who was family to her...and she is surprised and saddened when she finds that the body of Jesus has been taken away from the tomb. She is at a loss to know what has happened; while the gap that the absence of Jesus has opened up for her and the disciples seems so large.

Mary is crying. There is real sadness in her voice as she says to the person nearby (whom she thinks is the gardener), "They have taken away my Lord, and I do not know where they have put him!" Mary is at a loss. Similarly, you who have met to remember *Kate* are very conscious of all you have lost in the death of a *wife, mother, grandmother,* and family member.

There are elements of sadness and loss in our service *this morning,* but there is also another and different feeling. Mary encounters the risen Christ in the garden. "Who is it you are looking for?" he asks. Thinking it is the gardener, she says, "If you took him away, sir, tell me where you have put him!" And Jesus says, "Mary!" And Mary turns and joyfully recognizing Jesus says, "Rabboni, teacher!" And Mary runs to tell the disciples. You see, the other element in this story is joy.

(*A talk is now given by the daughters of the one who has died.*)

And you who meet to honour *Kate* have so much to remember joyfully of the life of this family-centred, *kind, and generous person.* We know how much you have lost, *Don,* in the death of such a caring and loving *wife,* someone who spent so many good times with you. *Mary* and *Brenda, Kate's daughters,* you made it so wonderfully clear when we talked, how your mother *was there for you all the time, a constant and reliable friend and confidant, and a wise guide in all the ups and the downs of family life.* There for your family members, too, *Don.* For *Kate, the home was central, the fixed point, the focus; she loved her home. She enjoyed nothing more than cooking for the family and their friends and keeping the place in apple-pie order!* And she gave shelter and a refuge from the storms of life to various family members over the years. For some people, it is the workplace where they make their mark, for some it is their social organizations, and for *Kate it was home!* And in the home no one was more important than you, *her grandchildren, Lamin* and *Joe.* Now I could say a whole lot about how your *Baba* felt about you, how *she* loved to give you a big hug, always ready to give you ice cream. I could say a lot, but *you, Lamin, wrote about your Baba, in a piece titled "The Person I Admire,"* and you have very kindly allowed us all to hear what you wrote, and that is much better!

(A short but touching letter by a grandson to his grandmother is read.)

Thank you, *Lamin,* that is quite a testimony to the *Baba* whom you loved. And I know there will be friends and neighbours in the congregation for whom *Kate* was such a strength, as *she was one to care for and visit the sick, even when she was sick herself.* And as you all know, *Kate* did get sick; and then so very suddenly you lost *her.*

You who are family members and friends have lost so much in the death of a *wife, a grandmother, a thoroughly good friend;* we feel for you today. And I would counsel you to face the feelings that are yours in *her* death, and put into words those most difficult to express, e.g., "I feel angry," even "I feel angry at God for *Kate* dying," "I feel so lonely now I can't go and see *her,*" "I feel frustrated that I couldn't say the things I wanted to say before *she* died," and share these feelings with a trusted one, a best friend, or minister, or counsellor. For it is in the sharing that peace and the ability to make a fresh start will come. In the words of our reading, "You truly do not walk alone." Be certain of one thing, all you family members are supported by the thoughts and prayers of those who are in the congregation this morning, and by many who could not be here be with us, but are with us in spirit. We are with you.

There is sadness in all you have lost, but there is joy in all the memories that come flooding back today. And there is an echo here of the disciples' joy in recognizing that their Lord is not dead but alive. *Kate* has, in the words of our reading, "passed over the horizon" and is greeted on another shore by those loved ones who have gone before. We rejoice that *Kate* had a strong and living faith. *She* was a regular worshipper at … *Church*, with you, *Don*.

"What can separate us from the love of God?" (see Romans 8, page 265) writes the apostle Paul. "Can death or life?" And we could say, "Could increasing infirmity?" "Can principalities or powers?" and we would say, "Can separation from the ones she loved?" No! "Nothing in all creation can separate us from the love of God as we know it in Christ Jesus our Lord." God's loved one, *Kate,* knows the wonderful truth of that now, and for *Kate,* God's servant, we give God thanks! Amen.

Meditation 8   *A Person Who Took Her Own Life*
Lynn took her own life. She was a deeply troubled young woman with underlying mental health problems. She was in her last year of high school. Her death took everyone by surprise.

Bible Readings
Out of the depths I cry to you, O Lord.
Lord, hear my voice!
Let your ears be attentive
to the voice of my supplications!
If you, O Lord, should mark iniquities,
Lord, who could stand?
But there is forgiveness with you,
so that you may be revered.
I wait for the Lord, my soul waits,
and in [God's] word I hope;
my soul waits for the Lord
more than those who watch for the morning,
more than those who watch for the morning.
O Israel, hope in the Lord!
For with the Lord there is steadfast love,
and with [God] is great power to redeem.
It is [God] who will redeem Israel
from all its iniquities.

(Psalm 130)

Jesus, the Way to God (see appendix 2, page 263)
(John 14:1–6, 8–14, 24, 27)

Life in the Spirit (see appendix 2, page 265)
(Romans 8:18, 31–32, 35, 37–39)

Meditation

"Out of the depths I cry to you, O Lord." It will be hard to take in any words this afternoon, hard to hear any words clearly. So deep are our feelings of grief over *Lynn* taking *her* own life, so intense is our sense of loss, so difficult to accept the fact that *she* will never be with us again. The ancient poet cries from the depth of his being, cries out to God because no one but God is able to hear clearly at this time of extraordinary loss. The psalmist cries out as if in deep water; we might say "He is out of his depth."

"Out of the depths I cry to you, O Lord." It is a cry from the heart, and you, *Roger and Tina (parents)*, those of you who are *Lynn's* family, those of you who were her friends, you know just where the writer is coming from. No words, certainly no words of mine, will measure up to the loss you have suffered, but words must be spoken.

"Out of the depths I cry to you, O Lord." And if no words can adequately express the loss felt by all of us this morning, neither are words adequate to describe the feelings of emptiness and futility that are the experience of some people who suffer from the illness of depression. This for years was the burden of *Lynn, clouding her loving and helpful personality, and curbing her enjoyment of friendship and competitive sports.* So often when the tragedy of a person taking *her* own life comes home to us, we are at a loss to understand why it happened. With *Lynn*, there is no doubt that *she* lost an unequal battle with the horrendous mental illness that is depression, an illness that *she* faced directly and bravely and sought help for over the years, an illness that, at the end of it all, *she* was unable to overcome.

And our hearts go out to you, *Roger* and *Tina,* in the loss of your precious *daughter,* and to you, *Jim,* in the loss of a well-loved *sister.* And we remember all of you who counted *Lynn* as a friend. You friends in particular will feel so bewildered and angry by *Lynn's* death; you will wonder "Is there anything I could have said, anything I could have done to help?" The questions will fill your minds; the answers that satisfy will be slow to come.

And I want to challenge each one of you here this morning to face the feelings that are yours, those feelings that you are least willing to put into words, to face these feelings and to share them with a trusted friend, or a minister, or a counsellor. Earl Grollman, rabbi and grief counsellor, gives good advice: "Say your deep feelings out loud, call them by their proper names: I feel so much loss, I feel angry at what has happened, I feel there was more I could have done"[2] for through the sharing, the first glimmer of hope will come.

For those of you who were classmates of *Lynn* I would direct you, if you feel down, to talk with (*names*), support counsellors who have assured me that they are ready and willing to hear you out and help in any way they can. For us as a community it is a challenge to get behind those who are working and lobbying to ensure that the *Mental Health Society Centre for Grangetown* is not just talked about but built, and the staff adequately funded.

And reach deeply into the faith that is yours to find strength in. For those of you who are Christians, it is good to remember that Jesus came to his own death by inner conviction, by the pressures from those who tested him yet knew God's love enfolding him. *Lynn* has been embraced, hugged tight, not by a stern, unfeeling, judging God, but by a God of unfailing tenderness, infinite understanding, and infinite compassion. *Lynn* is accepted; *she* is loved beyond any limits; *she* is with God.

"Out of the depths I cry to you, O Lord" writes the psalmist, but another ancient poet writes "Worship the Lord with gladness; come into [God's] presence with singing" (Psalm 100:2). There is sunlight behind the dark clouds; there is the sunlight of so many happy memories. You who have known *Lynn* well will have already begun to share them, and will continue to do so *downstairs after the service*. And we are so fortunate that *George* and *Frances* will share their memories with us, too.

(*Memories are shared.*)

Thank you, *George* and *Frances*. Your words have been grace to us. We are deeply grateful for a wonderful reminder that one positive thing we can do is to be there for each other in the days and the months that lie ahead—celebrating, sharing, remembering the good times, yet supporting and encouraging one another in the low moments.

At the end of the day, we do have hope. Our reading from the Gospel of John speaks of the house with many rooms where there is eternal joy, the heavenly home. We might better think of *Lynn* coming home to God where the darkness and despair of this world lie totally defeated by God's love. What can separate us from that love? What can separate *Lynn* from that wonderful love? "Can principalities, can heights and depths?" writes the apostle Paul, and we might add "Can the darkness of depression, can feelings of hopelessness and despair, the belief that there is no way out? Can anything in all creation?"

Nothing can separate us from the love of God as we know it in Jesus Christ our Lord, so let us go from here with the words of Jesus echoing in our ears: "Do not let your hearts be troubled, and do not let them be afraid" (John 14:27). Amen.

Meditation 9   *A Person Who Took Her Own Life (2)*
Rosie was a 43-year-old woman with a history of psychiatric illness.

Bible Reading
Jesus Calms the Storm

(Luke 8:22–25)

Meditation
The wind howls. The trees shake down to their roots. There is no mistaking a storm. Whether it is a winter storm complete with the blizzard conditions of blowing snow or a summer storm of pelting rain and fierce winds, the strong force of the weather is unmistakable. For most of *Rosie's* life, *she* lived the storm. *Her* body, mind, and spirit were in torment for so long. In spite of the incredible care given by *her* family, doctors, and other caregivers, in the end the anguish was just too strong, and *she* took her own life.

But for each one of you as well, the last few days have also been a storm of huge intensity. For some of you, it feels as if you have weak roots and you have been tested to the depths of your being. And for others the full force of *Rosie's* death is like a slap across your face. It stings—and all you can do is hurt. Your life feels turned upside down. But there are other emotions as well, for this is also a time of change and even relief. The anguish, the pain is finally over for *Rosie,* and we rejoice that *her* soul is finally at rest.

Either way, this is a surreal time. You have an endless number of questions and uncertainties, and answers are short in coming. But in the midst of the storm of loss, you carry priceless memories. *Rosie's* kindness, *her* compassion and understanding of others were gifts that you will treasure. *She* had a remarkable way of *worming her way into your heart*—often with *humour* and *always with openness. She* truly *wore her heart on her sleeve.* In many respects, *Rosie* was old for *her* age having a depth of *sensitivity and intelligence few could match. Rosie* was proud of the work *she* did as a peer counsellor and was open to sharing *her* tough life's story with *high school* and *college students.* Many of you knew *her* as a *soft-hearted, loving woman* who always wanted *to help others understand mental illness.* And *she* was so talented, *pouring out her feelings in poetry that touched the soul.*

And yet for all the joy and caring *she* brought, there were so many demons that *Rosie* fought. Between the physical agony and mental anguish that burdened *her,* the pain was excruciating. But even in the midst of pain, *her wicked sense of humour got her through,* and *she* would *come out with statements that caused you to chuckle.*

In the midst of this bewildering time, I urge you to support one another with sensitivity and compassion. Don't be afraid to speak of *Rosie's* life or of the way *she* died. It will be good to share your stories and memories of *Rosie.* For those of you who gather as friends and caring people from the community, your concern for one another will take different, practical forms. Be ready to share meals, listen deeply, or simply offer a shoulder to cry on. All of these gestures will help.

To find the right words for a day such as this is impossible. So instead, let us think about the truths and hope that scripture offers. I selected a particular passage of scripture with the hope that it might speak to our needs this morning.

In these warm months of the year, you look out over the lake and see numerous boats. On a calm day it is a scene of peace and tranquillity, but when the wind comes up out of nowhere and the white caps show, you fear for the safety of those on pleasure or fishing trips. Such was the setting for the memorable boating trip shared by Jesus and some of his disciples. It's the story we heard read earlier. "We are going to die, help us, save us!" the friends of Jesus cry out in fear. And the compassionate Christ offers safety and sustenance to his friends. The one who calmed the raging storm gives comfort and renewed peace.

As you mourn *Rosie*'s death, you may be feeling that like those friends of Jesus you are being tossed around like a boat in a storm. It seems as if you are crashing against an immovable force. Yet, just as Jesus calmed the storm and the disciples so long ago, be assured that your inner storms will also be calmed. By honestly acknowledging your need for comfort and consolation, the Holy One will support you. Know that God grieves right along with you and shares with the deepest love imaginable.

Rosie's storm is now past, and *she* has been embraced by the loving welcome of our Holy God. *Rosie* was accepted and loved by God in *her* life, and *she* is now in God's loving care in the time that begins when this time ends.

Thanks be to God that with death comes new life—eternal life. Amen.

Laura Turnbull (Adapted)

Meditation 10   *Older Woman (faith background)*
Lorna died slowly. She was much loved by her family.

Bible Reading
The Lord Is My Shepherd (see appendix 2, page 260)
(Psalm 23)

Meditation
The writer of Psalm 23 was a person who knew about loss, the loss of someone close and dear to him. The writer of Psalm 23 knew the feelings the loss aroused. It was in response to that loss that he wrote this memorable piece of religious poetry. Running through the whole psalm is the sense of God being with him, that in spite of the harshness of his suffering, God would go with him in time and beyond time.

We are gathered here this afternoon to say our final goodbye to *Lorna*, and we do so remembering that the word "goodbye" means "God be with you." There is the sense that God has gone with the psalmist in times past, and the imagery that he uses is of a shepherd going about his daily tasks: "[God] makes me lie down in green pastures, [God] leads me beside still waters." These are jobs that a shepherd would do, and we have a strong reminder here today of the variety and challenge in *Lorna's* life *of the work at the mill lab, the leisure pursuits, and the enjoyment of family that made up the life of this big-hearted woman.* There is also the strong sense that we have much to thank God for as we remember *her.* I know that some of you family members have words you would like to say, some thanksgivings to share at this time. Please feel free to do so.

(*Several family members come forward to share short eulogies.*)

Thank you all for your different insights into *Lorna's* life. *Lorna* was there for you, *her* family members, and I know *she* will be much missed within the family circle by you, *Garcia, Tami,* and *Freda* (*her children*). It has been hard for you to watch *your mum go down slowly but relentlessly over the last few years,* but you have stuck with *her* and you can rejoice that *she* has found the eternal peace *she* deserves. You told me that *she* was a most generous and loving *grandma,* and I know that the *grandchildren,* who have gained so much from *her unstinting presence,* will feel *her* absence in a special way. Our sympathetic feelings are there for you, *Naomi, Lucinda,* and *Clare.* And we are aware how much *her* passing will have meant to those who were *her* colleagues at work in the mill lab. You will remember *her* as a colleague whose outgoing generous nature changed the working climate for good. And those of you who were *her* friends will bring *her* to mind. Above all, our prayers are with you, *Jo,* in the death of a *wife/partner and best friend.*

To you who are family and friends, I would encourage you to share the feelings of loss that is yours in *Lorna's* passing, share especially with a best friend, or a minister, or a counsellor those feelings that are most difficult to speak about openly, for it is in this way that you will work through the loss that is naturally yours and experience the peace that you seek. The writer of Psalm 23 was working out his feelings of grief as he wrote this wonderful poem, and he is able to see as he does so, that the God in whom he believes is there for him in the valley of the shadow of death where he says he will fear no evil as "God's rod and staff—they comfort me."

The psalmist goes on to say that God "restores my soul" and that he "will dwell in the house of the Lord forever." Time would not be the end for the psalmist, for in God's strength he would overcome the ravages and the end of mortal time. *Lorna* would have believed that. *She* was a woman of faith, a faith that found expression in worship at church and its climax in the rising of Jesus. The rising of Jesus is there for *Lorna* and it is there for us as well!

Lorna would believe the apostle Paul when he wrote "What can separate us from the love of God? Can principalities or powers? Can heights or depths?" And we might add "Can infirmities or a slow and increasing illness?" "Nothing in all creation can separate us from the love of God, in Christ Jesus our Lord." God's servant, *Lorna,* now knows the glorious truth of that. *She* has passed from death to life and knows the peace of God, the peace of God that passes all human understanding, and for that, and for *her* good life, we give God thanks and praise. Amen.

Meditation 11   *Older Man (the "right time" to die)*
Bert was a man with many friends and was well-loved by his family. He died after a short illness, having exceeded his "three score years and 10" by 25. For Bert it was the "right time" to die.

Bible and Secular Readings
"Death Is Only an Horizon" by Bede Jarrett O.M. (see appendix 2, page 269)

Everything Has Its Time (see appendix 2, page 260)
                         (Ecclesiastes 3:1–8)

Now among those who went up to worship at the festival were some Greeks. They came to Philip, who was from Bethsaida in Galilee, and said to him, "Sir, we wish to see Jesus." Philip went and told Andrew; then Andrew and Philip went and told Jesus. Jesus answered them, "The hour has come for the Son of Man to be glorified. Very truly, I tell you, unless a grain of wheat falls into the earth and dies, it remains just a single grain; but if it dies, it bears much fruit. Those who love their life lose it, and those who hate their life in this world will keep it for eternal life. Whoever serves me must follow me, and where I am, there will my servant be also."
                         (John 12:20–26)

Meditation

For everything there is a season. As the writer of the Book of Ecclesiastes reminds us, there is a time to be born and a time to die. This is the time to say a final "goodbye" to *Bert, father, grandfather,* and *friend.* This is a time to measure our loss over one who has been important *in the family circle* and *in the community. His* fruitful life has come to an end, the unchanging cycle of the seasons is over for *him.*

As we experience the vista of changing colours of the leaves, we recognize the end of a season and we are reminded of the harvest where unless the wheat seed dies, it cannot bring new birth. This also is the time to remember our own limited lifespan, our own cycle of the seasons—the good years that have been ours and the end of this life that lies ahead for each one of us. This is the time to remember that the love of God embraces us through all the seasons of life and goes with us beyond the horizon we call death.

And this is the time when we think of various spheres of human endeavour, when we remember and thank God that *Bert* was able to be a part of them. The writer talks of "a time to plant and a time to pluck up" and in the agricultural society of the time, this would be a reminder of the work that people do. We remember that Bert was *a driver of heavy equipment for all of his working life.* But "planting and plucking up" also reminds us of gardening tasks, and *Bert loved his garden.*

[Note: "A time to…" phrases are about the contrasts of human life and they may be used as a framework to build a biographical section relating to the person who has died, the person for whom we give God thanks. "A time to tear and a time to sew" might be appropriate for another person. "A time for war and a time for peace" might be a lead-in for a former member of the armed forces. "A time to keep silence and a time to speak" might be appropriate for a community leader.]

But as the writer of Ecclesiastes reminds us, this is also "a time to mourn and a time to dance."

We do mourn the loss of *a good man.* You who are family are especially in our thoughts and prayers. We think first and foremost of you, *Jen,* in your loss of a *well-loved husband* and *friend* and all you shared of happy times and the challenges of life. We remember you, *Chuck* and *Rosemary,* and *your partners,* and the good times that were yours with *your dad.* And *Devin* and *Raleigh,* we know you will miss your *gramps* so much (*the grandchildren were young, and a few personal words were appreciated*).

For the author of Ecclesiastes writing in ancient times, the death of a person was pictured as one of the happenings in the natural order of things, but we know that there are deep feelings stirred by the loss of a loved one and that they have to be taken seriously. Feelings have to be acknowledged, have to be put into words, have to be shared with a trusted person to be gently worked through, for this is the nature of the grieving process. And I would charge you to take your grief work to heart. *Bert,* your loved one, was worth it!

"A time to mourn" it most certainly is, but it is also "a time to dance." Mourning is not only a sad and dismal process but also a celebration of the life of the person who has died. Find ways to celebrate *his* life. When you are in *his* favourite locations, talk of the time when *he* was there, what *he* did, and what *he* said. Get out the photo albums and share the stories, especially the stories that make you laugh and make you cry. You family members were telling me… (*This is a good time in the service to share with the congregation stories that the family members have shared with you, stories that highlight some key characteristics of their loved one.*)

Yes, you will miss *Bert. He* is lost from your sight, but be quite clear about this, *he* is not lost to God. John the gospel writer talks in terms of a seed being sown in the ground. Is the seed lost forever just because it is out of sight? Not at all. It is there all the time, unseen but ready to flower in a wonderful and quite unexpected way. This is one of the ways of explaining the resurrection—life does not come to an end when death happens; it goes on. How… we cannot be sure, where…we cannot be certain, but life goes on, the rising to life of Jesus is proof positive of that.

And so we rejoice that a new life has begun for *Bert. His* suffering is over, *he* is reunited with those family members who have gone before *him,* and *he* knows the peace of God, the peace of God that passes all human understanding; and for that, and for *his* good life, we give God thanks and praise. Amen.

Meditation 12   *Older Woman (faith community member)*
Paula had suffered ill health over a period of years; her earthly body was not serving her well. She died quite suddenly.

Bible and Secular Readings
"Gone Only from Our Sight" (see appendix 2, page 269)

So we do not lose heart. Even though our outer nature is wasting away, our inner nature is being renewed day by day. For this slight momentary affliction is preparing us for an eternal weight of glory beyond all measure, because we look not at what can be seen but at what cannot be seen; for what can be seen is temporary, but what cannot be seen is eternal.

For we know that if the earthly tent we live in is destroyed, we have a building from God, a house not made with hands, eternal in the heavens. For in this tent we groan, longing to be clothed with our heavenly dwelling—if indeed, when we have taken it off, we will not be found naked. For while we are still in this tent, we groan under our burden, because we wish not to be unclothed but to be further clothed, so that what is mortal may be swallowed up by life. He who has prepared us for this very thing is God, who has given us the Spirit as a guarantee.

(2 Corinthians 4:16—5:5)

Meditation
Paul talks in his letter to the Corinthians about the faithful life. He says, "We want to please God." He might have said, "We want to live a worthy life." And our first and joyful task this morning is to thank God for *Paula's* life, a faithful and a good life! Yet we come still suffering from shock that *she* has so unexpectedly, so quickly, gone from among us. It is difficult for those of you who, like myself, talked with *her* or saw *Paula in the week before she died, so full of life, in church, out shopping, talking to her friends in person and on the telephone, in touch with her family,* in short, doing the all the things *she* really enjoyed doing. It is so difficult to believe that *she* has gone from among us and that we will not see *her* again. Yet we do have to face the reality of this parting and so we have to come to this (*name*) Church, *Paula's* church, wishing that we could pass through the fragile but final barrier that is death and say our own heartfelt "goodbye" to her.

We do give thanks for *her* life and we are privileged that *Jim, her son-in-law,* will share family memories of this well-loved *mother, grandmother, former colleague,* and *very good friend. Jim* will guide our remembering and enable us to cast our own minds back to when *Paula* was a part of our lives.

(*The family member shares memories of the one who has died.*)

Thank you, *Jim*! It was good that you were able to share so much of the family experience and some of the family stories with us this morning and speak of the good times *Paula* shared with *her* friends. We have heard from *Jim* of so much in *Paula's* life to "please God," as Paul puts it.

I would encourage all you family members to share the sense of grief and loss that you feel, especially the aspects that are the most difficult to put into words, with someone you can trust absolutely, for it is in the sharing that peace will come.

The apostle Paul in our reading spends time considering this present existence. He deals with the reality of our humanity. He reminds us that our physical body is gradually decaying, and those of us (of you) who are getting up there in age are well aware of the creaks and protests of body parts as the days race by. But then Paul goes on to give us a different and wonderful reality when he writes, "Our spiritual being is renewed day after day." We are to fix our attention not on things that are seen, but on things that are unseen. "What is seen lasts only for a time," writes Paul, "but what is unseen lasts forever." What a wonderful statement from this good follower of Jesus Christ, and how completely out of step with the trends in modern society. We are encouraged by advertisers to think of our salvation in terms of what we can see right now—the new model car we can buy, the coffee shop we can frequent—while the apostle is pointing to another reality, to an unseen, eternal reality. It is so difficult for us to make this realty our own..."To leave our home in the body and make our home in the Lord," as Paul puts it. "It is not that we want to be rid of our earthly body," writes Paul, but it does wear out! You, friends and family members, are well aware, as I was, of the frustrating patches of ill health that Paula went through; we want to keep our earthly body, but it gets so that it doesn't function as well as it once did! But as Paul writes, "We want to have the heavenly body put on over us, so what is mortal will be transformed by life."

At the centre of the gospel is the hope that death is not an ending but a be-ginning. *Paula* was a long-time member of this congregation, *teaching Sunday school, a member of the choir, a former president of the women's group and a member of that organization until the time of her death, and a regular worship-per. She* shared that Christian cornerstone, that reality of resurrection hope, that faithful certainty that there is another sphere of life, spiritual life, which begins when we pass over the horizon that is death: where…we cannot be certain, in what form…we cannot be sure, but it is there ahead of us, where we will be embraced by the love of God known to us in Jesus Christ. God's peace will be certain and unending. God's faithful servant, *Paula,* knows the truth of that now, and one day so will we! Thanks be to God for *her* good life! Thanks be to God who has welcomed *her* home! Amen.

Meditation 13   *A Humble Woman*
Mary was one of this world's good people; she never made a fuss and could be relied on to help out whenever needed.

Bible Readings
He looked up and saw rich people putting their gifts into the treasury; he also saw a poor widow put in two small copper coins. He said, "Truly I tell you, this poor widow has put in more than all of them; for all of them have contributed out of their abundance, but she out of her poverty has put in all she had to live on."

(Luke 21:1–4)

When he noticed how the guests chose the places of honour, he told them a parable. "When you are invited by someone to a wedding banquet, do not sit down at the place of honor, in case someone more distinguished than you has been invited by your host; and the host who invited both of you may come and say to you, 'Give this person your place,' and then in disgrace you would start to take the lowest place. But when you are invited, go and sit down at the lowest place, so that when your host comes, he may say to you, 'Friend, move up higher'; then you will be honored in the presence of all who sit at the table with you. For all who exalt themselves will be humbled, and those who humble themselves will be exalted." He said also to the one who had invited him, "When you give a luncheon or a dinner, do not invite your friends or your brothers or your relatives or rich neighbors, in case they may invite you in return, and you would be repaid. But when you give a banquet, invite the poor, the crippled, the lame, and the blind. And you will be blessed, because they cannot repay you, for you will be repaid at the resurrection of the righteous."

(Luke14:7–14)

Meditation

The people who get noticed in this world are often the people who make a show of what they do. We encourage them. We follow the life and times of the stars (*name contemporary celebrities*); we read about them in the papers, we hear of their adventures from the tabloid headlines at the supermarket.

Today, we meet to remember *Mary* who probably only got into the papers with *her* wedding announcement and on *Tuesday* with *her* obituary. Yet, this unassuming and gentle person who was always there for *her* friends and neighbours deserved the headlines, deserved to have been publicly recognized. You, who have come to remember *her*, are fully aware of that.

If you look at the gospel record there is no doubt where the sympathy of Jesus lies, not with the power people of his time, the rulers and the Roman military controllers, not with the religious hierarchy, the High Priest, the scribes, and Pharisees, but with the unassuming and poor of this time. And so he notices the child who wants to come and see him when the disciples try to keep her away, and he notices the very poor widow who is dropping a couple of copper coins into the offertory chest of the Temple. "I tell you, this poor widow put in more than all the others," says Jesus. And Jesus makes the point, "the others offered their gifts from what they had to spare of their riches; but she gave all she had to live on."

We remember *Mary*, who had a hard time in this life but kept going, kept cheerful; who's well-loved husband, *Dennis,* died so young leaving *her* to bring up you, *her* so special children, *Brittany* and *Joe.* You, family members, have told me of the struggle to make ends meet that was *her* life, and the difficulty of balancing family responsibilities and that job at the store. You have told me how *she* wished the three of you could go on the sort of travelling holidays your friends went on (*include some stories of family life*). Mary also found time to volunteer at the *Food Bank on a Thursday evening; ironic really—she might well have been using it herself!* And if there was a bereavement in the street, or someone at work who had hit a patch of trouble, *Mary* would be the first one round with food and a shoulder to cry on.

If you do a whole lot for your family and friends, it stands to reason you will be much missed, and I know that *Mary* is much missed. And we know how much *she* is missed by you, *Brittany* and *Joe,* especially as you look back to your family times together and by the grandchildren *Nicholas* and *Emma…* your *Nana* was, I know, your greatest fan and supporter and went to all your *hockey/baseball games.* It will be very hard for you both to realize *she* will not be there to cheer you on anymore. And I know that you wider family members and friends will have so many good memories and stories. Well, don't hold back, share them over the coming days and months, and if there are feelings that you find difficult to share, memories that are painful, do not be afraid to seek out an empathetic person, counsellor, or minister who will listen and understand.

Mary, later on in life, got to the point where *she* didn't have to struggle anymore, but day-to-day living was never easy for *her.*

Our second reading, *this morning,* was about the guests who were invited to a wedding, and Jesus makes the point that in God's kingdom, those who are the people "at the top" will be humbled and the lowly ones will be recognized as great. The gospel record attests to the reality that the hope of the life that begins when this one ends has nothing to do with success in this world—quite the reverse. "You will be blessed if you invite the poor, the lame, and the blind to the feast," says Jesus. "God will repay you on the day good people rise from the dead." *Mary* is one of this world's good people. *She* is with God now; the testing times of this life are over and done with. *She* is embraced by God's love and *she* will be joyful for all eternity. For this and for *her* continual life of giving amongst us, we give God thanks! Amen.

Meditation 14   *A Backyard Event*
Ken died after being in the hospice for several weeks. He had an Easter and Christmas connection to the local faith community and had been visited by a staff person. His request was for "no funeral!" He wanted a family get-together—a barbeque and a celebration of his life. The family knew how to prepare for the barbeque, but not the celebration.

Ken had built a garden bench for his son. On this bench the family placed a handmade box containing his ashes, his golf clubs, and his Tilley hat. On a warm afternoon, the family gathered around the bench to remember Ken.

Readings
One of his sons opened with the first reading.
"Journey of Life" (see appendix 2, page 270)

The community visitor to *Ken* in the hospital then read two scripture passages that would be familiar to most people.
The Lord Is My Shepherd (see appendix 2, page 260)
(Psalm 23)

Life in the Spirit (see appendix 2, page 265)
(Romans 8:18, 31–32, 35, 37–39)

Meditation
Ken has gone from among us and will not return. This is our time to say our goodbye and to remember one who has touched us all and has been a central person in the family circle. And we rejoice that we can say our farewell in this beautiful spot, the place that *Ken* loved so much, with *his* significant stuff around us. It doesn't take much imagination to think of *him* here with us— unseen but lovingly present—perhaps smelling the barbeque and remembering so many good meals in times past!

We are glad that *he* was spared more suffering and trouble, the last *few weeks* were hard on *him* and hard on you who were family members. We are glad that *he* is at peace now.

Our reading reminds us of the journey that is the life of every person on this earth. The journey has its high spots and joyful moments, the journey has its time of loss and despair, the journey has its time of three steps forward and two back. This is the time for us to give God thanks for *Ken's* life. The life of this family-centred man who loved *his garden and the golf course!* I know some of you are prepared to do this…and we invite *Phillipa* and *Ian* to come forward now and talk about their *dad*. But it would be great if some other of you other family members who have something to share—a few words, a story—would come forward afterwards. We are all friends here!

(Philllipa and Ian talk about their dad. A couple of other family members talk briefly, and almost all the grandchildren share stories of the "fun times" with their grandpa.)

(The celebrant centres on the grandchildren when she resumes her meditation.)

We are all sorry that your *grandpa*'s life is over. We wish so much that *he* had not got sick and died; you shared so many fun times, but he loved you, loved your moms and dads, and you can keep that love going although *he* is not with you. I know you, family members, will miss *Ken* in your various ways, and feel *his* absence acutely. Keep on doing what you have been doing here this afternoon: remember *Ken* with good stories and laughter. And express all you have lost in *his* death openly and freely to a trusted one.

You, grandchildren, are probably wondering where your *grandpa* is, now you can't see *him*. Some people will tell you that *he* is up in the sky in a place called heaven; others will tell you that *he* is an angel among the stars. We can't be sure of that, but we believe that *Ken*, your *grandpa*, has been welcomed by God with a big loving hug, just like your mom or dad gives you when you come back from a trip away. One of our readings puts it this way: "What can separate us from God's love? Nothing in all the world!" That we are sure of!

Ken is at peace now, and we can go to eat our hotdogs, steaks, and hamburgers rejoicing that this is exactly what he would want us to do. Remember him and have a good time!

Meditation 15   *An Accidental Death*

Jean was an older and much-loved woman, a mother and grandmother. She died unexpectedly in a vehicle accident, and her death caused much grief in her family and friendship circle. When we talked with the family, grief was still intense and was likely to be so for some time. In the following meditation, I use the same basic approach as in Meditation 7, but focus on the intense feelings of Mary Magdalene as revealed in the account of John 20.

Biblical Reading

Mary and the Disciples Encounter the Risen Jesus (see appendix 2, page 264)

(John 20:1–21)

Meditation

We heard in our Christian scripture reading how Mary Magdalene comes to say her final goodbye to Jesus, her Lord, her good friend, the well-loved man who was family to her, and she is surprised and saddened when she finds that the body of Jesus has been taken away from the tomb. She is at a loss to know what has happened, and the gap that the absence of Jesus has opened up for her and the disciples seems so incredibly large…How was Mary feeling? She was feeling defeated, deeply disappointed that her beloved Jesus was no longer alive.

Mary is crying. There is sadness, even desolation in her voice as she says to the person nearby, whom she thinks is the gardener, "They have taken away my Lord, and I do not know where they have put him!" Mary is at a loss, and you who have met to remember *Jean* are very conscious of all you have lost in the death of a *wife, mother, grandmother,* and *family member.*

I know how frustrated and angry you will be feeling with *Jean* gone so shockingly fast from you. You will be numb; you will be angry that the terrible accident happened at all. It should not have happened! In his book, *Overcoming Life's Disappointments,* Harold Kushner quotes Victor Frankel, who survived the Holocaust concentration camp experience at Auschwitz; Frankel gave sound advice for all who are floored by terrible experiences as you have been. He encouraged people to place importance on how they were dealing with what has happened to them rather than on the experience itself.

And I know you are beginning to deal with the loss of *Jean,* the crushing loss of someone so central to your family. Your willingness to talk about *her,* to recount stories of *her* life, to reveal your deepest feelings, and to share the things hardest to talk about with a trusted friend—these facts are proof that you are making (*will make*) progress. I know you will not hesitate to contact a skilled counsellor if the need arises. Feel the pain of losing *Jean.* Don't shortcut your grief, but believe in your own ability to win through to better days. I do not underestimate the difficulty of all this because you loved *Jean* so much; you loved *this family-centred, hard-working woman who had such a terrific sense of humour.*

There is an element of sadness and loss in our service this morning, but there is also another and different feeling. Mary encounters the risen Christ in the garden. "Who is it you are looking for?" he says. She thinks he is the gardener, and she says, "If you took him away, sir, tell me where you have put him!" And Jesus says, "Mary." And Mary turns and joyfully recognizing Jesus says, "Rabboni, teacher!" And Mary runs to tell the disciples. You see, the other element in this story is joy. And we are fortunate this morning that *Harry, Jean's* uncle, will reflect the family's joyful memories of *her* in *his stories,* for there was so much joy in *her* life, and *she* was able to communicate that joy to all who came into contact with *her.*

(*Family member gives eulogy.*)

Thank you, *Harry,* your words have been grace to us! You have made *Jean's* way and *her* world come alive for us.

In our story from the Gospel of John, the focus of the account of Mary at the empty tomb and her encounter with the "gardener" is a simple one. It is to make clear to all who read the scriptures that the cross did not have the last word, that it was death itself that suffered defeat, that Jesus won through and eternally lives.

As we reflect on the death of *Jean*, we believe that the pattern holds true. Death is not the end for *her,* death is not a full stop for *Jean* anymore than death was the end for Jesus. There is a passage of scripture, which follows the one we have heard, that talks about the purpose of the gospel: "So that we may believe that Jesus is the Messiah and through faith in him you may have life."

Jean has gone from this life, and we desperately wish *she* had not, but *she* has begun another life, the eternal life that John speaks of, the life that never ends. In that joyful belief we will have the peace we seek, the peace that the disciples received when Mary came to them, the peace of God which passes all understanding. Amen.

Meditation 16 *Celebrating the Life of a Fisher (non-religious)*

Paulo was a family person and happily married to his wife, Beatrice, for 57 years. His job on the railroad provided a wage that enabled his three children to be raised comfortably, but his great joy was his weekend fishing expeditions. He especially loved to go fishing with his grandchildren and to introduce them to the sport, just as he had introduced his three children to fishing from the time that they had been able to walk. Paulo had once said that he wanted nothing more out of heaven than a perfect day when the fish were biting and some good buddies around to enjoy the sport with him. Paulo and Beatrice were married in church, but had only returned to church for the funerals of their friends.

The family enter, and members place fishing gear—rods, reels, a creel, boots—on a table on which there is also a picture of their loved one.

Time of Gathering

Celebrant: We gather to remember the life of *Paulo* who has died.
His life was *full of laughter* and *bad jokes.*
His life was never happy unless *he had family members around him.*
His life was enjoyed with *pizza* and *good red wine,*
especially enjoyed *when Beatrice made the pizza.*
His life was perfect when the sun was out, the fish were biting,
and his *grandchildren* were catching the fish.
His life was hard when *his* last illness kept him in pain and in bed.
We are all glad that this hard phase of *his* life is over and that *he* is at peace.

Celebrant: We are now going to ask his *son Peter* and *daughter Mary* to speak about their *dad*, and *friend* and *fishing partner Josh* to say a few words as well.

(Stories are shared.)

Celebrant: Thank you, *Peter and Mary,* your *dad* would have been proud of you! Thank you, *Josh,* and I am sure there were other fishing stories you could have told—about the ones that got away. And now two *grandchildren of Paulo* will read first a poem that speaks of how we feel now that *Paulo* is gone, and one that has a theme of fishing.

Afterglow

I'd like the memory of me
to be a happy one.
I'd like to leave an afterglow
of smiles when life is done.
I'd like to leave an echo
whispering softly down the ways,
of happy times and laughing times,
and bright and sunny days.
I'd like the tears of those who grieve
to dry before the sun
of happy memories
that I leave when life is done.

                                        Anon.

Heaven's Fishing Hole

For years, the riverbank was where
Your soul felt most at peace
Your heart was most content when there
With the fish and the geese
But then, your spirit came to rest
Where angels chose to roam
And once equipped with ten pound test
You made yourself at home.

The sky became your deep blue sea
The clouds became your shore
And there, for all eternity
You sat with friends galore
Each angel was a fisherman
Who had traded his pole
For golden wings and a game plan
At Heaven's Fishing Hole.

The tales you told about each catch
Its stature and its girth
Will live in memories unmatched

As days pass here on earth
Until we meet again, one day
Upon God's golden sand
We'll picture you, no other way
Than with a pole in hand.

Jill Eisnaugle[3]

Celebrant: And now in a few moments of silence I want you to close your eyes and think about *Paulo*. Remember *him* as *he* was in the family circle, around the family table, with *his* children and grandchildren. Think of *him* at his favourite fishing spot casting *his* line. Think of *him swapping jokes with his friends*. We remember *Paulo*.

(*time of silence; at least three minutes*)

(*announcement about refreshments*)

Celebrant: We remember *Paulo* and we go from here:
thankful for *his* life with all its joys and good catches,
rejoicing in all *he* shared within the family circle and with *his* good friends,
ready to comfort *his* family members in their grief and loss,
glad that *his* time of suffering is over and *he* is at peace.
We go from here cherishing our memories that will live
on in the days ahead to comfort and help us.
Paulo is gone, but *he* is not forgotten,
and will not be by you who are *his* family
and those of you who were *his* friends.

Meditation 17 *Celebrating the Life of an Artist (non-religious)*
Laura was an accomplished artist who lived on her own beside the lake. She loved her dog, Mike. Her paintings, which were recognized and collected in the area, were often of lakeside scenes. The celebration was held in the grounds of Laura's cottage beside the lake with the waves and the colour of the water changing as the ceremony took place. The breeze gently swayed the trees, and a squirrel, put out that his patch had been invaded, chattered throughout the ceremony. A few family members had been alerted to talk briefly about the aspects of Laura's life with which they were familiar.

There was a small group of family and friends sitting informally on picnic chairs, and there was a series of large rocks placed facing them. As the celebration began, family members, each carrying a canvas, came to the front, chose a rock, and propped up a painting.

Celebrant: We come rejoicing in the sky and the water, and we join with all creation in giving thanks for the earth (Mother Earth) and all it gives to us. We give thanks for its extraordinary beauty.

(*minute or so of silence*)

We gather as family and friends of *Laura*.

We come as family and friends feeling our sense of loss at *her* death, a death that has come far too soon.

We come to share our memories of *Laura* and to comfort one another.

We come remembering *Mike* (*pet Lab*) and how much *he* will miss an owner who spoilt him rotten!

We come feeling our own vulnerabilities and unease in the face of the death of someone we knew and loved.

Celebrant: Let's hear about *Laura* from two *family members, her nephew Kurt* and *her aunt Sophie*. We are also happy that *her friend Rose* will speak about her life.

(*The stories are shared.*)

Celebrant: We have been privileged to hear a good account of *Laura's* life from the people who meant a lot to her. I am going to ask you to get into small groups of two or three people and share your own stories and memories. (*Allow four to five minutes.*)

Celebrant: Now I am going to ask you to shout out a few words that ring true for you in the groups, e.g., "She had huge talent," "She could catch the colours of sky and the lake better than anyone else I knew," "She turned Mike into a fat dog," "Laura was my favourite auntie. She never forgot my birthday."

(*Allow time for words.*)

Celebrant: As we come to the end of this life celebration, let us hear a reading that speaks of *Laura* the artist, who calls on us to be the artist we are.

Are you an artist?
Does your spirit soar
Like an eagle in the sky?
Do you often wonder why
The sky is blue?
Well, me too.

Are you an artist?
Do you get bored easily
By trivial, mundane things?
Are you a wandering being?

Are you an artist?
Do you sing in the shower?
Oh, the horror of your voice,
Although, you secretly rejoice!

Are you an artist?
Do you feel like
Dancing for no reason?
Or maybe just to celebrate
The changing of the seasons?

Are you an artist?
Do you kiss adorable toddlers,
Cute cheek to sweet cheek?
Do you like to meet perfect
Strangers at odd hours?
Do you love
The smell of tender flowers?

Are you an artist?
Do you like to luxuriate
On a sandy beach?
Would you rather stay away
From those who preach?

Are you an artist?
Do you frequently lose your keys?
How about shooting the breeze?

Are you an artist?
Does "Investment Banking"
Sound too lame?
Why, you are not
Even in that game.

Are you an artist?
Do your feet
Dance to the beat
Of the Rhythm and Blues?
Well, put on your dancing shoes!

Are you an artist?
Do you fantasize and
Build castles in the air?
Why, even if people stare you down?
Who cares if they put on a frown?

Are you an artist?
Are you obsessed about
Shades, colours, and lights?
Do you love to fly kites?
Do you travel very light?

Are you an artist?
Do you often dream about
Making this world a better place?
And want to achieve that
By demonstrating aesthetic grace?

Achlan Mehta[4]

Closing Words

Celebrant: As we look at the waters of the lake, let us remember *Laura,* who has coloured our lives so beautifully.

(*time of silence*)

As we look up at the sky, let us remember *Laura,* who called the best, the highest out of us.

(*time of silence*)

As we look around us let us remember *Laura,* who has touched our lives in so many ways and will continue to influence us in the days ahead.

(*time of silence*)

We give thanks for *Laura,* our family member and friend; she has helped us paint the good canvas of our lives.

Meditation 18   *A Faithful Life with Many Changes*
José left Mexico for Toronto, Canada, in his early years. Originally a Roman Catholic, he met and married Rosemary in his late twenties and joined her church, The United Church of Canada. The two of them were faithful worshippers over the years. Rosemary and José had two children, and their life was marked by many changes in location as José followed his trade as a welder. They loved and were well-loved by their five grandchildren with whom they shared holidays, Christmas, Easter, and many weekends beside.

José died aged 85, just after Christmas, and one of his favourite scriptures was the story of the wise men. It seemed appropriate to use this story as one of the scripture passages for his funeral service.

Bible Readings
The Call of Abraham

(Genesis 12:1–9)

The Visit of the Wise Men

(Matthew 2:1–12)

Meditation
It is wonderful to be here together as a faith community, the faith community that *José* called *his* own, to celebrate *his* life. *José* was one of our faithful members who served this church so well in *his* retirement. We will miss *him,* all of us at *St. James* will miss *him,* as you, *Rosemary,* will miss *your husband* and *the boys will miss their grandpa.*

We only have to look around the church to see what season of the church year it is. The Holy Family figures are out on the table, and there are Mary and Joseph and the baby Jesus. The shepherds are looking on, and there in the background are the three wise men, the three persons who had gone on a long and hazardous journey, braving the wicked ruler Herod to find the king above all rulers, the wise one above all wise persons. *We have a banner at the back of this sanctuary that shows the wise men on their quest.*

The wise men's journey is a reminder for us of *José*, who was a man who took a risk, a huge risk when *he* left *his* homeland and went on a difficult journey that brought *him* to a new land, the land of his adoption—like Abraham leaving Haran. We heard about that journey in our Hebrew scriptures passage. And like Abraham, *José* made some other challenging journeys as *he* followed *his* chosen trade as a welder. Yet *he* also showed *his* willingness to adventure in leaving the faith of his family, the faith of *his* forebears, to become a member of The United Church of Canada. Not only do we say farewell this morning to a man beloved by *his* family, but also we come as members of the Christian family of *St. James* to say farewell to one of our own. Our faith family is poorer now that *José* has gone from among us, but rich in the faithful example *he* has left us.

We have two people who will speak to us this morning. First we will hear from *Travers, a grandson of José* and *Rosemary,* and then we will hear from *Bert Lucas, who served on church council with José.*

(*The stories are shared.*)

Thank you, *Travers*. Thank you, *Bert*. It was not easy for either of you to speak about someone who was close and well-loved…we are in your debt! When the journey of life comes to a close, when the journey of faith comes to its earthly end, it is good to have people who are ready to point out the key places along the way, and you have both done a great job for all of us. And you have challenged us to think about the times when our life and faith journeys have intersected with those of *José* and what a good experience that was.

We think especially of those who were *José's* companions along the journey, and first of all of *Rosemary, José's* wife of 53 years. *Rosemary,* you told me how you always dreaded unpacking the last mover's box because that was often the signal for *José* to say, "I just noticed this great welding job in Yellowknife…or

Halifax…or St. John's…or Regina…or…." Our hearts go out to you and to *Ricardo* and *Helen, his* children, in the loss of their *dad,* and to your families.

And as we remember those of you who were family to *José,* so we remember those of us who are in *his* family of faith. *Bert* has spoken and spoken well of *José*'s commitment to this church and *his* years of *heading up the property committee,* but I remember well *his* membership of the *Living the Faith group.* I remember *him* saying, *"I never stop growing in the faith and I never stop trying to work out my faith in practice."* And I remember *his* ability to *pose the simple question that everyone else was thinking but hadn't the courage to put into words.* I believe many of you in this faith community will come to be like *José,* asking the good questions and putting your faith into practice. We are going to miss *José* in so many areas of our church life, but we are thankful for all *he* has given us and other United Churches on *his* life's journey.

The journey theme is also a reminder that though your life's journey with your loved one has come to an end, your grief journey has only just begun. We all have our stories and we will make a start of sharing them at *the lunch that follows this service.*

It is interesting that in the gospel account, Matthew has those three wise individuals following a star to guide them to their destination. It is a reminder that in the journey that is loss and grief sometimes we need a "star" to help us when we get lost or distracted. That "star" might be a minister, counsellor, or best friend who listens carefully to our feelings and concerns to get us orientated, to get us "recalculated," to enable us to deal with our loss and put us on the right road again.

Did the three wise persons have any idea what they would find at the end of their faith journey? You bet they were surprised when they got to Bethlehem, surprised and delighted, that they had found the right person in the right place—even though the King of Kings wasn't at all the majestic ruler they had been expecting, but a tiny, vulnerable baby.

José is at one with the peace of God now. *His* life's journey is over, but as *he* was a full, participating, and enthusiastic member of this faith community it is good to think of *him* as beginning *his* journey as a member of the community of all of the joyful saints of all the ages, whose community we can't even begin to visualize but whose joy and whose worship know no end.

Thanks be to God, who in time and beyond time, journeys with us. Amen.

Meditation 19   *A Gifted, Challenged Person*

Louisa was a friendly and outgoing 28-year-old. She had many great gifts. She also had mental and physical challenges.

Bible Reading

The Beatitudes

(Matthew 5:1–10)

Meditation

To have encountered *Louisa* was a delight. To have known *her* was a blessing. You soon forgot *she* had some special needs, for to be in *Louisa's* presence was to be near a child of God.

It was a crowd of very different people, just like us, to whom Jesus spoke, and what he said was recorded in Matthew's gospel, the Bible reading we have just heard. The great teacher was on a mountainside when he gave this remarkable teaching, in verse, starting with "Blessed are..." and followed by "For they shall be...," the blessing verses that are now called "The Beatitudes." *Louisa* fitted very well into the definition of those who are counted among the blessed. Let's see how *she* measured up to The Beatitudes test...

"Blessed are the poor in spirit, for theirs is the kingdom of heaven" is the first couplet. Well, let's face it, there was nothing poor about *Louisa's* spirit. *She* would ask some of the most probing faith questions, and during the learning time with our younger folk in church, *she* always had a perceptive comment or two. *Louisa's* spirit was open and questioning.

"Blessed are those who mourn, for they will be comforted." Well, we are the ones who mourn. We can't quite believe that *Louisa* has died. We expect *her* to *show up at the hockey game, the bowling alley, library,* and *care centre.* Even though we will be hearing some of *her* music after the service, it won't be the same without *Louisa's head bobbing along to it.* Yes, we are mourning. We are sad, and our tears just keep coming. But we are promised that God will provide comfort in God's own time and we will be numbered with those who are the comforters and those who will be comforted.

"Blessed are the meek, for they will inherit the earth." *Louisa* had a wonderful blend of gentleness, compassion, and a boldness that stood *her* in good stead. I think this is what Jesus was referring to when he was describing "the meek." What a wonderful promise—to inherit the earth! With all the many places that *Louisa* has visited, it is true that *she* had much of the earth in her soul.

"Blessed are those who hunger and thirst for righteousness, for they will be filled." *Louisa* had a strong sense of what was right and what was wrong. I think that is partly why *she* so loved coming to church; it helped *her* to get *her* values sorted out. Each week, *Louisa* would come with prayer requests, seeking God's blessing and love, and *she* was deeply satisfied.

"Blessed are the merciful, for they will receive mercy." With all of *Louisa's* volunteering and *her* care for the young and the aged alike, we would definitely call *her* merciful. *She* shared *her* time and talents generously and graciously and brought love wherever *she* went. And in being merciful, it goes without saying, *she* did receive mercy.

"Blessed are the pure in heart, for they will see God." One of *Louisa's* greatest gifts was *her* purity of heart. *She* genuinely gave you who *she* was. *She* wasn't about putting on a false face or pretending to be someone *she* was not. *She* was the real thing. What a wonderful assurance to know that *she* sees God!

"Blessed are the peacemakers, for they will be called children of God." *Louisa* just wanted to be loved and accepted. Isn't that true for all of us? If we were to treat one another with the same tolerance and gentleness that *Louisa* showed to others, just imagine what a wonderful world we would have! And all of us would be called children of God!

"Blessed are those who are persecuted for righteousness' sake, for theirs is the kingdom of heaven." You will know better than I that there were times and situations where because of *her* challenges, *Louisa* was not treated with the respect, courtesy, and compassion that each of us deserves. And *Louisa* felt hurt and even a sense of being persecuted at times. But I do know that God was with *her* in all the situations and circumstances where *she* needed care and love. And I also know that the realm of heaven is for *her* now.

As Jesus sat on the mountain talking to the crowd, he spoke about being blessed. We have been blessed to have shared life with *Louisa*. Our lives have been richer because of *Louisa*. We miss *her*. How we miss *her*! But we hold onto the Good News that *Louisa* is in God's keeping. Amen.

Laura Turnbull (adapted)

Meditation 20   *A Respected Family Person (not churchgoer)*
This service was for Fred, a well-respected family and business person. He was not a churchgoer; his close family members were members of the faith community.

Bible Reading
The Beatitudes

(Matthew 5:1–10)

Building on Rock

(Matthew 7:24–27)

Meditation
This has been a year when everyone has been reading about or talking about basements. If yours wasn't flooded you will have known someone who has been mopping up or have read of the floods in *Calgary* or *New Jersey* where families have had to leave their homes because the water has come pouring in (*shares sample stories*). A torrential downpour tests a building, tests the water tightness of the windows, tests the soundness of the roof, and ultimately tests the construction of the basement.

"Everyone then who hears these words of mine and acts on them" we hear Jesus saying in the passage of scripture that has just been read, "will be like a wise man who built his house on rock." Then the rain, the river flooding, the wind can't shake it—can't find a way inside. Now Jesus was not using the concept of a solid foundation in a building construction sense; he was using it as an example of values that hold steady when everything else is crumbling—eternal values, true values, the ones that can be relied on in this life. We will hear of some of the values, these solid values, as we hear about the life of *Fred* from *his daughter, Jennie*.

(*Family member shares reflections about the one who has died.*)

Thank you, *Jennie*, you have given us a wonderful picture of *Fred* and the solid values, the solid foundation blocks, on which *his* life was built.

His integrity and organization in business, the building construction business!
His enjoyment and support of the sport of curling
His essentially giving nature
His insatiable curiosity about the world around him
His sense of the essential worth of family
His sense of humour, subtle but invigorating to experience

These were enduring qualities modelled by *Fred* that enabled others to lay down foundations for themselves. But your family foundations have been shaken by the loss of this good man *to cancer* far too soon. You have told me how your foundations have been shaken, and so I speak especially to you who are family members. To you, *Karen* and *Colin, his children;* to you, *Mary, his* so well-loved *wife of 45 years;* to the *grandchildren;* to those of you who his were *Fred's friends;* and to you, *his* wider family members.

"Blessed are those who mourn," says Jesus, for you will be comforted. Because you have lost so much love, so much good-humoured love and caring, each one of you, because you have lost so much as a family together, because you have lost so much as a *curling club* together, because you have lost so much as a *business group* together, you will feel the loss of *Fred,* feel it acutely, feel its pain. And I would counsel you to be good to yourselves. Give yourselves the time you need to do your grief work for *Fred.* If there are deep feelings to share, feelings of regret, feelings of distress, share them with someone you can trust absolutely, and don't delay! Share what is heartfelt. And it is good to remember that those of us who meet in this sanctuary are joined by many who could not be here today but are with us in spirit.

Jesus made clear, "The one who hears these words of mine and does them will endure." And Jesus lived out the solid and trusted values that he taught. Eventually it brought him in direct opposition to the power people of his time, to a cross, and to his own far-too-early death. But death was not the end for him; the gospel record makes that clear. The women at the tomb and the surprised disciples are aware that Jesus is alive again and that death has been overcome. We build our solid foundation of hope on this belief...that death was not the end for Jesus and it is not the end for *Fred.* Not only do *Fred's* values live on in those who knew and loved *him,* but also we believe that *Fred* lives on: where...we cannot be certain, how...we cannot be sure, but for *him* death has been defeated.

We mourn the loss of *a husband* and *father, a brother* and a family member. We mourn the loss of of one who served local communities well. But take heart! As the Bible tells us, mourning will be turned into laughter and sorrow into joyful dance.

Thanks be to God! Amen.

Meditation 21   *An Abusive Person*

Bertha abused her children and was disliked by them. However, planning a service was still important to them.

Bible Reading

The Story of Zacchaeus

(Luke 19:1–10)

Meditation

You did not want to get on the wrong side of a tax collector in the time of Jesus. Think Mafia and you are on the right track! Typically, these tax collectors were not nice guys. They had been sold a franchise by the Roman occupying authorities and were determined to make the most of it. Zacchaeus was one of these tax franchisees, and we know from the scriptures that he was one of those who charged more than he was entitled. Likely, if payment of tax was not made on time, he would send a couple of his friends round to apply some gentle persuasion. Tax franchisees like Zacchaeus lived well, in fact they lived luxuriously, but because of their profession and because they used force to get the money they were owed, were generally hated by the men and women of Jerusalem and the surrounding area.

You, family members, have told me that *your mother* was one who acted in line with the "spare the rod and spoil the child," way of parenting. *She* beat you often and later in life *she* abused you verbally and with venom. Visits to the family home after your *father* died were not to be welcomed but avoided at all costs. You told me that, and I know you didn't want to keep it a secret. Usually, we want to assure the family members of our concern for them as they grieve the loss of one they loved dearly. Today, we are with you in that sense of relief that you will not have to endure your *mother* and *her* abusive ways anymore.

Some of you in the congregation this morning will have seen a different side of *Bertha. Her* love for *her pet cat, Sammy,* certainly showed that *she* was capable of kindness and caring, and those of you who went to *bingo with Bertha* will have appreciated *her* friendly and sociable side. We don't want to forget that. We want to say, "Look at what *she* was capable of being," but it would be less than honest if we did not add, *"If only she had been as caring to her children and grandchildren."*

You, family members, had suggested to me that the origin of your *mother's* abusive behaviour was in *her* own troubled childhood, and I believe that this is true. Over a long period of time *Bertha* had learned that this was the way to raise children—to beat and abuse them. *She* had experienced this with *her* own parents and applied these techniques as *she* raised you. It wasn't good, it wasn't right, but it was what *she* knew and what *she* did.

But the story isn't over. We learned from our Christian scripture reading that Zacchaeus had a change of heart; he saw the light. He went out of his way to invite Jesus over for a meal and then showed that he was ready to pay back the money he had defrauded, and a whole lot more! And Jesus, for his part, made it clear that the new Zacchaeus was totally accepted by him—no judgment, no conditions, no lecture about how wicked Zacchaeus had been, just simple acceptance and an implied level of support as he began again.

Bertha died before there was any chance of *her* seeing the light of a new way. In this life it was not possible, but the God of ultimate compassion will not leave it at that; the God of ultimate compassion is infinitely bigger than refusing to receive *Bertha* anymore than the father of the lost, the prodigal son, was willing to shut him out of the family home.

"Nothing is able to separate us from the love of God as it is revealed in Jesus Christ," to quote the apostle Paul…not cruelty, not an abusive attitude, not despicable behaviours learned as a child. There is nothing in all creation, nothing at all! *Bertha* knows the eternal truth of that now. *Bertha* is at peace.

Thanks be to God. Amen.

Meditation (and service) 22   *A Well-Loved Pet*

Rocky, a border collie, was euthanized at aged 17 after cancer and other ailments had made life miserable for him. The family decided to bury him at the family cottage under a beautiful red pine tree.

Before the Service

The burial site has been located and a grave dug by family members. A large stone with the name "Rocky" carved on it has been placed close to the grave. The worship leader is chosen and volunteers requested to be readers of prayers, Bible readings, and other readings.

The Service

We walk around *Rocky's* favourite haunts in the cottage grounds, and some of the grandchildren throw sticks into the lake as they used to do when *Rocky* was healthy.

The worship leader welcomes everyone and then explains what will take place during the service.

Leader: It is good to be here to remember *Rocky*, who was our favourite pet and friend. *He* had a good life up to the last few months. *He barked and sniffed and chased cats and loved to have his ears scratched.* We are going to miss *him* because he was our *family dog* and our friend, but we are glad that for *him, his* suffering is over.

We are going to give thanks and praise to God, the Creator of all living things—flowers and trees, bees and butterflies, deer and elephants. We will especially thank God for *Rocky* and for all our good times shared with *him*.

During the service we will ask you to share briefly your favourite memory of *Rocky*.

We are going to *bury Rocky* in one of *his* favourite spots—where *he would bury precious bones*. And we will commend *Rocky* to God's love and care.

Call to Worship
Psalm 148 (adapted)
Praise the Lord!
Praise the Lord from the heavens;
Living things here on earth
Beings beyond time and space,
Praise God, praise God now and always.

The sun and the moon praise God!
Mountains and hills, praise God!
Fruit trees and forest trees, praise God!
Rivers, streams, and seas, praise God.
Wild animals and cattle, praise God.
Birds and reptiles, praise God!
Dogs and cats, (*names*), all our pets praise God!

Moms and dads, grandpas and nanas,
brothers and sisters, all our family praise God!

Prayer
Loving God, be with us this *morning/afternoon* as we say goodbye to
Rocky, our friend.
We know your love is for all living things and so we know that *this dog* will
be in your compassionate love and care for always and forever. Bless all who
will miss *him* especially now when we cannot see *him wag his tail* or *chase a
ball,* or *walk alongside us,* or *roll over waiting for his tummy to be scratched.*
We pray in the name of Jesus, the compassionate one. Amen.

Bible Readings
The God Who Cares for Birds and Flowers
(Luke 12:22–28)

Jesus Blesses Little Children
(Luke 18:15–17)

Remembering Rocky
Rocky's collar is passed around the family circle and as each family member receives the collar they share their favourite memory of *Rocky*. Only those who
wish to share need share their memories. At the end of this time there will be
a couple of minutes of silent remembering.

Meditation

As you have shown by your memories as we passed around *Rocky's* collar, we have so much to thank God for in having known this special pet. Because we have loved this *furry friend* so much, we will miss *him* so much.

Rocky's resourcefulness has been shown in (*name's story*).
His friendship has come clear in (*name's story*).
His patience has been revealed as we heard from (*name*).
His loyalty was disclosed in the incident about...that (*name*) told us about.

Our Bible reading from the Christian scriptures tells of Jesus blessing the children who the disciples would have had him ignore. And that is how we understand this wonderful man to be, one who showed compassion to the vulnerable and exploited. There are no *doggy* stories in the Christian scriptures, but the compassionate attitude of this wonderful teacher shows that there might have been some that went unrecorded. And there is a reminder here to be on the side of groups like the local animal shelter that rescue and support abused and abandoned pets.

It is also a reminder to show a caring attitude to those of us who are going to miss *Rocky* so much. Grief is not just something that happens when a well-loved human family member dies; it is there when a pet like *Rocky* is no longer with us. Take your grief for *Rocky* seriously. Share your stories, share your deepest feelings with a loved one or good friend, and don't expect your sadness for *Rocky's* death to go away just because it is six months since *Rocky* died or because there is another *dog* in the family circle. Grief for a *dog,* as with grief for a human, takes the time that it takes. Don't rush it!

Will *Rocky* now be *chasing birds in some doggy heaven?* Or *digging holes for bones* in some secret spot? Or *walking faithfully alongside a whistling angel?* We are not given to know these things. One thing we do know is that the God who cares for the birds of the air and the wildflowers will lovingly care for *Rocky* forever.

Rocky's suffering is over now, and we are glad of that.
Thanks be to God for *Rocky,* our faithful friend. Amen.

The Burial
(*pet's body or ashes*)

Committal
Into God's keeping and into God's unfailing love we commend *Rocky*.
We commit *his* body (*ashes*) to the ground, earth to earth, dust to dust,
believing that *he* is safe and happy forever and always.
(*The pet's body or the ashes container is lowered into the grave. Wildflowers or
mementoes are put in the grave. Family members shovel earth onto the body or
ashes container. The stone with the pet's name engraved is placed on the grave.*)

Prayer of Thanksgiving
Loving God, we thank you for *Rocky* and for all *he* meant to us over many
years.
He has been our companion in good times and hard times.
He has been there for us when we celebrated,
He has been there for us when others let us down.
He has unfailingly *greeted us with a wagging tail,*
and *his bark has warned us of the approach of friends and strangers.*
Now *he* has gone and we will miss *him*.
Be with us as we remember *his* presence with a laugh.
Be with us as we mourn *his* absence with a tear.
And be with us as we enjoy and treasure each of our pets in the coming days.
Amen.

Commissioning and Blessing
Care for all of God's creation,
each flower, each tree,
each frog, and each dragonfly.
Care for your human friends.
Care for your furry friends
and support them.

And the blessing of God, the Creator,
the blessing of Jesus the compassionate one,
the blessing of the Holy Spirit who calls us to action,
be with you and those you love, in time and beyond time. Amen.

Meditation 23   *A Prodigal Son*

Bruce had been addicted to drugs and alcohol, but had turned his life around and got a fulfilling job. He was loved by his family and grandchildren. Sadly, he died accidentally and tragically.

The scripture is woven in with the eulogy and worship leader's meditation. There are two voices: the Bible reader and the worship leader.

Bible Reading

Then Jesus said, "There was a man who had two sons. The younger of them said to his father, 'Father, give me the share of the property that will belong to me.' So he divided his property between them. A few days later the younger son gathered all he had and traveled to a distant country, and there he squandered his property in dissolute living."

(Luke 15:11–13)

Meditation

We come together to mourn *Bruce's* far too early death, most of us aware of *his* life's story, which was full of hard places and travels along some particularly dark roads. But we come certain that *he* had turned *his* life around, certain that when *he* died, *Bruce* was on a steady and healthy path. We are all going to miss *him* very much! *Son, Chris,* and *daughter, Megan,* you are especially in our thoughts as are the *grandchildren.* And you are, too, *Diane, Bruce's well-loved partner.* And we think also of you, *Doug and Elma, his so-supportive parents.* It is the toughest loss, the untimely loss of a child!

The passage of scripture chosen for the service is known as the "prodigal" or "lost" son, and you family members are conscious of the parallel with your experience with *Bruce.* The lost son in the story chose to abandon a steady but fulfilling area of work for a life of partying and easy living, and it is no secret that *Bruce,* too, went off the rails. *Drugs* were a problem and so was an *abuse of alcohol.* You, family members, have told me how *Bruce* was lost to you in much the same way as the prodigal son was lost to the father in the story. You have told me of the frustration and heartache caused by *him cutting himself off from you,* how you begged *him to come home but got no response.* But you have also told me that after some years *he* had a radical change in heart and action. Listen again to scripture.

"When he had spent everything, a severe famine took place throughout that country, and he began to be in need. So he went and hired himself out to one of the citizens of that country, who sent him to his fields to feed the pigs. He would gladly have filled himself with the pods that the pigs were eating; and no one gave him anything. But when he came to himself he said, 'How many of my father's hired hands have bread enough and to spare, but here I am dying of hunger! I will get up and go to my father, and I will say to him, "Father, I have sinned against heaven and before you; I am no longer worthy to be called your son; treat me like one of your hired hands."' So he set off and went to his father. But while he was still far off, his father saw him and was filled with compassion; he ran and put his arms around him and kissed him. Then the son said to him, 'Father, I have sinned against heaven and before you; I am no longer worthy to be called your son.'"

(Luke 15:14–21)

Bruce, like the prodigal son, came back home, and this was not the easy option. You have told me, *Diane,* how *he* struggled with *his addictions,* long after *he* was back in this city, and more than one of you *congregational members have recounted his experience as a member of Alcoholics Anonymous.* It was *his membership in AA* that was the foundation for his recovery and the strength from which *he* rebuilt *his* life. *He* was no churchgoer, certainly not a religious man, but *his* belief in a Higher Power and his willingness to put *his* hands in God's hands without reserve or conditions was the turning point in *his* recovery *from addictions.* Some of you may say, *"He* had no belief in heaven, no confidence in a life that begins when this one ends. How could *he* be counted a Christian?" This way of thinking is understandable, but can anyone who has enthusiastically borne witness to God walking with *him,* as *Bruce* has done, someone who embraced the spirit of God and felt *himself* to be embraced, held secure by that Loving Spirit, can anyone so alive in the Spirit be denied eternal joy and eternal bliss? I for one don't think so.

The scriptures continue:
"But the father said to his slaves, 'Quickly, bring out a robe—the best one— and put it on him; put a ring on his finger and sandals on his feet. And get the fatted calf and kill it, and let us eat and celebrate; for this son of mine was dead and is alive again; he was lost and is found!' And they began to celebrate."

(Luke 15:22–24)

We, too, have reason to celebrate, for *Bruce's* life when *he* got it under control was a rich and full one. *He* found vocational fulfillment in *his* job as a *pipefitter*. *His* love of *hockey* got *him* into the *training stream as a coach of beginning players*; and how those youngsters loved *him*! I know we have a team's worth of players with us this afternoon!

He loved *his grandchildren* and was loved by *them*. You have said how there was a peace about *Bruce* in these last few months that *he* had been lacking for many years. *His* life, as you have told me, was on a steady course and everything was looking good, but then that tragic *road accident* stopped *Bruce* in *his* tracks and has been devastating to you who are friends and close family members. You are in the thoughts and prayers of each person here and many who are far from here but who are with us in spirit.

And you have some emotions, some anxious feelings that are hard to deal with, hard to shift. When you are moved to tears, let them flow. When you are reluctant to share your deepest emotions, know that there are close friends who are willing to hear you out and keep what they hear to themselves. When you are tempted to mask your acute sense of loss, take a deep breath and look for another way, a healthy way.

Your loved one, *Bruce,* found peace at the end of *his* life. That peace has not left *him* in death. The Higher Power to whom *he* looked and on whom *he* relied has welcomed *him* to the eternal home, and peace, the peace that passes all human understanding, is *his*. Thanks be to the Loving God. Amen.

> (adapted from a meditation for a
> ministry colleague)

---

[1] From *Meditations of the Heart* by Thurman, Howard (adapted). Reproduced with permission of BEACON PRESS in a book via Copyright Clearance Center.

[2] From Rabbi Earl A. Grollman, DHL, DD *Living With Loss; Healing With Hope* audio visual tape. With permission from Global Distributions Networks, Inc.

[3] © 2006 Jill Eisnaugle's Poetry Collection. Used with permission.

[4] "Are You an Artist?" by Achlan Mehta. Used with permission of Son of the Sea, Inc., representing Drew Brophy Properties.

Checklists

Worship Leader's Checklist (own church)

Before the Service

☐ Arrive at least an hour before the service begins.

☐ Make sure you have all necessary notes and other liturgical materials and that they are placed on the lectern, pulpit, or other reading place. Check through to be certain that there are none missing. Do not *assume* you have brought everything you need.

☐ Make sure that the bulletins are ready and at the back of the sanctuary/ meeting place.

☐ Make sure that the parking spots for family members are reserved and that ropes are available to block off the pews used by family members. Or delegate this responsibility to others.

☐ Make sure that the sound system is up and running and that the "techies" are prepared for the service tasks. Do a spoken test, a few lines from a Bible will suffice, and have someone (who is willing to tell it the way it is) check from the back of the sanctuary to make sure you can be heard clearly.

☐ Liaise with the staff from the funeral home, giving them help and guidance about seating, sound, and the arrangement of photos, objects on the communion table, and family meeting place.

or

☐ Make sure that the ushers are well briefed. (See "Usher's/Funeral Helper's Checklist" on page 256.)

or

☐ Make sure that the designated funeral service helper/s is/are well briefed. (See checklist on page 256.)

☐ Make sure that the family members have a place where they are able to go and be with other family members and that the family members know the family room location.

☐ Liaise with family members and make sure that the family are able to use and put significant pictures on the communion table or other sanctuary furniture. Check that liturgical objects like the cross and candle are still in place and are visible.

☐ Make sure that family members who have a part in the service have arrived.

☐ Make sure that family members who have a part in the service know what is expected of them and the place in the service when they give their reading or eulogy. (For example, what do scripture readers say when they have finished reading?)

☐ Talk to the family of the need to decide who will sit with whom and where in the sanctuary. Talk also about the need to determine the order of family members going into the sanctuary/meeting area.

☐ Make sure that the Christ candle and other necessary candles are lit before the service begins.

☐ Make sure that the family has sufficient flower arrangement stands and advise on placement.

☐ Make sure that the refreshment coordinator has no problems.

☐ Make sure that the temperature of the sanctuary is between 21 and 23 degrees Celsius, 68–71 Fahrenheit. If it is warm and there is no air conditioning, make sure that the windows are open.

☐ Make sure that there are registers available to be signed by congregants, and that the ushers direct people to sign them.

☐ Make sure that baskets or other receptacles are placed beside the registers to accept the cards of sympathy and donations to charities. If specific charities have been named, it is helpful to have envelopes obtained from the local branch available and some appropriate literature. The helpers/ushers who are by the registers should be aware of the charities that the family has chosen.

☐ Make sure that there is water and that there are tissues for family members in the family room. Also, ensure there are tissues in the family seating area in the sanctuary.

☐ Make sure that there is water located conveniently in the sanctuary for the worship participants.

☐ Make sure that the musician is present and has no problems with her location or with the service music.

☐ Make sure that there are sufficient paper supplies in the washrooms and that the washrooms are clean.

☐ Make sure that the cheques for the service participants are available and are distributed to them.

☐ Offer a prayer with the family just before the service after first checking that this will be helpful to them.

Just Before and During the Service

☐ Advise people of the need to turn off their cellphones and other electronic devices.

☐ Focus on the liturgy and the needs of presenting the liturgy.

☐ Be aware of sound needs and how sound quality might be improved.

☐ Be aware of family personal concerns and how they can be met.

At the End of the Service
☐ Make sure that the family is led out of the sanctuary first or lead them out yourself.

☐ Make sure that the family members are situated in the hall or outside the sanctuary so that friends may greet them. Or, reserve a family table where congregational members may greet family members.

☐ Make sure that the refreshments are readily available and that a grace is offered if this is the custom of the place.

☐ Make sure that you are visible so that congregants may greet you, offer you their feelings about the service, and express their feelings around the death of their friend or their feelings about the death of one of their family members or loved one.

Clearly it is going to help the worship leader if as many of these tasks as possible are delegated to other church personnel; she will have enough to do in preparing for the worship liturgy. However, the responsibility rests with her and a quick check will not go amiss. On one occasion, my check for the musician revealed his absence; I phoned his home to see if he was there, and was told that he was "at the grocery store." His wife put his music in the family car, found him at the meat counter, and rushed him to the church where the service was due to start in two minutes. He put a gown over his shorts and played without missing a beat.

The responsibility for the service and service personnel, their presence, and their capability rests with the worship leader. Pilots have a checklist to go through as their aircraft readies for take-off. Worship leaders will do well to prepare a checklist that may include the above items plus some local needs.

Usher's/Funeral Service Helper's Checklist
☐ Report to the worship leader at least 45 minutes before the service. Introduce yourselves. See if he has any special instructions. Be available to help the worship leader at any time before, during, or after the service

☐ Check that there is parking for the family members and that it has been designated or blocked off.

☐ Make contact with the family member who has responsibility for preparing the sanctuary for the service. Does he/she need help with the flowers or to organize the placement of pictures or other items at the front of the sanctuary?

☐ Find out the location of the washrooms. You will be asked.

☐ Check for the location of the place where the family members will gather.

☐ Make sure that the family area in the sanctuary is reserved.

☐ If the service will be projected on a screen, check with the worship leader to determine if there are places in the sanctuary where the view will be obscured and point these out to the congregants.

☐ Find out if there will be bulletins for the service and arrange for them to be given out to family members and friends as they arrive. Take a suitable number to the family meeting place.

☐ Make sure that the registers for those who are attending the service are in place and that you direct incoming family and friends to sign them.

☐ Make sure that the baskets or other receptacles for cards and donations to specified charities are available. If possible, have literature relating to the charities close by. Some people will want to make a contribution on the spot, so know to whom or to what charity the cheque should be made out.

☐ Make sure that there is someone with a cellphone present or that you know where the nearest land line is located. You may need this if there is a medical emergency.

☐ Be aware of seats for those who have physical or developmental challenges. Know where wheelchairs should be located and whether there are special seats or amplifiers for those who are hearing impaired.

☐ Be available to direct congregants to their seats. This is especially important if there is a limited number of seats. Offer an arm to those who need a steadying presence and help them park their walkers.

☐ Be available to help latecomers. Your work is not finished when the service begins.

- [ ] Be alert and available to help any congregant during the service.

- [ ] Tidy up the sanctuary after the service. Collect up bulletins and tissues and tidy hymn books.

- [ ] Make sure that cards, donations, and the registers are given to the appropriate family member.

- [ ] Be available for any other duties as delegated by the worship leader or family members.

Worship Leader's Checklist (other location)

Before the Service
- [ ] Arrive at least 40 minutes before the service begins.

- [ ] Make sure you have all necessary notes and other liturgical materials and that they are placed on the lectern, pulpit, or other reading place. Check through to be certain that none are missing. Do not assume you have brought everything you need.

- [ ] Make sure that the bulletins are ready at the back of the sanctuary/meeting place.

- [ ] Make sure that the sound system is up and running and that the "techies" are prepared for the service tasks. Do a spoken test, a few lines from a Bible will suffice, and have someone check from the back of the sanctuary to make sure you can be heard clearly.

- [ ] Liaise with the staff from the funeral home. Make sure that you agree about when the service will start and what signals will be given to you to begin. Make sure you agree about what will happen at the end of the service.

- [ ] Greet and assist the family members, giving them help and guidance about seating, the arrangement of photos and objects on the communion table, and the family meeting place.

- [ ] Make sure that family members who have a part in the service have arrived.

☐ Make sure that family members who have a part in the service know what is expected of them: at what stage they go to the front to give their reading or eulogy, and what they say at the end of the scripture passage.

☐ Talk to the family of the need to decide who will sit with whom and where. Talk also about the need to determine the order of family members going into the sanctuary/meeting area.

☐ Make sure that the Christ candle and other necessary candles are lit before the service begins.

☐ Make sure that there is water located conveniently in the sanctuary for the worship participants.

☐ Make sure that the musician is present and has no problems with his location or with the service music.

☐ Offer a prayer with the family after first checking that this will be helpful to them.

Just Before and During the Service

☐ Advise people of the need to turn off their cellphones and other electronic devices.

☐ Focus on the liturgy and the needs of presenting the liturgy.

☐ Be aware of sound needs and how sound quality might be improved.

☐ Be aware of family personal concerns and how they can be met.

At the End of the Service

☐ Make sure that the family is led out of the sanctuary first or lead them out yourself.

☐ Make sure that the family are conveniently situated in the hall or outside the sanctuary so that friends may greet them.

Readings

Bible Readings

Ecclesiastes 3:1–8

For everything there is a season, and a time for every matter under heaven:
a time to be born, and a time to die;
a time to plant, and a time to pluck up what is planted;
a time to kill, and a time to heal;
a time to break down, and a time to build up;
a time to weep, and a time to laugh;
a time to mourn, and a time to dance;
a time to throw away stones, and a time to gather stones together;
a time to embrace, and a time to refrain from embracing;
a time to seek, and a time to lose;
a time to keep, and a time to throw away;
a time to tear, and a time to sew;
a time to keep silence, and a time to speak;
a time to love, and a time to hate;
a time for war, and a time for peace.

Psalm 23

The Lord is my shepherd, I shall not want.
[God] makes me lie down in green pastures;
[God] leads me beside still waters;
[God] restores my soul.
[God] leads me in right paths
for [God's] name's sake.

Even though I walk through the darkest valley,
I fear no evil;
for you are with me;
your rod and your staff—
they comfort me.

You prepare a table before me
in the presence of my enemies;
you anoint my head with oil;
my cup overflows.
Surely goodness and mercy shall follow me
all the days of my life,
and I shall dwell in the house of the Lord
my whole life long.

Psalm 23, A First Nations Translation

The Great Father is a Shepherd Chief: I am [the Shepherd Chief's] and with [the Shepherd Chief] I will not want.

[The Shepherd Chief] throws out to me a rope and the name of the rope is love, and [the Shepherd Chief] draws me and [the Shepherd Chief] draws me, and [the Shepherd Chief] draws me to where the grass is green, and the water is good, and I eat and lie down satisfied.

Sometimes my heart is weak and falls down, but the Shepherd Chief lifts it up again, and draws me into a good road. [The Shepherd Chief's] name is wonderful.

Sometimes my heart is very weak and falls down, but [the Shepherd Chief] lifts it up again,

And draws me into a good road. [The Shepherd Chief's] name is Wonderful.

Sometime, it may be soon, it may be longer, it may be a long, long time, the Shepherd Chief will draw me into a place between mountains. It is dark there, but I'll not draw back. I'll not be afraid, for it is there between the mountains that the Shepherd Chief will meet me and the hunger I have felt in my heart, all through this life, will be satisfied. [The Shepherd Chief] gives me a staff to lean on.

(continued)

The Shepherd Chief spreads a table before me with all kinds of food. [The Shepherd Chief] puts [the Shepherd Chief's] hand on my head and the "tired" is gone. My cup is filled until it runs over.

What I tell you is true. I do not lie. These roads that are a way ahead will stay with me through this life, and afterwards I will go to the "Big Teepee" and sit down with the Shepherd Chief forever.

Psalm 139:1–2, 7–12
O Lord, you have searched me and known me.
You know when I sit down and when I rise up;
you discern my thoughts from far away.

Where can I go from your spirit?
Or where can I flee from your presence?
If I ascend to heaven, you are there;
if I make my bed in Sheol, you are there.
If I take the wings of the morning
and settle at the farthest limits of the sea,
even there your hand shall lead me,
and your right hand shall hold me fast.
If I say, "Surely the darkness shall cover me,
and the light around me become night,"
even the darkness is not dark to you;
the night is as bright as the day,
for darkness is as light to you.

Luke 24:13–20, 28–35
Now on that same day two of them were going to a village called Emmaus, about seven miles from Jerusalem, and talking with each other about all these things that had happened. While they were talking and discussing, Jesus himself came near and went with them, but their eyes were kept from recognizing him. And he said to them, "What are you discussing with each other while you walk along?" They stood still, looking sad. Then one of them, whose name was Cleopas, answered him, "Are you the only stranger in Jerusalem who does not know the things that have taken place there in these days?" He asked them, "What things?" They replied, "The things about Jesus of Nazareth, who was a prophet mighty in deed and word before God and all the people, and how our chief priests and leaders handed him over to be condemned to death and crucified him."

As they came near the village to which they were going, he walked ahead
as if he were going on. But they urged him strongly, saying, "Stay with us,
because it is almost evening and the day is now nearly over." So he went in to
stay with them. When he was at the table with them, he took bread, blessed
and broke it, and gave it to them. Then their eyes were opened, and they
recognized him; and he vanished from their sight. They said to each other,
"Were not our hearts burning within us while he was talking to us on the
road, while he was opening the scriptures to us?" That same hour they got up
and returned to Jerusalem; and they found the eleven and their companions
gathered together. They were saying, "The Lord has risen indeed, and he has
appeared to Simon!" Then they told what had happened on the road, and
how he had been made known to them in the breaking of the bread.

John 14:1–6, 8–14, 24, 27

"Do not let your hearts be troubled. Believe in God, believe also in me. In
[God's] house there are many dwelling places. If it were not so, would I have
told you that I go to prepare a place for you? And if I go and prepare a place
for you, I will come again and will take you to myself, so that where I am,
there you may be also. And you know the way to the place where I am going." Thomas said to him, "Lord, we do not know where you are going. How
can we know the way?" Jesus said to him, "I am the way, and the truth, and
the life. No one comes to [God] except through me."

Philip said to him, "Lord, show us [God], and we will be satisfied." Jesus
said to him, "Have I been with you all this time, Philip, and you still do not
know me? Whoever has seen me has seen [God]. How can you say, 'Show
us [God]'? Do you not believe that I am in [God] and [God] is in me? The
words that I say to you I do not speak on my own; but [God] who dwells in
me does [God's] works. Believe me that I am in [God] and [God] is in me;
but if you do not, then believe me because of the works themselves. Very
truly, I tell you, the one who believes in me will also do the works that I do
and, in fact, will do greater works than these, because I am going to [God]. I
will do whatever you ask in my name, so that [God] may be glorified in the
Son. If in my name you ask me for anything, I will do it.

"Whoever does not love me does not keep my words; and the word that you
hear is not mine, but is from [God] who sent me…Peace I leave with you;
my peace I give to you. I do not give to you as the world gives. Do not let
your hearts be troubled, and do not let them be afraid."

John 20:1–10

Early on the first day of the week, while it was still dark, Mary Magdalene came to the tomb and saw that the stone had been removed from the tomb. So she ran and went to Simon Peter and the other disciple, the one whom Jesus loved, and said to them, "They have taken the Lord out of the tomb, and we do not know where they have laid him." Then Peter and the other disciple set out and went toward the tomb. The two were running together, but the other disciple outran Peter and reached the tomb first. He bent down to look in and saw the linen wrappings lying there, but he did not go in. Then Simon Peter came, following him, and went into the tomb. He saw the linen wrappings lying there, and the cloth that had been on Jesus' head, not lying with the linen wrappings but rolled up in a place by itself. Then the other disciple, who reached the tomb first, also went in, and he saw and believed; for as yet they did not understand the scripture, that he must rise from the dead. Then the disciples returned to their homes.

John 20:11–18 Jesus Appears to Mary Magdalene

But Mary stood weeping outside the tomb. As she wept, she bent over to look into the tomb; and she saw two angels in white, sitting where the body of Jesus had been lying, one at the head and the other at the feet. They said to her, "Woman, why are you weeping?" She said to them, "They have taken away my Lord, and I do not know where they have laid him." When she had said this, she turned around and saw Jesus standing there, but she did not know that it was Jesus. Jesus said to her, "Woman, why are you weeping? Whom are you looking for?" Supposing him to be the gardener, she said to him, "Sir, if you have carried him away, tell me where you have laid him, and I will take him away." Jesus said to her, "Mary!" She turned and said to him in Hebrew, "Rabbouni!" (which means Teacher). Jesus said to her, "Do not hold on to me, because I have not yet ascended to the Father. But go to my brothers and say to them, 'I am ascending to my Father and your Father, to my God and your God.'" Mary Magdalene went and announced to the disciples, "I have seen the Lord"; and she told them that he had said these things to her.

John 20:19–21

When it was evening on that day, the first day of the week, and the doors of the house where the disciples had met were locked for fear of the Jews,

Jesus came and stood among them and said, "Peace be with you." After he said this, he showed them his hands and his side. Then the disciples rejoiced when they saw the Lord. Jesus said to them again, "Peace be with you."

Romans 8:18, 31–32, 35, 37–39

I consider that the sufferings of this present time are not worth comparing with the glory about to be revealed to us.

What then are we to say about these things? If God is for us, who is against us? [God] who did not withhold [God's] own Son, but gave him up for all of us, will [God] not with him also give us everything else?

Who will separate us from the love of Christ? Will hardship, or distress, or persecution, or famine, or nakedness, or peril, or sword?

No, in all these things we are more than conquerors through him who loved us. For I am convinced that neither death, nor life, nor angels, nor rulers, nor things present, nor things to come, nor powers, nor height, nor depth, nor anything else in all creation, will be able to separate us from the love of God in Christ Jesus our Lord.

1 Corinthians 13

If I speak in the tongues of mortals and of angels, but do not have love, I am a noisy gong or a clanging cymbal. And if I have prophetic powers, and understand all mysteries and all knowledge, and if I have all faith, so as to remove mountains, but do not have love, I am nothing. If I give away all my possessions, and if I hand over my body so that I may boast, but do not have love, I gain nothing. Love is patient; love is kind; love is not envious or boastful or arrogant or rude. It does not insist on its own way; it is not irritable or resentful; it does not rejoice in wrongdoing, but rejoices in the truth. It bears all things, believes all things, hopes all things, endures all things. Love never ends. But as for prophecies, they will come to an end; as for tongues, they will cease; as for knowledge, it will come to an end. For we know only in part, and we prophesy only in part; but when the complete comes, the partial will come to an end. When I was a child, I spoke like a child, I thought like a child, I reasoned like a child; when I became an adult, I put an end to childish ways. For now we see in a mirror, dimly, but then we will see face to face. Now I know only in part; then I will know fully, even as I have been fully known. And now faith, hope, and love abide, these three; and the greatest of these is love.

2 Corinthians 4:16—5:9

So we do not lose heart. Even though our outer nature is wasting away, our inner nature is being renewed day by day. For this slight momentary affliction is preparing us for an eternal weight of glory beyond all measure, because we look not at what can be seen but at what cannot be seen; for what can be seen is temporary, but what cannot be seen is eternal. For we know that if the earthly tent we live in is destroyed, we have a building from God, a house not made with hands, eternal in the heavens.

For in this tent we groan, longing to be clothed with our heavenly dwelling—if indeed, when we have taken it off we will not be found naked. For while we are still in this tent, we groan under our burden, because we wish not to be unclothed but to be further clothed, so that what is mortal may be swallowed up by life. He who has prepared us for this very thing is God, who has given us the Spirit as a guarantee.

So we are always confident; even though we know that while we are at home in the body we are away from the Lord—for we walk by faith, not by sight. Yes, we do have confidence, and we would rather be away from the body and at home with the Lord. So whether we are at home or away, we make it our aim to please [God]. For all of us must appear before the judgment seat of Christ, so that each may receive recompense for what has been done in the body, whether good or evil.

Philippians 1:3–11

I thank my God every time I remember you, constantly praying with joy in every one of my prayers for all of you, because of your sharing in the gospel from the first day until now. I am confident of this, that the one who began a good work among you will bring it to completion by the day of Jesus Christ. It is right for me to think this way about all of you, because you hold me in your heart, for all of you share in God's grace with me, both in my imprisonment and in the defence and confirmation of the gospel. For God is my witness, how I long for all of you with the compassion of Christ Jesus. And this is my prayer, that your love may overflow more and more with knowledge and full insight to help you to determine what is best, so that in the day of Christ you may be pure and blameless, having produced the harvest of righteousness that comes through Jesus Christ for the glory and praise of God.

Secular Readings

Love Crosses the Gulf between the Generations
In a house that becomes a home
one hands down and another takes
up the heritage of heart and mind,
laughter and tears, musing and deeds.
Love, like a carefully loaded ship,
crosses the gulf between the generations.
Therefore we do not neglect the ceremonies
of our passage, when we wed, when we die,
and when we are blessed with a child...
We live, not by things but by the meaning of things.
It is needful to transmit the passwords from generation to generation.

Antoine de Saint-Exupéry[1]

God Does Not Close the Gap
You have to simply carry on and win through.
There is a huge gap created when a loved one dies,
God does not fill the gap but keeps it open
even at the cost of pain.
The more precious the memories the harder the separation.
The determination to keep on going after
the death of the flesh of your flesh,
bone of your bone, involves the hardest battle there is on earth,
but victory can be won.

Dietrich Bonhoeffer[2]

The Cost
Death is not too high a price to pay
For having lived. Mountains never die
Nor do the sea or rocks or endless sky.
Through endless centuries of time, they stay
Eternal, deathless. Yet they never live!
If choice there were, I would not hesitate
To choose mortality. Whatever fate
Demanded in return for life I'd give,
For never to have seen the fertile plains

Nor heard the winds, nor felt the warm sun on sands
Beside the salty sea, nor touched the hands
Of those I love—without these, all the gains
Of timelessness would not be worth one day
Of living and of loving; come what may.

Dorothy N. Monroe

Meditations of the Heart

We share with you the hard place of your grief,
The anguish of your heart finds echo in our own.
We cannot enter all you feel
Nor bear with you the burden of your pain;
We can only offer what our love does give;
The strength of caring,
The warmth of those who seek to understand,
The loss of (*name*)
This we do in quiet ways,
That on your lonely path
You may not walk alone.

Howard Thurman[3]

Remembering

Everyone loves to be remembered.
But if we want to be remembered
We have a duty also to remember.
Memory is a powerful thing
Wrongly used it can bring death rather than life.
Rightly used it is a form of immortality.
It keeps the past alive.
Those who remember never die.
They continue to walk and talk with us.
Their influence is still felt among us.
There is nothing stronger,
There is nothing more helpful
Than a good remembrance.

Flor McCarthy[4]

A Statement about Death

It seems to me that to face death we need to make the most of life and to do our best to enable others to enjoy it more. To move through the enjoyment of life to the enjoyment of God, the source of all life.

To face death we need to begin to experience the renewal of life day by day, which promises the fuller life ahead.

Geoffrey Lampe (adapted)

Death Is Only an Horizon

We give them back to you, O Lord,
who first gave them to us.
And as you did not lose them in the giving,
so we do not lose them in return.
Not as the world gives do you give,
O lover of souls.
For what is yours is ours also
if we belong to you.
Life is unending as love is undying,
and as the boundaries of this life are but an horizon,
and an horizon is but the limit of our vision.
Lift us up Living God,
that we can see farther.
Strengthen our faith that we may see beyond the horizon.
And while you prepare a place for us
as you have promised,
prepare us also for that happy place;
that where you are we may be also
(with those we have loved, forever).

Bede Jarrett from a prayer by
William Penn[5]

Gone Only from Our Sight

I am standing on the seashore.
Suddenly a ship at my side spreads her white sails to the morning breeze
and starts out for the blue ocean.
She is an object of beauty and of strength;
and I stand and I watch her until at length she is only a ribbon of white
cloud just above where sea and sky mingle with each other.

Then someone at my side says,
"There, she's gone."
Gone where?
Gone from my sight, that's all.
For she's just as large in mast and hull and spar as she was when she left my
side; and just as able to bear her load of living freight to the place of destination. Her diminished size is in me, not in her; and just at that moment when
someone at my side says,
"There, she's gone,"
there are other voices on the far and distant shore ready to take up the
glad shout, "Look, she has arrived!"

Colonel Marcus [6]

Journey of Life
For each of us life is like a journey.
Birth is the beginning of the journey,
and death is not the end but the destination.
It is a journey that takes us
from youth to age,
from innocence to awareness,
from ignorance to knowledge,
from foolishness to wisdom,
from weakness to strength and back again,
from offence to forgiveness,
from loneliness to friendship,
from pain to compassion,
from fear to faith,
from defeat to victory and from victory to defeat,
until, looking backward or ahead,
we see that victory does not lie
at some high point along the way,
but in having made the journey stage by stage.

Traditional Hebrew Prayer

Memories
In the faint glow of dawn
I will remember the day's beginning
When we rose in the parting dark,
and stood hand in hand beside the misty lake.

In the smell of sizzling bacon,
I will remember the gathered family,
Loudly breakfasting, fearlessly
fighting over the last pancake.

In the peace before an afternoon nap,
I will remember the two of us together
Swapping stories of the morning apart
Agonizing over a crossword clue.

As drowsy sleep embraces me
I will remember the bed we shared,
the dreams that came surprisingly,
and an awakening to a day of promise.

I will remember, how could I forget?

David Sparks

If I Should Go Before the Rest of You
If I should go before the rest of you
Break not a flower nor inscribe a stone
Nor when I'm gone speak in a Sunday voice
But be the usual selves that I have known
Weep if you must
Parting is hell
But life goes on
So sing as well.

Joyce Grenfell[7]

Hospital
When I remember lying in my tiny room,
I remember heat, darkness, pain, and fear
And the constant cheerfulness of the nurses.
Why are dying people so calm?
I was scared and unwilling.
I'm a Christian so I shouldn't be afraid,
But I didn't want to leave yet.
I didn't want to be told
Or not to be there when my parents came

Or not to finish the things started.
So I prayed long and desperately
and I knew God heard,
And I felt God with me.
I can't say that I wasn't afraid any more
but at least there was hope,
And now I give thanks;
To the doctor who knew what to do,
To the nurses that cared and were calm
To the blood donors who came out at midnight,
But most of all to God.

Julie Nash[8]

To Lose a Child

Grief is the loneliest of all human experiences.
Losing a child is the hardest thing in life to bear.
There is no antidote,
no cure,
no end,
no one has any answers.

It is a long hard battle,
but there are no enemies.
It is a long and winding path,
but there are no signs to guide you.
It is an overbearing weight,
but no one can see the burden you carry in your heart.
It is unimaginable anguish,
but no one else perceives the half of it.
It is the most sad of all sad deaths,
but the world has enough sadness of her own.
It is the end of your world but you have to go on living.

Marilyn Shawe [9]

Grief Is a Process, Recovering Is Your Choice

Grief is a process. Recovering is your choice. Grief is the price you pay for love, but you don't have to go on paying forever. Time does not automatically heal your pain. It is your willingness to touch your pain—to accept it, to work with it, to understand your change of moods and behaviour, and then to begin to reorganize your life. Healing happens as you allow feelings to happen. Time does not completely heal a broken heart; it only teaches you how to live with it.

Earl A. Grollman [10]

Do Not Go Gentle into That Good Night
Do not go gentle into that good night,
Old age should burn and rave at close of day;
Rage, rage against the dying of the light.
Though wise men at their end know dark is right,
Because their words had forked no lightening they
Do not go gentle into that good night.
Good men, the last wave by, crying how bright
Their frail deeds might have danced in a green bay,
Rage, rage against the dying of the light.
Wild men who caught and sang the sun in flight,
And learn, too late, they grieved it on its way,
Do not go gentle into that good night.
Grave men, near death, who see with blinding sight
Blind eyes could blaze like meteors and be gay,
Rage, rage against the dying of the light.
And you, my father, there on the sad height,
Curse, bless me now with your fierce tears, I pray.
Do not go gentle into that good night.
Rage, rage against the dying of the light.

Dylan Thomas[11]

A Poem
Whatever happens,
those who have learned
to love one another
have made their way
to the lasting world
and will not leave,
whatever happens.

Wendell Berry[12]

Pilgrim's Epitaph

My sword I leave to him
who shall succeed me
in my pilgrimage,
and my courage
to him who can get it.
My marks and scars
I carry with me
to be my witness
that I have fought God's fight
who now will be my rewarder.

John Bunyan[13]

A Dimension beyond Each Season

Harsh shadows,
cast in icy darkness by moonlight
Across a crisp blanket of new snow,
Sudden burst,
of compressed energy in an indigo sky
When Sirius rises brightly at sunset,
Sudden stillness,
as the fiery orb rests in reflection
Upon the glassy surface of a quiet lake.
Undulating waves,
Of more mature grass stirred by a whisper as time passes.
Certain constancy,
of a dimension beyond each season.
You are my friend.

Anon.

Remember Me

To the living, I am gone.
To the sorrowful, I will never return.
To the angry, I was cheated,
But to the happy, I am at peace,
And to the faithful, I have never left.
I cannot be seen, but I can be heard.
So as you stand upon a shore, gazing at a beautiful sea—remember me.

As you look in awe at a mighty forest and its grand majesty—remember me.
As you look upon a flower and admire its simplicity—remember me. ·
Remember me in your heart, your thoughts, your memories of the times we
loved,
the times we cried, the times we fought, the times we laughed.
For if you always think of me, I will never be gone.

Margaret Mead[14]

---

[1] Antoine de Saint-Exupéry (1900–1944). In public domain.

[2] Dietrich Bonhoeffer (1906–1945). In public domain.

[3] From *Meditations of the Heart* by Thurman, Howard (adapted). Reproduced with permission of BEACON PRESS in a book via Copyright Clearance Center.

[4] "Remembering" by Flor McCarthy. Permission granted by Dominican Publications, Dublin, Ireland, www.dominicanpublications.com.

[5] "Death Is Only an Horizon" by Bede Jarrett (1881–1934) from a prayer by William Penn (1644–1718) Permission granted by Dominican Publications, Dublin, Ireland, www.dominicanpublications.com.

[6] Words found in the wallet of Colonel Marcus of the Israeli Army, when he was killed in action on June 11, 1948. In the public domain.

[7] "If I Should Go Before the Rest of You" by Joyce Grenfell, © The Joyce Grenfell Memorial Trust 1980. Reproduced by permission of Sheil Land Associates Ltd.

[8] "Hospital" by Julie Nash who died from Leukaemia, July 22, 1976, aged 17.

[9] "To Lose a Child" from *Enduring, Sharing, Loving* by Marilyn Shawe ©1992; Darton, Longman, and Todd Publishers. Used with permission.

[10] From Rabbi Earl A. Grollman, DHL, DD *Living With Loss; Healing With Hope* audio visual tape, with permission from Global Distributions Networks, Inc.

[11] By Dylan Thomas, from THE POEMS OF DYLAN THOMAS, copyright © 1952 by Dylan Thomas. Reprinted by permission of New Directions Publishing Corp.

[12] Copyright © 2005 by Wendell Berry from *Given*. Reprinted by permission of Counterpoint.

[13] From *The Pilgrim's Progress* by John Bunyan (1628–1688). In the public domain.

[14] "Remember Me" by Margaret Mead. Used with permission of the American Anthropological Association.

Other Resources

A Matter of Life and Death by Charles Hoffacker (Cowley Publications). Good "how to preach" information and sample funeral sermons.

Accompany Them with Singing by Thomas Long (Westminster/John Knox Press). The contemporary classic on how to plan and conduct meaningful and theologically sound Christian funerals.

Being With Dying by Joan Halifax (Shambalha Boston). A Buddhist approach to death by one who has extensive experience of being with those who are dying, their families, and their friends.

Celebrate God's Presence, A Book of Services for The United Church of Canada (United Church Publishing House). A treasure house of prayers, scripture readings, and services for celebrations and funeral services.

I Don't Know What to Say by Robert Buckman (Key Porter Books). A commonsense and practical guide for those who help and support people who are dying.

In Memoriam by Edward Searle (Skinner House Books). A planning guide for those who want practical advice on how to put together a meaningful service or celebration. Edward Searle draws on many years of experience as a Unitarian minister.

Inspiring Funeral and Memorial Resources by Wendy Haynes (First Edition). Haynes is a secular celebrant in Australia.

Life/Earth Prayers: 365 Prayers, Poems, and Invocations from Around the World by Elizabeth Roberts and Elias Amidon (HarperOne). An eclectic resource of prayers and secular readings for the worship leader.

Living When a Loved One Has Died by Earl A. Grollman (Beacon Press). Wise words on feelings when a loved one has died and on the process of grief.

Talking About Death by Virginia Morris (Algonquin Books). How to face death and take the fear and anxiety out of life's ending moments.

Transitions in Dying and Bereavement, A Psychosocial Guide to Hospice and Palliative Care, Victoria Hospice Society (Health Professions Press). How to meet the needs of those who are dying, their families, and their caregivers.

Understanding Your Grief: Ten Essential Touchstones for Finding Hope and Healing Your Heart by Alan D. Wolfelt Ph.D. (Companion Press). Explains the important difference between grief and mourning.

What Helped Me When My Loved One Died, Earl A. Grollman (ed.) (Beacon Press). The stories of wives, husbands, children, and friends who have mourned the death of a loved one.

Online

After a Suicide: Recommendations for Religious Services and Other Public Memorial Observances by David Litts, Suicide Prevention Resource Center (www.edc.org). A site that gives much good information about this major cause of death, including how you create services and the language you use.

British Columbia Bereavement Helpline (www.bcbereavementhelpline.com). A resource for those who are grieving (primarily for residents of British Columbia, Canada).

Canadian Virtual Hospice (www.virtualhospice.ca). A website with a wealth of information for individuals or families.

Funeral Helper (www.funeralhelper.org). An online source of readings and poems.

UNITED CHURCH
PUBLISHING HOUSE

We'd love to hear what you thought of this book. Please add your review at UCRDstore.ca or e-mail your comments to bookpub@united-church.ca.

www.ingramcontent.com/pod-product-compliance
Lightning Source LLC
Chambersburg PA
CBHW060837280326
41934CB00007B/822